Applying Anzalduan Frameworks to Understand Transnational Youth Identities

Framed by the theoretical work of Gloria Anzaldúa, this volume focuses on the cultural and linguistic practices of Mexican-origin youth at the U.S. border to explore how young people engage in acts of "bridging" to develop rich, transnational identities.

Using a wealth of empirical data gathered through interviews and observations, and featuring perspectives from multinational and transnational authors, this text highlights how youth resist racialized and raciolinguistic oppression in both formal and informal contexts by purposefully engaging with their heritage culture and language. In doing so, they defy deficit narratives and negotiate identities in the "in-between." As a whole, the volume engages issues of identity, language, and education, and offers a uniquely asset-based perspective on the complexities of transnational youth identity, demonstrating its value in educational and academic spaces in particular.

This text will benefit researchers, academics, and educators with an interest in the sociology of education, multicultural education, and youth culture more broadly. Those interested in language and identity studies, as well as adolescence, schooling, and bilingualism, will also benefit from this volume.

G. Sue Kasun is Associate Professor of Language and Cultural Theory, Georgia State University, U.S. She is also the Director of the Center for Transnational & Multilingual Education.

Irasema Mora-Pablo is Professor of Applied Linguistics, University of Guanajuato, Mexico.

Routledge Research in Educational Equality and Diversity

Books in the series include:

Global Perspectives on Microaggressions in Schools
Understanding and Combating Covert Violence
Edited by Julie K. Corkett, Christine L. Cho and Astrid Steele

Working-class masculinities in Australian higher education
Policies, pathways, progress
Garth Stahl

Indigenous Identity Formation in Chilean Education
New Racism and Schooling Experiences of Mapuche Youth
Andrew Webb

Supporting Children of Incarcerated Parents in Schools
Foregrounding Youth Voices to Improve Educational Support
Whitney Q. Hollins

The Hidden Academic Curriculum and Inequality in Early Education
How Class, Race, Teacher Interactions, and Friendship Influence Student Success
Karen Phelan Kozlowski

Applying Anzalduan Frameworks to Understand Transnational Youth Identities
Bridging Culture, Language, and Schooling at the US-Mexican Border
Edited by G. Sue Kasun and Irasema Mora-Pablo

For more information about this series, please visit: www.routledge.com/Routledge-Research-in-Educational-Equality-and-Diversity/book-series/RREED

Applying Anzalduan Frameworks to Understand Transnational Youth Identities

Bridging Culture, Language, and Schooling at the US-Mexican Border

Edited by G. Sue Kasun and Irasema Mora-Pablo

NEW YORK AND LONDON

First published 2022
by Routledge
605 Third Avenue, New York, NY 10158

and by Routledge
4 Park Square, Milton Park, Abingdon, Oxon, OX14 4RN

Routledge is an imprint of the Taylor & Francis Group, an informa business

© 2022 selection and editorial matter, G. Sue Kasun and Irasema Mora-Pablo; individual chapters, the contributors

The right of G. Sue Kasun and Irasema Mora-Pablo to be identified as the authors of the editorial material, and of the authors for their individual chapters, has been asserted in accordance with sections 77 and 78 of the Copyright, Designs and Patents Act 1988.

All rights reserved. No part of this book may be reprinted or reproduced or utilised in any form or by any electronic, mechanical, or other means, now known or hereafter invented, including photocopying and recording, or in any information storage or retrieval system, without permission in writing from the publishers.

Trademark notice: Product or corporate names may be trademarks or registered trademarks, and are used only for identification and explanation without intent to infringe.

Library of Congress Cataloging-in-Publication Data
A catalog record for this book has been requested

ISBN: 978-1-032-04350-0 (hbk)
ISBN: 978-1-032-04354-8 (pbk)
ISBN: 978-1-003-19157-5 (ebk)

DOI: 10.4324/9781003191575

Typeset in Sabon
by Apex CoVantage, LLC

To our seres queridos en ambos lados, en todos lados. Especially for Maya and Kai (from Sue) and Mom, Dad, Troy, Emma, and Gema (from Irasema).

Contents

List of Figures and Tables   ix
List of Contributors   x
List of Abbreviations   xiii
About the Editors   xiv
Foreword   xv
ANGELA VALENZUELA
Acknowledgments   xvii

Introduction: When the Bridge Could Build Itself—
Without Permission—Through Mexican-Origin
Transnational Youth   1
G. SUE KASUN AND IRASEMA MORA-PABLO

PART 1
Resistance, Language, and Identity Among
Mexican-Origin Transnational Youth   **17**

1 *Travesía* and Resistance Across Borders. Achieving
   Nepantilism?   19
   NELLY PAULINA TREJO GUZMÁN

2 *Nepantla* as Resistance for Transnational Youth in
   Northern Mexico   37
   SANDRA CANDEL

3 Nations Within Nations: The Heterogeneity of Mexican
   Transnationals of Indigenous Descent From Anzalduan
   Lenses   52
   DAVID MARTÍNEZ-PRIETO

PART 2
Formal Schooling and Transnationalism From an Anzalduan Lens · · · 69

4   Navigating Multiple *Fronteras*: The Transnational Experiences of Latina Second-Generation Immigrant College Students · · · 71
JANETH MARTINEZ-CORTES

5   Language as Boundary, Language as Bridge: The Linguistic Paths of Children of Return Migrants in Mexican Schools as Reported by Adults · · · 91
KATHLEEN TACELOSKY

PART 3
Theorizing Transnationalism With Anzaldúa · · · 111

6   Double *Mestiza* Consciousness: *Aquí y Allá* · · · 113
COLETTE DESPAGNE AND MÓNICA JACOBO-SUÁREZ

7   It's All Gone *South*! Applying Anzalduan Frameworks to Metonymy, Metaphor, and Mythologies to Understand the Language About Transnational Youth · · · 133
STEVE DANIEL PRZYMUS AND JOSÉ OMAR SERNA GUTIÉRREZ

8   Malinche's Move From Traitor to Survivor: Recasting Mexico's First Indigenous Woman to Reframe Mexican-Origin Transnationals Returning Home · · · 155
G. SUE KASUN AND IRASEMA MORA-PABLO

Conclusion: Expanding Transnational Bridges for a World Where Many Worlds Fit · · · 173
IRASEMA MORA-PABLO AND G. SUE KASUN

Index · · · 178

Figures and Tables

Figures

4.1	*Ni de aquí, ni de allá* (neither here, nor there)	79
7.1	Section labels at a bookstore in Texas, U.S.	141
7.2	Transnational funds of knowledge water cycle	151

Tables

4.1	Participants' pseudonym and demographic information	76
7.1	Mythifying the Malinche myth with three semiological chains	147
7.2	Mythifying the common water metaphors/myths	148

Contributors

Sandra Candel, Ph.D., is a mother scholar of color born in Guadalajara, Mexico. As a Mexican immigrant, she is an avid advocate for the rights of undocumented immigrants and an ally to the LGBTQIA+ community. She obtained her doctoral degree in curriculum and instruction with an emphasis in cultural studies, international education, and multicultural education at the University of Nevada, Las Vegas (UNLV). Candel is currently an instructor at the Department of Interdisciplinary, Gender and Ethnic Studies at UNLV, where she teaches women's study courses. Her research focuses on the educational trajectories of U.S.-born transnational students who were forced to attend schools in Mexico due to parental deportation.

Colette Despagne has a Ph.D. in language education. She is an associate professor in postgraduate studies in language sciences at the Research Institute for Social Sciences and Humanities at the Benemérita Universidad Autónoma de Puebla (BUAP). Her main research focus is on critical applied linguistics and bi- and plurilingualism where she mainly analyzes questions related to language, power, and identity in the Mexican context. Over the last decade, she has collaborated with Mexican migrants in the United States and Mexico, transnational students, and Indigenous people in Puebla. She has published in English, Spanish, and French in several international journals.

José Omar Serna Gutiérrez holds a master's degree in applied linguistics in TESOL from the University of Guanajuato, Mexico. His research has focused on the academic and social (re)insertion of transnational students and in-service English as a Foreign Language teachers in Guanajuato, Mexico. His current research interests reside in the nexus between language education and transnationalism. He teaches English as Second Language at Tarrant County College and the Refugee Education Program at Catholic Charities Fort Worth. Omar is also Associate Editor for the MEXTESOL Journal.

Mónica Jacobo-Suárez has a Ph.D. in public policy and international development. She is Associate Professor in the Interdisciplinary Program on Policy and Educational Practices at the Center for Research and Teaching in Economics. Her areas of expertise include transnational students, return migration in Mexico, language programs for migrants, and education policy for minority students. Over the last years, she has collaborated with Mexico's federal government to amend education regulations and thus facilitate transnational students' right to education. She has collaborated with Mexico's Ministry of Education and the National Institute for Educational Evaluation to generate migration statistics within schools nationwide.

Janeth Martinez-Cortes received her Ph.D. in culture, literacy, and language from the University of Texas at San Antonio in May 2020. In her dissertation titled "Second-Generation Immigrant Latinx/a/os and Their First-Generation College Experience: Counterstories of Success and Belonging," she examined the educational experiences of Latinx/a/o students navigating higher education. Her research interests focus on issues related to Latinx/a/o first-generation college students, higher education, and second-generation immigrant education. She has worked with refugee students in the non-profit sector. She is a postdoctoral research fellow at the University of Texas at San Antonio.

David Martínez-Prieto is Assistant Professor in the Department of Bilingual and Literacy Studies at the University of Texas Rio Grande Valley. David holds a Ph.D. in culture, literacy, and language from the University of Texas at San Antonio. David has taught ESL and bilingual pre-service teachers in Mexico and the United States. His area of concentration relates to the ideological impact of U.S. curricular ideologies among Mexican transnational pre-service language teachers.

Steve Daniel Przymus, Ph.D., is Assistant Professor of Educational Linguistics at Texas Christian University. Steve teaches courses in TESOL, bilingual special education, sociolinguistics, and bilingual education in the TCU College of Education. Steve researches conceptual metonymy and metaphor in schoolscapes, translanguaging methods for bilingual education, translanguaging in language sample analysis for distinguishing language difference from disability, the use of online gaming for language and identity development, and community-based biliteracy development in Indigenous Mexican communities.

Kathleen Tacelosky, Ph.D., is Professor of Spanish at Lebanon Valley College in Annville, Pennsylvania, U.S. Dr. Tacelosky has received two Fulbright Scholar grants to Mexico. Her ongoing research regarding the linguistic and educational realities of the children of return migrants in Mexico is the topic of numerous publications and presentations as well as a TEDx Talk. Dr. Tacelosky has taught Spanish, English as a Second Language, and linguistics in the United States, Mexico, Japan, and Puerto Rico.

Nelly Paulina Trejo Guzmán holds a doctoral degree from the University of Exeter, United Kingdom. She is Professor at Universidad Autónoma de Tamaulipas, México. Her research interests include the analysis of personal and professional identities of bilingual and bicultural communities. Her works have been published by *Language and Intercultural Communication*, the *International Journal of Bilingual Education and Bilingualism*, the *International Multilingual Research Journal*, and *Latino Studies*.

Abbreviations

BA	Bachelor of Arts
CDA	Critical Discourse Analysis
DACA	Deferred Action for Minor Arrivals
DHS	Department of Homeland Security
DREAM	Development, Relief, and Education for Alien Minors
DWA	Domestic Workers' Association
EFL	English as a Foreign Language
ELT	English Language Teaching
ESL	English as a Second Language
GED	General Education Development
HSI	Hispanic Serving Institution
ICELT	In-service Certificate in English Language Teaching
NEPBE	National English Program in Basic Education
PNIEB	*Programa Nacional de Inglés en Educación Básica* (National English Program in Basic Education)
PROBEM	*Programa Binacional de Educación Migrante* (Binational Education Program for Migrants)
SEP	*Secretaría de Educación Pública*
TESOL	Teaching English to Speakers of Other Languages

About the Editors

G. Sue Kasun, Ph.D., is Associate Professor of language education and culture at Georgia State University in Atlanta, Georgia, U.S. She is the Director of the Center for Transnational & Multilingual Education at the same institution. Kasun has been researching the transnationalism of Mexican-origin immigrant and returnee communities' ways of knowing and being on both sides of the border for over a decade. Her research, published and presented in journals and universities throughout the U.S. and Mexico, supports the development of a critical transnational awareness that supports multilingualism, multiculturalism, and transliteracies as assets for learning in order to build and become bridges. Her latest work has engaged Indigenous ways of knowing and decolonial approaches to education and living. She is the mother of two beautiful children; she is raising them bilingually and biculturally.

Irasema Mora-Pablo holds a Ph.D. in applied linguistics from the University of Kent, England, and an MA in applied linguistics by the Universidad de las Américas-Puebla, Mexico. She is a full-tenured Professor at the University of Guanajuato, Mexico, in the Department of Languages. She currently coordinates the MA in applied linguistics in English language teaching. She leads the research group of Applied Linguistics in English Language Teaching, recognized by the Ministry of Education in Mexico and awarded with funding to conduct research, focused on transnational students, with the University of Tamaulipas (Mexico) and the University of Texas at San Antonio, U.S. Her teaching experiences shape her areas of interests: bilingualism, transnationalism, and identity formation of second-language teachers. She has conducted research and published on these issues in the United States, Colombia, Iran, and Spain. She is part of the Editorial Board of *HOW Journal* (Colombia) and the Editor of the *International Journal of Multicultural Education*. She has been an Invited Professor at different universities in Mexico.

Foreword

It is my pleasure to read this edited text which has connected two entities who are very close to me—the visionary theorist Gloria Anzaldúa with transnational, Mexican-origin youth. While this book is written predominantly in English, I have enjoyed the various ways authors have engaged usages of language similar to how transnational and multilingual people are in the world—hybridized, playful, and always working to both convey and extend meaning. The authors represented here are also, as the young people portrayed in the studies, *nepantleras* in their own right. As Anzaldúa (2015) explained about these thresholders creating personal and spiritual transformation, "*la nepantlera* leads us in celebrating *la comunidad soñada*, reminding us that spirit connects the irreconcilable warring parts *para que todo el mundo se haga un país*, so that the whole world may become *un pueblo*" (p. 149). The chapter authors come predominantly from Mexico and have often resided on both sides of the border and beyond. It comes as a relief to read about individuals residing in the Global South who are written about by those from the Global South—geographically and otherwise—as Anzaldúa herself was arguably from the Global South. It is time to engage more scholarship from the points of view which have so much to teach and to help co-create with respect to this "dreamed-of" community.

In *Applying Anzalduan Frameworks to Understand Transnational Youth Identities: Bridging Culture, Language, and Schooling at the US-Mexican Border*, the chapters bridge the practices of young people with theory in ways that deeply honor Anzaldúa while also at times challenging and extending her ideas. Indeed, the young people portrayed in these chapters are refracted mirrors of the kind of existence she led in so many ways. They are liminal, in-between people who at times feel that they must hide aspects of who they are. The border and the institutions challenge them on either side of the border in ways they sometimes resist, embrace, or overcome. What is in some ways most remarkable is the level or resilience demonstrated as young people come into deep knowing (what Anzaldúa described as *conocimiento*) because their parents had been deported, because they endured miseducation in their schooling, and because they activated their decisions to act rather than react. Several of the young people demonstrate linguistic genius, and yet we also see the limits of language on what and who people get to become because of language and the myths and metaphors embedded therein. By engaging Anzaldúa so purposefully, the authors directly challenge these limits and open bridges and pathways toward greater depths of possibility in identity, language, and culture.

For me, this book is also personal. I, too, have lived my own transnational journey, first engaging my family in Guerrero, Mexico, during a year-long Fulbright Award after establishing my professional career as an activist and policy leader for the Latinx community in the U.S. I, too, found myself gravitating toward Anzaldúa, toward her revered Aztec goddess figures of both mother-of-creation, Coatlicue, and toward her dismembered, moon-goddess daughter, Coyolxauhqui. While my personal struggles and discoveries were of course distinct, I can relate on so many levels to the varied senses of mestiza consciousness engaged in these chapters, of seeing the world through multiple lenses at once, of resistance to oppressive dominant narratives, and of wanting to create change through *conocimiento*.

For scholars of return migration, transnationalism, and bilingualism, this book revitalizes the discussion around Mexican-origin transnational youth and reaffirms the importance of critical analysis and advocacy in this field. It is my hope that this book indeed creates the space that Kasun and Mora-Pablo try to create. This is a nurturing, enriching space that "talks back" to the combined forces of fear-mongering, division, and exclusion by building bridges toward much-needed understanding in a deeply polarized, frequently anti-immigrant, political context and world. Toward the end of her life, Anzaldúa (2002) left us a blueprint for knowing titled, "now let us shift . . . *conocimiento* . . . inner works, public acts." Indeed, this book is part of that knowledge shift. I, for one, am impressed with the multidimensional, situated ways of knowing exemplified here so that we might "be" the vision of which Anzaldúa wrote.

Angela Valenzuela

Acknowledgments

G. Sue Kasun

This book would not be possible without the generosity and warmth of so many people of Mexican origin who have allowed me into their lives on both sides of the border. That generosity has changed my life into one that is bilingual and multicultural, and I continue to watch this hospitality play out into the next generation with my two children, Maya and Kai. My depth of understanding of transnationalism, specifically from the Mexican side, grew in great measure thanks to a Fulbright-Robles Award I received for teaching and research at the Universidad Autónoma del Estado de Hidalgo, Mexico (2017–2018), where I was again welcomed graciously. My colleagues there, as well as my transnational students, taught me so much, and their ideas undergird my understandings in this book. I maintain special affection for the four Mexican families from my initial dissertation work. Finally, I am grateful to so many mentors, from my advisor at the University of Texas, Dr. Luis Urrieta, Jr., to others I consider my elders in many ways (even when they are sometimes agemates). I remain in gratitude to all these teachers.

Irasema Mora-Pablo

I would like to thank my family for their endless encouragement and continuous support. Also, I appreciate the invaluable contributions of all the authors whose perspectives have added much to the area of transnationals and return migrants. I owe a huge debt of gratitude to those students who allowed me to know their stories, who were sharp, insightful, and committed to every project we embarked together. Your testimonios have taught more than you could ever imagine.

Introduction
When the Bridge Could Build Itself— Without Permission—Through Mexican-Origin Transnational Youth

G. Sue Kasun and Irasema Mora-Pablo

We offer this book as a corrective—a corrective to the misunderstandings of who transnational youth, especially Mexican-origin transnational youth, are. To assist in this effort, we enlist the wisdom of border theory/ Chicana feminist scholar Gloria Anzaldúa to frame the chapters found in this text, authored by a multiplicity of voices of those who have lived in the borderlands and those who have studied them, and from all sides. Anzaldúa spent her career engaging and cultivating interconnected theories of borders, identity, mestizaje, and knowledge (Keating, 2015)—all issues that are engaged in varying ways by border-crossing youth. As Anzaldúa was as wise as she was often misunderstood, we see a similar phenomenon among transnational, Mexican-origin youths. These youths are often well-equipped with culture-crossing skills and yet commonly misunderstood on both sides of the border that their bodies cross—the Mexican–U.S. border. We refer specifically to Mexican-origin, transnational youths, the subjects, and focus of this book. We recognize these young people in possession of far-reaching abilities that are linguistic, cultural, and emotional. These skills are learned, generally, through practice among peers and families.

Transnational youth also learn such skills because transnational life circumstances push these young people to different limits, thresholds, and frontiers. This recognition led us to engage Anzaldúa as a theorist whose work then contextualizes these subjects' experiences, a theorist who was an expert in similar events and who heavily theorized the potentiality of the in-between. Anzaldúa may be best known for work as a borderland theorist and her hallmark text, Borderlands/La Frontera (1987), in which she theorized the complexities and suspensions of living multiple identities when they are not always recognized and welcomed by others, themes she continued to take up through her life's work until she passed in 2005. Indeed, Anzaldúa explained:

> Necesitamos hacer teorías that will rewrite history using race, class, gender, and ethnicity as categories of analysis, theories that cross

DOI: 10.4324/9781003191575-1

borders, that blur boundaries—new kinds of theories with new theorizing methods.

(p. xxv)

In this book, we offer the application of Anzalduan theories to consider transnational Mexican-origin youth identities and experiences on and from the different sides of the border. We also extend and, at times, even question her theories thanks to the extraordinarily complex realities the youth navigate.

We highlight some of our research-based observations to illustrate the different and rich experiences these transnationals go through. For example, a transnational Mexican young person in a small pueblo often knows how to be respectful with town elders while also carrying the knowledge of how to engage African–American neighbors she used to live next door to in Clearwater, Florida. A Mexican-origin child in the Washington, D.C., area knows how to take the metro throughout the city while also knowing how to do traditional dances for annual patron saint festivals to which he has returned to attend. Meantime, their teachers on both sides of the border and many loved ones generally have little understanding of how profound their abilities are. Quietly, via the Internet, some transnational youths continue to listen to genres of music from the country they most recently left in a language "foreign" to their newest residence. They may study the language of the country they left via Internet apps and videos. They sort out how to share cultural codes with some individuals and not others as a way to stay safe emotionally. As one participant commented when she was in college during Kasun's research in the early 2010s, "Why do universities tell us to do study abroad when I've already lived it?" To that, we respond, "Indeed."

Why do "important" institutions such as universities and businesses try to groom and cultivate skills that millions of young people already possess, yet in a hidden-in-plain-sight way? To be sure, part of the answer is the racialized/raciolinguistic oppression heaped on by the dominant culture's willful ignorance (Alim et al., 2016; Flores & Rosa, 2015). Here, we recognize the importance of Anzaldúa's work in answering this question—we are failing to recognize the skills and resourcefulness of those who live in the borderlands, in part due to colonial/genocidal heritages and in part due to their residues in the forms of capitalism, patriarchy, and greed (Anzaldúa, 1987). When we allow our focus to shift in that direction, we can start to tease out the giftedness/strength and the resilience of these transnational youths. In the following, we offer some insights of Anzaldúa's theorizing and then our own brief autohistorias to help illustrate our points of entry into this work and this edition. We then explore the present state of research related to Mexican-origin transnational youth, followed by the unique contributions of the authors of the chapters in this book.

Anzalduan Insights and Theories

While there are conferences and volumes devoted to Anzaldúa's vast, interdisciplinary work (e.g., Keating, 2005; Keating & González-López, 2011), we encapsulate some of her critical concepts to foreground the work done in the chapters which follow. First, Anzaldúa was anything but a conventional scholar. Neither her dissertation writing nor her approach to this, in general, was conventional, and she published about the labors, birthings, and rituals related to her writing process. Her most significant contribution—her writing—is thus unmasked in terms of process. She is clear, too, that writing is never objective and without an author full of ideas, spirit, hope, and contradictions. For her, writing was her art, a form of spiritual transformation, as painful as it was brilliant. Her scholarly texts can at times read so elegantly that the reader could miss the depth of scholarship and attribution to other authors and world spiritual and literary traditions which undergird the work. She explained:

> Why am I compelled to write? . . . Because the world I create in the writing compensates for what the real world does not give me. By writing I put order in the world, give it a handle so I can grasp it. I write because life does not appease my appetites and anger . . . To become more intimate with myself and you. To discover myself, to preserve myself, to make myself, to achieve self-autonomy.
>
> (1985, p. 222)

Anzaldúa, we believe, more deeply embraced her varying senses of (often unaccepted) identities—from queer to Chicana, to multilingual hybrid speaker to decolonial theorist through her processes of writing. She thus delivered a rich set of understandings weaving the past within the present in terms of meshing belief systems, creating space for *conocimiento* (knowing) wherein ways of being that led toward social transformation and liberation were welcome and where forms of further violence and oppression were indeed not. She drew heavily from Aztec symbology and especially the goddess Coatlicue and her dismembered daughter, Coyoalxhaqui. All duality of these symbol systems undergirded her senses of the elliptical nature of shadow's and creation's interwoven processes. As to why she endeavored in this direction, she explained:

> By creating a new mythos—that is, a change in the way we perceive reality, the way we see ourselves, and the ways we behave—la mestiza creates a new consciousness. The work of mestiza consciousness is to break down the subject/object duality that keeps her prisoner and to show in the flesh and through the images in her work how duality is transcended.
>
> (1987, p. 102)

For Anzaldúa, a mestiza consciousness allowed one to see through multiple lenses at once because of her numerous positionings as a woman, Chicana, and due to the joys and sufferings experienced in that person's life. It allowed for non-Western (and by that nature limiting) framings of understandings. It helped undo the nefarious deficit perspectives about who and how people like Anzaldúa were. Indeed, Anzaldúa recognized the rich spaces of possibility afforded by the collisions of those who could engage mestiza consciousness with the hegemony of the West and its patriarchy, racism, capitalism, and heteronormativity, among other oppressions. Specifically, Anzaldúa (1987) recognized the border's historical role in this potential, "The U.S-Mexican border es *una herida abierta* where the Third World grates against the first and bleeds. And before a scab forms it hemorrhages again, the lifeblood of two worlds merging to form a third country—a border culture."

As Anzaldúa continued her work into the following decades, she further developed senses of how we might connect and build bridges despite the complex nature of such work toward her theory of *conocimiento*. She leaned heavily into her unique concept of nepantla, a Nahuatl word meaning the in-between, one that she recognized as fraught and yet full of potential toward allowing space for those who embraced it to become nepantleras, those who worked toward spiritual transformation and change (2002). These individuals would thus fit into the interwoven spaces of belonging she described as "el mundo zurdo," the left-handed world of space for those from the margins as well as the "new tribalism" (Saavedra & Nymark, 2008), which allowed for people of multiple backgrounds to build the new kind of belonging which the Zapatistas in Mexico describe as "a world where many worlds fit." We are provoked, inspired, and at times clinging to these visions offered by Anzaldúa in a world that can look wildly hopeful when we consider rich autonomous social movements and impossibly necrophiliac when we observe the savage smash-and-grab end-of-capitalism. This end-of-capitalism is exhibited by the men leading multinational corporations, planning for annihilation, with their bunkers in New Zealand and other far-flung locales where they and their loved ones might live out another couple generations if the nihlisitic end they and those like them imagine actually comes to pass. Rather than being prescriptive, we embrace the dualistic sense Anzaldúa (1987) offers about engaging these realities on the interior and exterior before turning briefly to our own autohistorias:

> I am an act of kneading, of uniting and joining that not only has produced both a creature of darkness and a creature of light, but also a creature that questions the definitions of light and dark and gives them new meanings.
>
> (pp. 102–103)

Next, we provide our autohistorias to better understand our positionality.

Editor's Autohistorias

Sue

In my adult life, it was the year I was most able to be fully me—a formerly working-class White monolingual (until adulthood) who through the grace of loving caregivers valued difference and other cultures, values they instilled in me as educators, youth leaders, and activists. I had arrived to interior Mexico on a Fulbright Award from 2017 to 2018 to teach and research about transnationalism for an entire academic year with both my young children. The culture I was born into—*el norte*, the U.S.—was generally appreciated in this second culture context of Pachuca, Mexico (despite the then-recent inauguration of a bloviating, Mexican-insulting U.S. president the year prior—Mexicans have perhaps too often been forgiving of the U.S.). I was able to live bilingually/translanguagingly *todos los días* with these public university pre-service English teachers, almost all of whom were, like me, first generation. While the context of the school expected me to use English nearly exclusively, I filled my lungs and exhaled in both languages as I taught, as I interacted with my students, *tan queridos*, as I learned to be differently in my 40s in a translingual environment as I watched my own flesh and blood children take on ways of being in their Spanish-only elementary school.

Many of my university students helped organize a Freirian (e.g., Freire, 2008) English language teaching program, which centered on social justice at a youth prison in our one-on-one teaching. It was a small miracle we were about to enter so quickly and do the work, as prisons are complicated spaces for which to gain entry (Castro, 2017). We waited together every Tuesday morning to be allowed entrance, intermingling our banter and ways of being in our multiculturality. Our liminal spaces mixed in the passageway through metal detectors, among prison guards, among youths on the inside who drank up what we brought, who in turn filled us with an understanding that meaningful exchange is the substance of life. The pretext of sharing English melded into the goal of creating liminal zones of contact. Right there, we were our own mundo zurdo for a semester.

I then picked up my young children from their Spanish-speaking elementary school daily. They would tell exciting stories about many animals on the grounds (intentionally placed there as part of an interconnected web of being and learning) and about cleaning out the fragrant *hierbas* from the *huerta* where they harvested the herbs for cooking, and we then engaged multilingually around the city and through nearby lands. Some of my university students got to know my children in all their multilingual connections. My own kids returned to the U.S. fully expecting the best teachers to be always fluent in Spanish, to be loving in Spanish, with caution when their teachers were only monolingual in English. The interwoven nature of that lush transnational year for me remains a glimmer of a promise about how translingual ways of being can be when a *mundo zurdo* is allowed for. As full of privilege as my experience was, the privilege allowed me to consider ways of weaving richness of identities, of bridge-building with those most marginalized in society, of those with the most promise as young university students, and in various domains of creation with animals, the land, and beyond.

Irasema

Originally from Mexico, I grew up bilingual, having Spanish as my mother tongue and early exposure to English. I was always intrigued about how people learn languages and how they decide which language to use in which context. My educational background has taken me to Mexico, the U.S., and England. My graduate studies led me to applied linguistics and it was when I was a full-time teacher at a public university in central Mexico that I started to have contact with young return migrants.

These young return migrants had come back to Mexico due to different reasons: deportation, family reasons, unable to continue their college degrees in the U.S., because of their migratory status. They had found a place where they felt a sense of belonging in a BA in English language teaching in central Mexico. Most of them did not have as a first choice to become English teachers, but their circumstances took them to this professional path. I started to conduct research with them and analyze their life experiences as migrants. I found out that most of them had arrived in the U.S. at a very early age, without knowing English and having troubles adapting to the new community. However, as years passed, they developed a high proficiency in English, and, in some cases, they prefer it over Spanish. When coming back to Mexico, they had a linguistic capital that was in demand (English). Yet, even when this was an advantage over their Mexican English teacher counterparts, they experienced discrimination, bullying, and stigmatization for their accent when speaking in Spanish. That is when I found that they were constantly struggling, not knowing when their linguistic capital was considered valuable and when they had to hide it to avoid problems. In addition, they often had an identity conflict. When being in the U.S., they did not meet the expectations of the American society (they "looked" Latinx). When they were in Mexico, they did not meet the expectations of the Mexican society either (they were considered foreigners).

This profound complexity related to identity is what Zentella (2002) has called "*ni de aquí ni de allá*" (neither from here nor from there). In this book, we embrace the idea that we need to acknowledge the experiences these transnationals have lived on both sides of the border and allow them and recognize them to be "from here and from there" (Kasun & Mora-Pablo, 2021) and co-existing among multiple forms of identity, as Anzaldúa has correctly steered us.

Weaving Anzaldúa Into Transnational Scholarship About Mexican Youth

Drawing on empirical contributions, this book foregrounds the experiences of transnational Mexican youth, highlighting an appreciation of their complexities primarily through the lens of Gloria Anzaldúa's theorizing on the importance of bridging among cultures and understanding the negotiation of living the "in-between" (Anzaldúa, 2000, 2002). These Mexican-origin youths on both sides of the border are portrayed in their experiences of formal education, language, and culture—a vision of creating new ways of being in the collection—which Anzaldúa advocated in her work.

At the core of the book, researchers from both sides of the U.S.–Mexico border show how transnational youth navigate educational, linguistic, and cultural-identic borders. These are the primary challenges that transnational Mexican-origin youth face. The research in this book and elsewhere indicates that these are the most interrelated factors in transnational youth's adaptation and senses of success in their transnational lives. As part of this, contributions explore how transnationals engage education toward bridge-building and the support they receive (or not) to make sense of their language learning and their maintenance of bridge-building identities. We present cases in Mexico and the U.S., providing a picture of how complex the mobility in this area can be and the impact this has on transnational youth.

Prior Research About Transnational Youth of Mexican Origin: A View From Both Sides

This book presents scholars from Mexico and the United States focusing on a topic of extensive interest on both sides of the border. However, the intention is to analyze this through Anzalduan lenses. The purpose was to bring both Mexican and U.S. scholars together to explore the lives of Mexican-origin youth differently from how research has examined this phenomenon over the years. As we will see in the chapters, these authors have investigated transnational youth from both sides of the border, which adds a richer view to this phenomenon.

Varying concepts have been used to address these young transnational return migrants. Returnees are defined as those born in Mexico, who migrated to the United States at an early age, and then returned to

Mexico (Petrón, 2009). "American–Mexicans" is a term used by Zúñiga and Hamann (2015, p. 172) to refer to the Mexican-heritage youth born in the United States and migrating to Mexico for the first time (Jacobo-Suárez, 2017; Jensen et al., 2017). On the other hand, transnationals can be defined as those who "hold strong family and friendship links in both countries and have developed an identification with either one or both cultures" (Mora et al., 2018, p. 3). The scholars included in this book provide comprehensive research addressing these different conceptualizations to portray the complex dynamics around the lives of young migrants.

The transnational research on youth of Mexican origin has influenced studies across different disciplines such as sociology, education, applied linguistics, and economics, to mention a few. Studies in Mexico and the United States generally have focused on migratory transition points in their lives. For example, some studies have addressed the socioeconomic aspects that surround the re-insertion of return migrants into the Mexican labor market and their job opportunities (Fundación BBVA Bancomer, 2015; Massey, 1987; Massey & Riosmena, 2010; Padilla & Jardón Hernández, 2015; Rivera Sánchez, 2013). Others have addressed educational issues and how these migrants adapt to the educational systems, in Mexico and the United States, or become "invisible" (Hamann et al., 2006; Hamann & Zuñiga, 2011; Jacobo & Jensen, 2018; Ocampo, 2014; Román González & Zúñiga, 2014; Sánchez García & Zúñiga, 2010; Zúñiga & Hamann, 2013). Other studies have reported on the challenges these migrants face and that are caused by linguistic barriers, social stigmas, and prejudices (De la Rosa, 2015; Despagne, 2018; Despagne & Jacobo, 2019; Despagne & Manzano-Munguía, 2020; Hamann et al., 2006; Hazán, 2018; Kasun, 2016). Other studies have focused on the sense of belonging of "American–Mexicans" (Bybee et al., 2020; Zúñiga & Hamann, 2015). Another area of analysis has been the one dedicated to those return migrants who find a way to survive in Mexico by becoming English language teachers, and analyze their professional identity (Christiansen et al., 2017; Kasun et al., 2020; Mora-Pablo et al., 2015; Mora et al., 2016; Petrón, 2009; Petrón & Greybeck, 2014; Rivas, 2013; Trejo Guzmán et al., 2016). Research in these areas has provided important insights into the understanding of Mexican-origin youth's experiences on both sides of the border. In our book, we aim to recount how the transnational youth navigate different borders—educational, linguistic, and cultural—and how they engage or resist their heritage. We look at their transnational spaces and what we have learned from both sides of the border, and the actions we can take in order to become more understanding and proactive when encountering these transnationals in our educational spaces.

Weaving in Prior Research Toward Hybridized Understandings

Other publications address the complexities transnationals go through during their lives. Some of them have focused on the lives of transnational children and the challenges they face when accessing education (Jensen & Sawyer, 2012). Additional scholars have addressed the issue from a more global perspective (Capstick, 2020) and also how to prepare educators to address the constant mobility of these transnationals (e.g., Gándara & Jensen, 2020). Other scholars have centered their discussion around the sociopolitical relationship between Mexico and the U.S. (Boehm, 2012; Segura & Zavella, 2007). This book centers deeper theorizing of transnationals' experiences toward helping readers embrace the central experience of being in-between in a growing increasingly complex world. We also include a chapter that centers Indigenous transnationals' experiences, an often-overlooked area.

The Structure of the Book

This book engages issues of identity, language, and education, drawing on Anzaldúa's work and how contributors can theorize transnational practices through Anzalduan lenses. The authors in this book recount how transnational youth navigate different borders—educational, linguistic, and cultural—and how they engage or resist their heritage. We look at their transnational spaces and what we have learned from both sides of the border, and the actions we can take in order to become more understanding and proactive when encountering these transnationals in our educational spaces. Our multinational and transnational authors from both sides of the border provide unique insights extending prior research. This text offers three parts focusing on empirical research that bridges with Anzaldúa's theory—one on resistance, language, and identity; another on schooling through Anzalduan lenses; and, finally, the third part where theory is extended regarding these transnational youths and Anzaldúa.

In the first part, "Resistance, Language, and Identity Among Mexican-Origin Transnational Youth," we offer contributions spanning borders with authors who have lived on both sides, and a final contribution which in many ways transcends borders with its focus on Indigenous youth. The section begins with Nelly Paulina Trejo Guzmán's, "Travesía and Resistance Across Borders. Achieving Nepantilism?" In it, she analyzes the life histories of four transnationals who, at different points of their lives, embarked on the "return odyssey to the historical/mythological Aztlan" (Anzaldúa, 1987). The participants' discourses reveal how recalling and verbalizing significant memories of their multiple journeys across borders enable them to connect with their continuously shifting identities. Her analysis provides a deeper understanding of how movements across cultural and linguistic borders cause some of the participants to remain in *la resistencia* while others embark on *la travesía* to achieve a mental state of nepantilism in unique ways. Throughout the chapter, each participant's *mestiza* ways are outlined to witness both stagnation within inherited and learned oppressions and ruptures with old selves that lead to transformed understandings of who they are. In the following, Sandra Candel describes the challenges and identic strains and strengths of two returning boys to Mexico in "Nepantla as Resistance for Transnational Youth in Northern Mexico." Two participants in her study, Hans and Peter, use language and nationality to navigate a space in which they have to adapt to their new reality in Mexico, accepting and rejecting aspects of their identity to help them find a sense of belonging and acceptance, while at the same time using identity as a way of cultural survival. They are perceived as being "*del norte*," and, as such, they are expected to display specific attributes while, at the same time, being excused for certain behaviors. Their "otherness" is a *nepantla* state that is at the same time restricting and liberating, and school is the site where this *nepantilismo* takes place. This qualitative study uses the Anzalduan concept of *nepantla* to explore the experiences of two U.S.-born youths who were forced to live in a Mexican city near the U.S.–Mexico border after their mother's deportation. While identity creates problems in academic spaces due to negative stereotypes, language gives them access to a reserved status available only to native English speakers. Findings also revealed that being "*del norte*" carried a set of expectations and assumptions. The study concludes with a reflection of how, with a change in paradigm, *conocimiento*, the Anzalduan concept of "knowing" has the potential to turn defiance into personal and social transformation.

David Martínez-Prieto takes a different and sorely needed turn in the research by engaging connections to identity and the tools and limits of Anzaldúa's work on indigeneity in "Nations Within Nations: The Heterogeneity of Mexican Transnationals of Indigenous Descent From Anzalduan Lenses." He calls for a better understanding of the historical and political factors that impact the identities of Mexican transnationals of Indigenous origin. Based on data collected during three investigations with transnational (pre)service teachers from Indigenous communities in the Mexican states of Puebla (2017), Tlaxcala (2017), and Oaxaca (2018), Martínez-Prieto analyzes the pertinence of Anzaldúa's framework in understanding the subjugation and internal differences of Indigenous transnational populations.

The second part, "Formal Schooling and Transnationalism From an Anzalduan Lens," highlights the skills and challenges faced in two distinct educational contexts—higher education in the U.S. and Mexican K-12 education. In the first chapter by Janeth Martinez-Cortes, "Navigating Multiple *Fronteras*: The Transnational Experiences of Latina Second-Generation Immigrant College Students," the transnational experiences of Latina second-generation immigrant college students at a Hispanic-Serving Institution (HSI) in South Central Texas are highlighted. The author draws on the theoretical concept of the "mestiza consciousness" (Anzaldúa, 1987) wherein Latinx/a/o students reject the either/or duality and reconcile multiple cultural identities (Anzaldúa, 1987) while navigating cultural, linguistic, and academic borders. Drawing on a qualitative research approach, the data collection consisted of semi-structured interviews and *pláticas* with the women attending college. Analyses of responses from interviews with students illustrate the ways Latinas developed their cultural identities, maintained family ties across borders, and formed understandings of education as the children of immigrants. Implications of this study include the need for practices that recognize and value the continuous transnational experiences of second-generation immigrants, as these experiences can translate to their lives as first-generation college students. In the following, Kathleen Tacelosky engages the importance of language from Anzalduan lenses for Mexican youth returnees in "Language as Boundary, Language as Bridge: The Linguistic Paths of Children of Return Migrants in Mexican Schools as Reported by Adults." In this chapter, grounded in 10 years of ethnolinguistic research, Tacelosky explores the intersection of language and education in the context of Mexican schools. She traces the trajectory of students who begin their linguistic journey with Spanish at home, encounter school in English, and move to Mexican schools where they must bridge the space between home and school by repurposing their home Spanish for academic coursework. The stories of three young adults shared here serve as the basis for an understanding of transnational educational experiences in the U.S.–Mexico context. Following an analysis of how these women have traversed the spaces they inhabit, exhibited agency, and engaged meaningful identities, she concludes that they embody the kind of integrated interconnectedness that Anzaldúa calls mestizaje (1987).

The final section, "Theorizing Transnationalism With Anzaldúa," has three unique contributions that engage mestiza consciousness, language, and decolonial identity approaches. In a similar vein of engaging *mestiza* knowing as Trejo Guzmán contributed, Colette Despagne and Mónica Jacobo-Suárez offer "Mestiza Consciousness: *Aquí y Allá*," engaging that forbidding sense of not being from either side and reframing it. They present an in-depth analysis of two Mexican migrants, Ana in New York, and Javier in Guadalajara, who break down dualistic hegemonic paradigms that impose culturally determined roles in which they feel rejected. This work analyzes how Ana and Javier defy the pre-established norms of their immediate contexts and how they create their own *mundo zurdo* by creating their own definitions of what it means for them to be Mexicans on both sides of the border. Steve Prysmuz and José Omar Serna Gutiérrez offer a thoughtful engagement of language production and disruption in "It's All Gone South! Applying Anzalduan Frameworks to Metonymy, Metaphor, and Mythologies to Understand the Language About Transnational Youth." Their chapter is centered around the testimonios of four transnational individuals who share stories of developing multilingual and multicultural strengths while growing up, when others looked down on them. In applying Anzalduan frameworks to metonymy, metaphor, and mythologies, the authors unearth implicit messaging in common language about transnational youth, in order to re-appropriate this rhetoric for a new consciousness. The authors' critical discourse analysis exposes multiple directional, spatial, and other conceptual metonymies, metaphors, and myths that act to position transnational youth as having problematic identities. Left unquestioned, these deficit-based narratives get repeated, normalized, become invisible to scrutiny, and convert into the new truth discourse about these youths. Following Anzaldúa's call to create and recognize a new language and a new consciousness, the chapter concludes with an exercise in semiotically dismantling existing myths with new ways of talking about and thinking about transnational youth.

We author the last chapter as a correction to the historic understanding of Mexico's female first-traitor figure titled, "Malinche's Move From Traitor to Survivor: Recasting Mexico's First Indigenous Woman to Reframe Mexican-Origin Transnationals Returning Home." By engaging Anzalduan and postcolonial theory, this chapter recognizes how Mexicans inside Mexico have a righteous anger toward further colonization. We argue that the nationalist myth of the first conquerors' Indigenous partner, Malinche, as a traitor misguides this decolonial tendency. Casting a woman with her sights upon survival as a simplistically sketched traitor further oppresses Mexicans who are mostly trying to survive when they live in the U.S. and later return to Mexico. By using the myth of Malinche, we recognize her for her historic strengths and then map that onto returning transnationals. The main argument derives from the Mexican transnational youth returnees with whom the authors have researched for several years and who have shared stories of intense pain and confusion about how their identities were or were not embraced upon return to Mexico. At the same time, they often demonstrated a self-awareness in which they claimed a rich form of varying hybridities about their identity. The chapter calls for the need of the discourse to shift and that the hybridity returnees bring is one from which we can all learn toward better engaging an increasingly multicultural world. The afterword highlights the common ground in the chapters that we hope will encourage educators, policy makers, families, and transnational youth to discuss the complexities around living "in-between."

We are excited about the contributions of the authors in this book as well as the spaces of possibility their work opens. We see the mapping of incredibly complex work on language, identity, and survival from Anzaldúa into the promise of potentialities for educators, scholars, and community members toward creating greater spaces where a *mundo zurdo* can exist more than just in the interstices of some select transnational youth. We embrace a vision of the future where human movement is free in a world where a new tribalism exists. We are proud to include multinational voices and scholarship from both sides of the border, providing what we believe is a glimpse into our own *nepantla*-style scholarship in this collective work.

References

Alim, H. S., Rickford, J. R., & Ball, A. F. (Eds.). (2016). *Raciolinguistics: How language shapes our ideas about race*. Oxford University Press.

Anzaldúa, G. E. (1985). On writing. In C. West (Ed.), *Words in our pockets: The feminist writers' guild handbook on how to gain power, get published & get paid* (pp. 215–229). Dustbooks.

Anzaldúa, G. E. (1987). *Borderlands/La frontera: The new Mestiza*. Aunt Lute.

Anzaldúa, G. E. (2000). Making alliances, queerness, and bridging conocimientos: An interview with Jamie Lee Evans (1993). In A. Keating (Ed.), *Interviews/Entrevistas/Gloria E. Anzaldúa* (pp. 195–210). Routledge.

Anzaldúa, G. E. (2002). Now let us shift . . . the path of conocimiento . . . inner work, public acts. In G. E. Anzaldúa & A. Keating (Eds.), *This bridge we call home: Radical visions for transformation* (pp. 540–578). Routledge.

Boehm, D. A. (2012). *Intimate migrations*. New York University Press.

Bybee, E. R., Feinauer Whiting, E., Jensen, B., Savage, V., Baker, A., & Holdaway, E. (2020). "Estamos aquí pero no soy de aqui": American Mexican youth, belonging and schooling in rural, central Mexico. *Anthropology & Education Quarterly, 51*(2), 123–145.

Capstick, T. (2020). *Language and migration*. Routledge.

Castro, E. (2017). Personal communication.

Christiansen, M. S., Trejo Guzmán, N. P., & Mora-Pablo, I. (2017). 'You know English, so why don't you teach?' Language ideologies and returnees becoming English language teachers in México. *International Multilingual Research Journal.* https://doi.org/10.1080/19313152.2017.1401446

De la Rosa, R. (2015). *Migración de retorno y educación*. www.controlescolar.sep.gob.mx/work/models/controlescolar/Resource/archivo_ppt/5-Migracion_de_Retorno.pdf

Despagne, C. (2018). Language is what makes everything easier: The awareness of semiotic resources of Mexican transnational students in Mexican schools. *International Multilingual Research Journal, 13*(1), 1–14.

Despagne, C., & Jacobo, M. (2019). The adaptation process of transnational children into Mexico's school. *Latino Studies, 17*(4), 428–447.

Despagne, C., & Manzano-Munguía, M. C. (2020). Youth return migration (US-Mexico): Students' citizenship in Mexican schools. *Children and Youth Services Review, 110,* 104652.

Flores, N., & Rosa, J. (2015). Undoing appropriateness: Raciolinguistic ideologies and language diversity in education. *Harvard Educational Review, 85*(2), 149–171. https://doi.org/10.17763/0017-8055.85.2.149

Freire, P. (2008). *Pedagogy of the oppressed* (M. Bergman Ramos, Trans. 30th Anniversary ed.). Continuum.

Fundación BBVA Bancomer. (2015). *Situación Migración México. Primer Semestre 2015.* BBVA Research México.

Gándara, P., & Jensen, B. (Eds.). (2020). *The students we share: Preparing US and Mexican educators for our transnational future.* SUNY Press.

Hamann, E. T., & Zuñiga, V. (2011). Schooling and the everyday ruptures of transnational children encounter in the United States and Mexico. In C. Coe, R. R. Reynolds, D. A. Boehm, J. M. Hess, & H. Rae-Espinoza (Eds.), *Everyday ruptures: Children, youth, and migration in global perspective* (pp. 141–160). VUP.

Hamann, E., Zúñiga, V., & Sánchez, J. (2006). Pensando en Cynthia y su Hermana: Educational implications of US/Mexico transnationalism for children. *Journal of Latinos in Education, 5*(4), 253–274.

Hazán, M. (2018). *Understanding return migration to Mexico: Towards a comprehensive policy for the reintegration of returning migrants. Matt, leading the conversation together. Mexicans and Americans thinking together.* www.matt.org/wp-content/uploads/2018/07/Understanding-Return-Migration-to-Mexico-White-Paper.pdf

Jacobo, M., & Jensen, B. (2018). *Schooling for US-Citizen students in Mexico.* Civil Rights Project, UCLA. Conference paper: The impact of immigration enforcement policies on teaching and learning in America's Public Schools, Washington, DC on February 28, 2018. www.researchgate.net/publication/327235483_SCHOOLING_FOR_USCITIZEN_STUDENTS_IN_MEXICO

Jacobo-Suárez, M. (2017). De regreso a "casa" y sin apostilla: estudiantes mexicoamericanos en México. *Sinéctica,* (48), 1–18.

Jensen, B., Mejía Arauz, R., & Aguilar Zepeda, R. (2017). Equitable teaching for returnee children in Mexico. *Sinéctica,* (48).

Jensen, B., & Sawyer, A. (2012). *Regarding educación: Mexican-American schooling, immigration, and bi-national improvement.* Teachers College Press.

Kasun, G. S. (2016). Interplay of a way of a knowing among Mexican-origin transnationals: Chaining to the border and to transnational communities. *Teachers College Record, 119*(9), 1–32.

Kasun, G. S., Hernández, T., & Montiel, H. (2020). The engagement of transnationals in Mexican university classrooms: Points of entry towards recognition among future English teachers. *Multicultural Perspectives, 22*(1), 37–45.

Kasun, G. S., & Mora-Pablo, I. (2021). El anti-malinchismo contra el mexicano-transnacional: Cómo se puede transformar esa frontera limitante. In *Anales de Antropología, 55*(1), 39–48.

Keating, A. (2005). Introduction: Shifting worlds, una entrada. In A. Keating (Ed.), *EntreMundos/among words* (pp. 1–12). Palgrave.

Keating, A. (2015). Re-envisioning Coyolxauhqui, decolonizing reality: Anzaldúa's twenty-first-century imperative. In A. Keating (Ed.), *Light in the dark luz en lo oscuro: Rewriting identity, spirituality, reality/Gloria E. Anzaldúa* (pp. ix–xxxvii). Duke University Press.

Keating, A., & González-López, G. (2011). *Bridging: How Gloria Anzaldúa's life and work transformed our own*. University of Texas Press.

Massey, D. S. (1987). *Return to Aztlan: The social process of international migration from Western Mexico*. University of California Press.

Massey, D. S., & Riosmena, F. (2010). Undocumented migration from Latin America in an era of rising US enforcement. *Annals of the American Academy of Political & Social Science, 630*(1), 294–321. https://doi.org/10.1177/0002716210368114

Mora, A., Guzmán, N. P. T., & Mora-Pablo, I. (2018). 'I was lucky to be a bilingual kid, and that makes me who I am:' The role of transnationalism in identity issues. *International Journal of Bilingual Education and Bilingualism, 24*(5), 693–707.

Mora, A., Trejo, N. P., & Roux, R. (2016). The complexities of being and becoming language teachers: Issues of identity and investment. *Language and Intercultural Communication, 16*(2), 182–198. https://doi.org/10.1080/14708477.2015.1136318

Mora-Pablo, I., Lengeling, M., & Basurto Santos, N. M. (2015). Crossing borders: Stories of transnationals becoming English language teachers in Mexico. *Signum: Studios da Linguagem, 18*(2), 326–348. https://doi.org/10.5433/2237-4876.2015v18n2p326

Ocampo, A. C. (2014). The gay second generation: Sexual identity and family relations of Filipino and Latino gay men. *Journal of Ethnic and Migration Studies, 40*(1), 155–173. https://doi.org/ 10.1080/1369183X.2013.849567

Padilla, J., & Jardón Hernández, A. E. (2015). Migración y empleo: Reinserción de los migrantes de retorno al mercado laboral nacional. *Instituto de Estudios y Divulgación sobre Migración, A.C*. Distrito Federal, México. http://ri.uaemex.mx/handle/20.500.11799/65207

Petrón, M. (2009). Transnational teachers of English in Mexico. *The High School Journal, 92*(4), 115–128. www.jstor.org/stable/40364009?seq=1#page_scan_tab_contents

Petrón, M. A., & Greybeck, B. (2014). Borderlands epistemologies and the transnational experience. *Gist: Education and Learning Research Journal*, (8), 137–155.

Rivas, L. (2013). Returnees' identity construction at a BA TESOL program in Mexico. *Profile Issues in Teachers' Professional Development, 15*(2), 185–197. https://revistas.unal.edu.co/index.php/profile/article/view/39071/42067

Rivera Sánchez, L. (2013). Migración de Retorno y Experiencias de Reinserción en la Zona Metropolitana de la Ciudad de México. *Revista Interdisciplinar de Mobilidad Humana, 21*(41). https://doi.org/10.1590/S1980-85852013000200004

Román González, B., & Zúñiga, V. (2014). Niños de Retorno de Estados Unidos a México: ¿Escuela, Dulce Escuela? *Migraciones Internacionales, 7*(4),

277–286. www.scielo.org.mx/scielo.php?script=sci_arttext&pid=S1665-8906 2014000200010

Saavedra, C. M., & Nymark, E. D. (2008). Borderland-Mestizaje feminism: The new tribalism. In N. K. Denzin, Y. S. Lincoln, & L. T. Smith (Eds.), *Handbook of critical and indigenous methodology* (pp. 255–276). Sage.

Sánchez García, J., & Zúñiga, V. (2010). Trayectorias de los Alumnos Transnacionales en México. Propuesta Intercultural de Atención Educativa. *Trayectorias, 12*(30), 5–23. www.redalyc.org/articulo.oa?id=60713488002

Segura, D. A., & Zavella, P. (Eds.). (2007). *Women and migration in the US-Mexico borderlands: A reader*. Duke University Press.

Trejo Guzmán, N. P., Mora Vázquez, A., Mora-Pablo, I., Lengeling, M. M., & Crawford, T. (2016). Learning transitions of returnee English language teachers in Mexico. *Lenguas en Contexto, 13*, 1–13.

Zentella, A. C. (2002). Latin@ languages and identities. In M. Suárez Orozco & M. Páez (Eds.), *Latinos: Remaking America* (pp. 321–338). University of California Press.

Zúñiga, V., & Hamann, E. T. (2013). Understanding American Mexican children. In B. Jensen & A. Sawyer (Eds.), *Regarding Educación: Mexican-American schooling, immigration, and bi-national improvement* (pp. 172–188). Teachers College Press.

Zúñiga, V., & Hamann, E. T. (2015). Going to a home you have never been to: The return migration of Mexican and American-Mexican children. *Children's Geographies, 13*(6), 643–655, https://doi.org/10.1080/14733285.2014.936364

Part 1

Resistance, Language, and Identity Among Mexican-Origin Transnational Youth

Chapter 1

Travesía and Resistance Across Borders. Achieving Nepantilism?

Nelly Paulina Trejo Guzmán

Introduction

The Mexico–U.S. border represents a unique case of international migration. It has been, for several decades, the largest and most active border in the world. According to Durand (2000), the massive migratory flows across both countries have created a complex interdependence among them that has been characterized as a set of deeply intertwined symbolic and material inequalities. Heyman (2017) contends that societies along the Mexico–U.S. border cannot be any longer viewed as discrete homogeneous cultural entities that coexist on each side of a geopolitical border. These societies have created complex networks of interactions in multiple arenas generating a space filled with tensions, contradictions, connections, and diversity. Similar assertions were made in the late 1980s by Anzaldúa (2012) in her foundational work "Borderlands/La Frontera: The New Mestiza," where she defined this space as "una herida abierta where the Third World grates against the first and bleeds. And before a scab forms it hemorrhages again, the lifeblood of two worlds merging to form a third country—a border culture" (p. 25). Her writings proved to be so empowering for those of diverse backgrounds that they were among those banned in Arizona's public school system.

Cantú and Hurtado (2007) succinctly put forward the idea that Anzaldúa's literature "is dangerous only because it has the power to change minds, to disturb complacencies" (p. 3). It is that power that I intend to use to better understand the transnational experiences of four young people. The present chapter employs an Anzalduan analytical framework to investigate the life histories of four transnationals whose lives have taken place on both sides of the border. It specifically applies El camino de la mestiza/The Mestiza Way metaphor to depict the identity transformations that participants undergo during each migratory transition in their lives. The present chapter includes a reflection that revolves around the following questions:

What impact do the discourses regarding language and nationality that young migrants encounter across borders have on their individual identities?
What characterizes the selves and subjectivities of young migrants who remain in *la resistencia*?
What characterizes the selves and subjectivities of young migrants who embark *on la travesía* (an increment of consciousness, a step forward) to achieve nepantilism?

A Blurred Border

Traditionally, much emphasis has been placed on the migratory movements of Mexicans to the United States. A search in databases revealed vast amounts of information on this issue. The most salient topics include illegal immigration (Hanson, 2006; Donato & Perez, 2017), drug-related violence (Borges et al., 2011; Heyman, 2018), language learning and educational attainment (Miller, 2016; Feliciano & Lanuza, 2017), and high-skilled migration (Tuirán & Ávila, 2013; Wise, 2015). In addition, there is a binational project run by Universidad de Guadalajara and Princeton University which has investigated Mexican migration to the U.S. for almost 40 years (https://mmp.opr.princeton.edu).

In contrast, little attention is paid to the flows of U.S. citizens to Mexico. A search in the same databases showed scarce results. Most of the research found focuses on the U.S.-born children from Mexican parents who returned to the country in large numbers since 2009 (Jacobo & Jensen, 2018; Masferrer et al., 2019; Montoya Zavala et al., 2020), and retirees (Dixon et al., 2006; Lizárraga Morales, 2008). However, an important issue is being overlooked by the literature: U.S. citizens have been the largest immigrant population in Mexico for more than 30 years (Montaño & Cervantes, 2017). According to the most recent statistics regarding the number of international immigrants to Mexico, authorities registered a total of 1,705,462 immigrants in the country (Encuesta Nacional de la Dinámica Demográfica [ENADID], 2018). The ENADID points out that 75% of immigrants in Mexico are U.S. citizens, making a total of 799,123 persons, and most of these are young people under 20. However, the U.S. State Department estimates that 1.5 million U.S. citizens live in Mexico (www.state.gov/countries-areas/mexico/). The reasons behind this sharp difference have not been investigated by academia, but several press publications have reported that many of these U.S. citizens may be living illegally in Mexico with an overstayed tourist status (Knobloch, 2020; Mark, 2019). This issue has been known to Mexican authorities since 2015, as government official data and Mexico's Foreign Affairs Secretary confirm (Consejo Nacional de Población [CONAPO], 2016; Sheridan, 2019; Fry, 2019; Rojas, 2019). In contrast to the data reported by ENADID (2018), press sources indicate that U.S. citizens in Mexico are currently employed, belong to age groups between 35 and 50, and have created strong bonds among themselves and Mexican citizens (Knobloch, 2020; Fry, 2019; Rojas, 2019; Sheridan, 2019).

This analysis brings light into a phenomenon that is not sufficiently highlighted by the prevailing discourse in academia, which is the fact that large numbers of both Mexican and U.S. populations perceive the neighboring country as a place where they have the possibility to improve their quality of life, and that both populations, documented or undocumented, are making significant economic, social, and cultural contributions to their receiving countries. This circumstance that is taking place despite borders, migratory regulations, and discourses of difference among Mexicans and U.S. citizens bears similarity with Anzaldúa's concept of *nepantla*, through which she celebrates the possibility of cultural and spiritual hybridity through fruitful and eclectic alliances (Anzaldúa, 2012; Cantú et al., 2010). Anzaldúa uses the Nahuatl word *nepantla* or *mental nepantilism* to mean "torn between ways" (p. 100). In line with this *mental nepantilism*, previous research on transnationals has pointed out that the place of birth does not determine the ascribed nationality of individuals (Mora Vázquez et al., 2018). These findings highlight the possibilities of nepantilism that subsist within individuals that are in contact with more than one language and culture.

However, a word of caution is similarly valid here to not romanticize nepantilism. Transnationals, or those who migrate across borders, face racialized and gendered discourses (Bourdieu, 1991; Lotman, 2009) that shape their identities and levels of agency (Block, 2013; Norton, 2013). The experience of a white middle-class Anglo individual migrating to another country stands in structural asymmetry with that of a multiracial working-class Spanish-speaking person, regardless of whether this migration takes place northward or southward, legally or illegally. There is ample evidence in the literature of the historical repression and racism experienced by Mexicans in the U.S. (e.g., Brack, 1970; Menchaca, 1993), the institutional racism prevailing in immigration law enforcement (Provine, 2013), and the impact of racial barriers on the identities of Mexican-Americans (Ortiz & Telles, 2012). Similar issues are faced by dark-skinned people in Mexico (Aguilar Pariente, 2011).

El Origen de La Frontera

Bourdieu (1991) makes a critique about the origin of borders, and regional and ethnic identities. He understands them as social constructions that are imposed on societies by groups in power "to *make and unmake groups*" (p. 221). Furthermore, he places special emphasis on the role played by educational systems in the production of cultural differences and the legitimation of an "*official* language" (p. 45), all these with the pretense of erasing historical memories and creating consensus around the idea of sharp differences among social groups on each side of "a legal act of delimitation" (p. 222) of a non-existent natural border that is initially constructed ideologically. Borders are therefore the result of power struggles in which the political will of the most powerful, in this case the white Anglo, is imposed to erode historically constructed cultural and linguistic realities.

To better understand the reasons behind transnationals' interpretations of their individual histories, it is necessary to look at them through Anzaldúa's eyes. Her historical reconstruction of the events which took place during the 1800s along the Mexico–U.S. border helps us to revolutionize the hegemonic perspectives that we have learned from official history curricula and look for alternative and more empowering narratives that can lead to transformed understandings of La Frontera's social and cultural dynamics.

El destierro (Anzaldúa, 2012) recounts the illegal invasion of Anglos into Texas, which at that time was Mexican territory. She describes how "all manner of atrocities" (p. 28) were perpetrated against Tejanos to drive them away from their lands. Moreover, after defeating Mexican forces in 1846, Anglos seized the territory that today constitutes the states of Texas, New Mexico, Arizona, Colorado, and California. Despite signing a treaty that recognized Mexican's ownership of the lands, it was never respected. "The Gringo, locked into the fiction of white superiority, seized complete political power, stripping Mexicans and Indians of their land while their feet were still rooted in it" (p. 29). This stands in sharp contrast with the Anglocentric depiction of the Battle of the Alamo, in which Mexicans are portrayed as cowards and villains and has served as a historical narrative to legitimize the invasion of Mexican territory. In Mexico, official textbooks (free texts that are distributed across the country that contain the national curricula for basic education) tell the story of a war that ends after a villain sold more than half of our territory to the U.S. in 1848, the country's former president Antonio López de Santa Anna. This narrative leaves out important details that precipitated this war, such as the occupation of Mexican territory by undocumented farmers and adventurers from the U.S. since 1823, and how, in 1845, U.S. authorities offered to pay an alleged debt from the Mexican government to U.S. citizens who claimed that Mexican citizens who were the original owners of the land were in debt with them.

Anzaldúa (2012) questions the dominant narrative regarding the understandings of Mexican migration to U.S. territory, whether this is documented or undocumented and conceives it as "the return odyssey to the historical/mythological Aztlán" (p. 33), since she undertakes a historical analysis of this phenomenon without excluding events that took place before 1820 (Alcaraz et al., 1980). Anzaldúa additionally speaks strongly against rigidity or stagnation of the self, "*la resistencia*—resistance to knowing, to letting go" (p. 70), which entails avoiding the possibility of gaining knowledge and a better understanding of the self, condemning it to "death" (p. 100). She highlights that flexibility and the capacity of continuous transformation are two attributes that lead to increased levels of agency and stronger identities: "it is not enough to stand on the opposite riverbank, shouting questions, challenging patriarchal, white conventions" (p. 100). The mestiza consciousness transforms the ways individuals perceive reality and, therefore, the ways they act upon their world.

Methodology

This study adopts a phenomenological approach to analyze the ways in which young transnationals' identities are transformed as a result of migratory transitions in their lives. Phenomenological studies enable deep understandings of common lived experiences of individuals (Moustakas, 1994). In this case, the phenomenon under study is the contact transnationals have with languages, discourses, and cultural practices across borders.

Data for the present study come from several conversations I held during the years 2018 and 2019 with former students of a B.A. program in applied linguistics and colleagues from a language center where I worked at the beginning of my career. These conversations were part of ongoing research that a group of colleagues and I from three different public higher education institutions—two in Mexico and one in the U.S.—had been carrying out on transnationalism, bilingualism, and interculturality. The participants whose conversations are analyzed in this chapter were selected due to the ample details they provided about their experiences and the depth of the reflections they made about those experiences. The interviews took place in different settings that participants chose: two of them were interviewed in a coffee shop and the other two in the home of a mutual friend. Each interview lasted between two and three and a half hours.

My Positionality as a Researcher

As a researcher, I need to disclose the closeness I felt with each of the participants, whom I had known for more than four years at the time of the research. I myself grew up as a child in a multinational community, where speaking English was a gatekeeping tool to have access to privileged learning opportunities. Therefore, when I met students with similar experiences, I became interested in trying to understand the different ways in which migration transitions impacted their lives, their sense of self, and their capacity to act upon their context.

Data Analysis Procedure

To ensure an accurate representation of participants' experiences, Creswell's (2013) simplified version of the Stevick—Colarzzi—Keen method was used. Even though this six-step process involves identifying central themes and then grouping these into categories as most qualitative data analysis procedures, the remaining steps enabled me to reflect on my personal experiences with multilingual communities and leave them aside to focus on the participants' perspectives. In addition, this procedure facilitated the writing of life episodes that included "textural descriptions" (p. 193) of what took place during these meaningful events and "structural descriptions" (p. 194) of how participants experienced these events within a particular context.

Participants

The participants of this study are four young people who, at different stages of their lives, crossed the Mexico–U.S. border: Rosaura and Paloma, who currently live in the U.S. and work as bilingual teachers, and Fernando and Josué, who now live in Mexico and work as interpreters.

Rosaura was born in México and was in constant contact with the language and culture of Texas's southern Rio Grande Valley, since she lived in a city near the border. She studied elementary school in Mexico, and when she was halfway through middle school, her parents registered her at a private school in the U.S. Rio Grande Valley where she interacted with Mexican and American children from middle-class backgrounds. She returned to study her undergraduate degree in Mexico, and after graduating, she began to work for a large transnational company. She moved to the U.S. after marrying a U.S. citizen, and a couple of years later, she began to work as a bilingual teacher. She is currently the Head of the Human Resources Department of a large educational district in Texas, where she has been responsible for bilingual teachers' recruitments for several years.

Paloma was born in a border city in the northeastern region of Mexico. Hers was a low-income family, and her father was a farm worker in southern Texas. When Paloma turned ten, her parents decided to move to the U.S. Texas Rio Grande Valley area. Initially, Paloma and her mother entered the U.S. without immigration documents, but they became legal residents and then U.S. citizens several years later. Paloma was a hard-working committed student. When she finished high school, she actively searched for an opportunity to go to college despite her migratory situation. At that time, she had a work permit that allowed her to remain legally in the U.S., but it did not give her access to student loans or reduced school fees. Paloma looked for help from her school counselors and was awarded a full scholarship for college studies as an international student due to her excellent academic record. She is currently a bilingual primary teacher in southern Texas.

Josué is the second of three siblings and was born in the capital city of a border state in the northeastern region of Mexico by chance. Josué's brothers were born in the U.S., but his parents, who worked in the U.S., had to come to Mexico to take care of a sick relative, which led to an early delivery. Josué's parents remained in Mexico until they could take him to the U.S. when he turned four, where he spent most of his life living in a small town in central Texas. He recalls enjoying school because it was the place where he could play with friends. His home, in contrast, was frequently a lonely place. Josué was forced to return to Mexico in 2012. He was accompanied by his mother and "ended up back in the same *colonia*" where he was born. She helped him settle and tried to find options to take him back to the U.S. However, after several months of living in Mexico, he decided to "stop living in fear," remain in Mexico and major in applied linguistics. This undergraduate program gave him some relief from the emotional shock he reported experiencing after returning to Mexico. He particularly enjoyed being considered a linguistic authority by his peers and helping them learn English. Josué currently works as a translator and interpreter in a state of the northern region of Mexico.

Fernando was born in Mexico and has experienced several migratory movements across the Mexico–U.S. border. He lived in a city near the beach in Mexico until he was three. He and his family moved to a state on the northeastern border of the U.S., where he lived until he turned 11. Fernando recalls being a shy boy full of insecurities because English was not his first language. At 11, he moved back to the northeastern border of Mexico where he faced similar challenges to the ones he faced when moving to the U.S. because he was now fully proficient in English, but his writing and reading skills in Spanish were insufficient to help him succeed in school. After a year and a half, Fernando and his family returned to the U.S., but this time they moved to the Texas Rio Grande Valley where he studied one and a half years of middle school and one year of high school. They returned to Mexico for Fernando's senior year of high school. Like Josué, Fernando majored in applied linguistics. He currently works as an EFL teacher and interpreter in a large city in central Mexico.

El Camino de la Mestiza/The Mestiza Way

The data analysis revealed four larger themes that describe the different stages participants underwent, as they attempted to cope with the challenges that migrating to another country entails. Anzaldúa's (2012) *El camino de la mestiza*/The Mestiza Way represents an analogy of the transformational experiences that the selves of young transnationals endure because of migratory transitions in their lives. Each of the categories presented in the following illustrates distinct stages of participants' selves. The first category depicts how at a certain point of their lives, the participants remained bound to *la resistencia*, denying transformation, experiencing the sharp pain of being an *atravesado*. The second category illustrates that for some of the participants, *taking inventory, despojando, desgranando, quitando paja*, eventually seemed like an almost natural unproblematic event that is experienced without pain.

The third category includes other participants who lived painful ruptures that required *Botar lo que no vale . . . a conscious rupture with all oppressive traditions*. Their narratives include one or several episodes of identity transformation that result from effort and reflection processes. It is through these processes that participants construct stronger identities that enable them to reconfigure their visions of themselves and the world they inhabit. The last category illustrates how participants *transform the small "I" into the total Self. Se hace modeladora de su alma*. Here is where most of the participants' life episodes narrate how they successfully achieved a state of mental nepantilism that makes them feel comfortable with their mestiza identities and embrace the linguistic and cultural wealth that results from this process.

La Resistencia, Ser un Atravesado

Josué vividly recalls being aware that he was an *atravesado* at a very tender age. He started school a couple of months after arriving in the U.S. and describes the experience as "horrible;" he recalls not being understood and feeling distressed because of that "the first three months I was always crying." He felt as an oddity in his school, since most of the students and teachers were white and only two other kids were of Mexican origin in a school of more than 100 students. Going home did not make things easier for Josué, he narrated the following memories:

> At home it was very lonely, because . . . at that time it was only me and my parents. Friends at home were hard to come by, because all the neighbors were . . . white, they were American . . . we were always . . . when I got older, I knew why they were always afraid, we were always . . . precautious, because, um . . . we were illegally

there . . . I just wanted to play, I just wanted to be outside and play but I didn't know there were consequences, if some authorities started asking questions . . . and because of all the racial, the ethnic issues that that country has, that's why they were afraid of interacting with Americans. Because if we do something wrong, the authority comes and everything just goes away.

As Josué narrated more episodes of his life in the U.S., it became clear that schoolteachers and authorities did not understand his personal circumstances. He mentioned that he felt he always struggled with everything because, "at home there's no internet, there's no books, there's no . . . there's nothing, there's just me, what I know and my parents helping." Josué's mother did not finish elementary school and his father only finished the second grade of middle school. As such, it was very challenging for them to help their child learn in a foreign language. The following quote illustrates this issue, "after the first three months, I mean I of course. I can understand people, but you never stop hitting a wall, it's just . . . my walls were always horrible."

Fernando's childhood was similarly difficult and led him to experience feelings of inadequacy and insecurity, since he was always aware that he "did not speak like a native." He was so anxious about himself and his ability to speak "proper" English that he even put his life at risk because of these insecurities as the following extract suggests:

People would ask me, "Do you know how to swim?" But I didn't say anything because I didn't want to speak to anybody because I was nervous. Well, I remember I jumped twice [on the springboard] and then I jumped [into the pool] and all I saw was just water around me . . . I remember when I was drowning, I would see people like playing and jumping in the pool . . . all of a sudden somebody pulled me, I mean he jumped in with clothes . . . I didn't want to speak to anybody because I didn't want to look weird in front of other people.

Josué and Fernando's testimonies illustrate how, at a very tender age, both boys had internalized that their language and culture were different from those of the people in power. They were both native speakers of a language that had been defeated in the late 1800s and the educational system was highly effective "to induce the holders of dominated linguistic competencies to collaborate in the destruction of their instruments of expression" (Bourdieu, 2003, p. 49). This had serious implications for their future lives, as they continued to assimilate into a monolingual linguistic community and gradually stopped learning their mother tongue. The following excerpt illustrates how returning to Mexico made

Fernando feel incapable of learning, since he had stopped developing his Spanish skills:

> But I never did my homework, I mean, first of all because I didn't understand, and secondly, because I didn't know when was *jueves*—Thursday, I mean, I didn't even know what was *jueves*. And I remember Thursday a lot because I was like this for one week, and the teacher saw that my performance was very low and that I did not read or participate, I never raised my hand, I was very insecure . . . and I became even more insecure [Original in Spanish, author's translation].

In Fernando's case, we will analyze in a subsequent category how he is able to overcome his insecurities through conscious reflection in order to get rid of the idea of Anglo superiority he had acquired as a child.

In contrast, Josué shared several memories that can help us better understand the place Anglo and Mestizo identities held in his life. He recalled that in his schools, most of the teaching and managerial positions were held by Anglos while Hispanics were, "the typical janitor or cook." In another life episode, he narrated how he felt "awesome" when he found out that he could use English in the applied linguistics undergraduate program where he had just registered in Mexico. At the time of the interview, Josué continued to resist being in contact with Spanish, even after having lived for more than five years in Mexico and having no plans to return to the U.S., as the following life episode suggests:

> I can't stand staring at the cable and just hearing Spanish it just is just too much. So, I just look for something online [when] it's in English. I talk to my brothers in English, and I just watch like movies or the History channel but it's all in English.

This hampers his possibilities for complete integration into his native country. Josué seems to be avoiding the pain that results from knowing. According to Anzaldúa (2012), it entails gaining conscience, moving forward, and transforming the self. By remaining in *la resistencia*, Josué clings to the language and culture he considers superior and avoids embracing mental nepantilism.

Taking Inventory, *Despojando, Desgranando, Quitando Paja*

Taking inventory, *irse despojando de lo innecesario,* seemed to be an easier task for those participants who moved to the U.S. at a later age such as Rosaura and Paloma. Their transition seemed less traumatic than that of Josué and Fernando. Both participants reported experiencing difficulties during their first year of school, but they easily developed strategies that helped them to cope with the challenges they were facing. For example, Paloma recalls that when she first arrived in the U.S. at the age of ten, she was placed in a monolingual classroom where she began to have difficulties. However, she was promptly transferred to a bilingual class where she took classes in both languages.

Rosaura's experience was also similar because some of her classmates came from Mexico, just like her. During her interview, Rosaura expressed that she always felt curious about *"el otro lado"* and seemed to be very aware that the U.S. was not her country, and she was a stranger there:

> And as I mention it here, we are the stranger ones. We don't . . . we are coming to a place, we are like the intruders, aren't we? And for them, the strange ones, the weird ones are us, so, where do they set their eyes? On us. [Original in Spanish, author's translation].

This excerpt expresses Rosaura's willingness to reinvent herself, to get rid of what is unnecessary to become part of this new society, though perhaps at the cost of some sort of historical amnesia, which is not an Anzalduan recommendation. Her initial reflections revolve around the role of language in placing newcomers as insiders or outsiders of a community.

> The accent, that is a tremendous insecurity for most of the people, they don't want to speak, not everyone, but we don't want to speak. At the beginning it is a very strong barrier for most of us. But then they feel. What do they feel? What happens with the accent? I mean, embarrassment, we are ashamed of the accent, and . . . the syntax too, we say things in the wrong order [Original in Spanish, author's translation].

Rosaura never seemed to question the linguistic and cultural hierarchies established by Anglos in Texas during the 1800s; on the contrary, she seemed to fully embrace the current status quo and clearly identified the strongest cultural and linguistic barriers toward her integration into the community; this enabled her to take steps to actively address these issues to transform "living in the Borderlands from a nightmare to a numinous experience" (Anzaldúa, 2012, p. 95). A similar perspective is expressed by Paloma, who describes the process of looking for funding for her undergraduate studies assuming an empowered position despite her circumstances:

> My parents could not help me in that way, and everything depended on me asking questions. In fact, my mom did not know how to read,

she knows a little more now because I am teaching her. I was the one who had to translate and fill out the paperwork [Original in Spanish, author's translation].

Cortina (2010) interprets Anzaldúa's proposal throughout her work is to take what will help you be better and fulfilled and reject anything that restricts or annuls you, *despojar, quitar paja*. She similarly places emphasis on helping others once you have helped yourself. This is precisely what Paloma managed to achieve even though at that time her migratory situation was far from ideal. She decided to overlook her challenging circumstances and focus on her good grades and bilingual proficiency to obtain a full scholarship as an international student.

Bota lo que no Vale . . . A Conscious Rupture With All Oppressive Traditions

In this category, participants reflect on how they opted for making oppressive ideas aside, and how this led to stronger selves that acted upon their contexts more confidently. In this extract, Fernando describes the role that English and Spanish have played in the construction of his identity. Each language occupies a unique space and serves a particular purpose in his life; English is the language for learning, while Spanish is the language for socializing and developing a unique self.

> I see English as more "formal," I do not know if [it is a] "requirement" or "intellectual." The thing is that when I started going out more, and having more friends, I became very sociable in Mexico. The United States was more academic, I did have friends and all, but to be honest we didn't talk much. I never needed the language in the United States as much as I needed it in Mexico, I used to be more to myself there, as if . . . I had no identity [Original in Spanish, author's translation].

Just like Fernando in Mexico, Paloma and her colleagues in Texas decided to overlook discriminatory attitudes and developed a strong support community to face issues such as racism in their working environments. Hispanic teachers (as they identified themselves) constituted a close-knit collaborative community that centered its attention on helping their students overcome the challenges that this borderland imposed on them.

> They are Anglo teachers from regular classrooms, sometimes I do not know if it is jealousy or they are a little bit racist but [the behaviors range] from laughing of the way we pronounce or if we said the wrong word up to [saying], "look your kids seem very filthy," and

discrimination will always exist, always and everywhere, and schools are no exception. Our kids receive less help in the remedial programs they develop. They tell us, "No, your kids cannot attend because they do not understand English, your exams are not in English," therefore we need to look for support in parents. They are just like Mexican parents, you know how they are, as family [Original in Spanish, author's translation].

Anzalduan works challenged hegemonic discourses; specifically, the Nepantla construct is synchronous with fruitful and eclectic alliances such as the ones these teachers seem to be creating to empower their learning communities (Cortina, 2010). This transnational learning community opted for avoiding "shouting questions, challenging patriarchal, white conventions," (Anzaldúa, 2012, p. 100) and instead reinvented itself as an empowered learning community.

Transform the Small "I" Into the Total Self. Se Hace Modeladora de su Alma

The last category highlights two excerpts in which participants reflect upon how life events led to identity transformations. These processes were experienced with varying degrees of pain and rupture and led both Fernando and Rosaura to achieve a state of mental nepantilism where they could embrace both cultures and languages.

In Fernando's case, his ability to reconstruct painful and traumatic events enabled him to bestow these memories with new meanings that not only helped him heal, but also brought him joy and the possibility to help others (Anzaldúa, 2012).

> *Creo que mi vida batallando con el idioma fue lo que influenció mi deseo de ser intérprete . . .* [I think that my life struggling with language was what influenced my desire to become an interpreter . . .] because I had a lot of like I don´t know if it was like psychological problems like due to like . . . acceptancy and like I don't know like insecurities and stuff like that. At the end of the day, it's like wow okay all of this happened for a reason and it's incredibly cool how I understand people [who struggle learning a language], I kind of know what they're going through.

Fernando's childhood insecurities are transformed into feelings of empathy and understanding now that he has become an interpreter and is frequently faced with English language teaching situations. The reinterpretation he makes of those memories highlights the fluid nature of identities. This excerpt similarly seems to indicate that Fernando's next step to achieving an empowered identity is to help his students overcome the fear of acquiring a new language.

Rosaura's identity journey toward mental nepantilism seemed less difficult. Since she had less pain to heal from her memories, her nepantilism was accompanied by a desire to help others who may be embarking on a similar journey.

> Latinos, believe me, come with a tremendous strength, that is why I want them to take out that strength and express it in the ways they act, in the ways they speak, they shouldn't feel ashamed . . . the most important is for us to be connected to the culture of our bilingual students, and that we are willing to integrate the new culture, embrace both cultures and develop self-esteem in children, they need to feel that they belong and love both cultures, that they belong there but they also occupy a special place here [Original in Spanish, Author's translation].

This last excerpt seems to recall Anzaldúa's words in Joysmith and Lomas' (2005) text "this country's real battle is with its shadow—its racism, propensity for violence, rapacity for consuming, neglect for its responsibility for global communities and the environment, and unjust treatment of dissenters and disenfranchised, especially people of color" (p. 93). Rosaura, as someone who is married to an Anglo, seems to be actively making her part of tending bridges across cultures and helping her own community feel capable and empowered within the Borderlands.

Conclusions

Anzaldúa's *El camino de la mestiza*/The mestiza way metaphor facilitated the identification of the range of individual identity configurations that can occur from participants' contact with various discourses about language and race. After migrating to the U.S., all participants faced racism, discrimination, and otherization. They were likewise socialized in cultural and linguistic contexts where their mother tongue was associated with defeat, powerlessness, and lack of education, whereas English was assigned the role of power and education. This discourse negatively impacted the selves and subjectivities of those participants who were in touch with it at earlier ages and for longer periods of time. These participants not only stopped learning their mother tongue but actively decided to remain monolingual in English even after returning to Mexico. Participants who decided to remain in *la resistencia* faced more significant difficulties with integrating into their new social communities fully. They also seemed unwilling to engage in reflection that enabled them to transform their understandings of "living in the Borderlands from a nightmare to a numinous experience" (Anzaldúa, 2012, p. 95).

In contrast, those participants who decided to embark on *la travesía* were more willing to reinvent themselves by identifying the strongest linguistic barriers toward their integration into a new society. These participants seemed to be better equipped to take inventory, get rid of the unnecessary, and assume empowered positions despite their personal circumstances. Oppressive ideas regarding Anglo superiority and Mestizo inferiority were actively resisted and put aside by these participants. This led to stronger selves that acted upon their contexts more confidently. Another salient characteristic of young migrants who embarked on *la travesía* was the little power they gave to the discriminatory and racist discourses and attitudes they encountered at the Borderlands; they decided instead to use their agency to construct bridges and reinvent themselves as a learning community that seemed to lead to the empowerment of all its members, their pupils, and parents.

Sadly, something that remained absent in participants' narratives was the bridge that could connect Mestiza and Anglo cultures. These participants seemed to be tending bridges among Mestizos, but there was no evidence of any kind of connection to Anglos other than now they inhabited their territory. Let us not forget Anzaldúa's words "abre los ojos, North America, open your eyes, look at your shadow and listen to your soul" (Joysmith & Lomas, 2005, p. 94). This phrase invites us to reflect on the implications of research carried out within Anzaluduan analytical frameworks for our understandings of identity and education.

The testimonies shared by participants in this research highlight the power that childhood language learning experiences have on the construction of identity. The participants whose mother tongue and culture were made invisible during educational experiences seemed to have suffered more traumatic learning events at the expense of their levels of agency. In contrast, those who were educated in bilingual and bicultural programs were more capable of resisting racism and otherization and of creating empowered communities. The disadvantage of bilingual/bicultural approaches to education is that they place emphasis on two cultures and languages coexisting in the same territory, creating a divided society such as the one described by participants.

It is therefore of utmost importance to reflect on the importance that intercultural, multilingual, and transnational educational approaches could have for both countries. Educational approaches within these perspectives may help to overcome the division that currently exists between Mestizos and Anglos, people of color and whites, Spanish and English, by generating shared identities that are constructed through learning experiences that stem from more egalitarian notions of knowledge construction where heterogeneity is celebrated (Schmelkes, 2006). This is a highly complex task, since it entails a thorough involvement with the specific characteristics of each context. MacDonald and O'Regan (2012) have suggested that an emphasis on the constitution of "locales" and the power struggles that emerge from "the historical and discursive forces in which the participants are embedded" (p. 564) may shed further light not only into the shaping of learning experiences, but also on the methodological approaches that are employed to investigate the impact of such experiences on learners identities.

References

Aguilar Pariente, R. (2011). *Social and political consequences of stereotypes related to racial phenotypes in Mexico*. CIDE.

Alcaraz, R., Barreiro, A., Castillo, J. M., Escalante, F. M., Iglesias, J. M., Muñoz, M., Ortiz, R., Payno, M., Prieto, G., Ramírez, I., Saborio, N., Schiafino, F., Segura, F., Torrescano, P. M., y Urquidi, F. (1980). *Apuntes para la historia de la guerra entre México y los Estados Unidos*. (Edición facsimilar de la de 1848). Siglo XXI.

Anzaldúa, G. (2012). *Borderlands: The new mestiza: 25th anniversary*. Aunt Lute Books.

Block, D. (2013). The structure and agency Dilemma in identity and intercultural communication research. *Language and Intercultural Communication, 13*(2), 126–147. https://doi.org/10.1080/14708477.2013.770863

Borges, G., Breslau, J., Orozco, R., Tancredi, D. J., Anderson, H., Aguilar-Gaxiola, S., & Mora, M. E. M. (2011). A cross-national study on Mexico-US migration, substance use and substance use disorders. *Drug and Alcohol Dependence, 117*(1), 16–23.

Bourdieu, P. (1991). *Language and symbolic power*. Harvard University Press.

Bourdieu, P. (2003). *Language and symbolic power*. Harvard University Press.

Brack, G. M. (1970). Mexican opinion, American racism, and the War of 1846. *The Western Historical Quarterly, 1*(2), 161–174.

Cantú, N. E., Gutiérrez, C. L., Alarcón, N., & Urquijo-Ruiz, R. (2010). *El mundo zurdo: Selected works from the meetings of the society for the study of Gloria Anzaldúa 2007 & 2009*. Aunt Lute Books.

Cantú, N. E., & Hurtado, A. (2007). Introduction to the fourth edition. In G. Anzaldúa (Ed.) (2012). *Borderlands: The new mestiza: 25th anniversary*. Aunt Lute Books.

Consejo Nacional de Población [CONAPO]. (2016). *Prontuario sobre movilidad y migración internacional*. Dimensiones del fenómeno en México. www.gob.mx/cms/uploads/attachment/file/192258/Prontuario_movilidad_y_migraci_n_internacional_Parte1.pdf

Cortina, G. (2010). Andamos huyendo, Gloria. Academia, fronteras y la nueva mestiza. In N. Cantú, C. Gutiérrez, N. Alarcón, & R. Urqijo-Ruiz (Eds.), *El mundo zurdo. Selected works from the meetings of the society for the study of Gloria Anzaldúa* (1st ed., pp. 43–56). Aunt Lute Books.

Creswell, J. (2013). *Qualitative inquiry and research design: Five different approaches*. Sage.

Dixon, D., Murray, J., & Gelatt, G. (2006). America's emigrants: US retirement migration to Mexico and Panamá. *Migration Policy Institute.* www.migrationpolicy.org/pubs/americas_emigrants.pdf

Donato, K. M., & Perez, S. L. (2017). Crossing the Mexico-US border: Illegality and children's migration to the United States. *RSF: The Russell Sage Foundation Journal of the Social Sciences, 3*(4), 116–135.

Durand, J. (2000). Tres premisas para entender y explicar la migración México-Estados Unidos. *Relaciones Estudios de Historia y Sociedad, 21*(83), 18–35.

Encuesta Nacional de la Dinámica Demográfica [ENADID]. (2018). *ENADID 2018-Migración Internacional.* www.gob.mx/conapo/documentos/enadid-2018-migracion-internacional-202155

Feliciano, C., & Lanuza, Y. R. (2017). An immigrant paradox? Contextual attainment and intergenerational educational mobility. *American Sociological Review, 82*(1), 211–241.

Fry, W. (2019). *Americans make up Mexico's largest demographic of immigrants.* The San Diego Union Tribune. www.sandiegouniontribune.com/news/border-baja-california/story/2019-06-15/americans-make-up-mexicos-largest-demographic-of-immigrants

Hanson, G. H. (2006). Illegal migration from Mexico to the United States. *Journal of Economic Literature, 44*(4), 869–924.

Heyman, J. (2017). Contributions of US-Mexico border studies to social science theory. In C. G. Vélez-Ibáñez & J. Heyman (Eds.), *The US-Mexico transborder region: Cultural dynamics and historical interaction* (pp. 44–64). University of Arizona Press.

Heyman, J. (2018). *The shadow of the wall: violence and migration on the US-Mexico border.* University of Arizona Press.

Jacobo, M., & Jensen, B. (2018). Schooling for US-citizen students in Mexico. *Civil Rights Project, UCLA.* www.civilrightsproject.ucla.edu/research/k-12-education/immigration-immigrant-students/when-families-are-deported-schooling-for-us-citizen-students-in-mexico/Schooling-for-US-Citizens_Jacobo-and-Jensen_June19.pdf

Joysmith, C., & Lomas, C. (Eds.). (2005). *One wound for another/Una herida por otra. Testimonios de latinos in the US through cyberspace (11 de septiembre de 2001–11 de marzo de 2002).* CISAN—UNAM/The Colorado College/Whittier College México, Colorado Springs and Whittier.

Knobloch, A. (2020). *Cada vez más estadounidenses se mudan a México.* DW. www.dw.com/es/cada-vez-m%C3%A1s-estadounidenses-se-mudan-a-m%C3%A9xico/a-52614792

Lizárraga Morales, O. (2008). La inmigración de jubilados estadounidenses en México y sus prácticas transnacionales: Estudio de caso en Mazatlán, Sinaloa y Cabo San Lucas, Baja California Sur. *Migración y Desarrollo,* (11), 97–117.

Lotman, J. (2009). *Culture and explosion.* Walter de Gruyter.

MacDonald, M. N., & O'Regan, J. P. (2012). A global agenda for intercultural communication research and practice. In *The Routledge handbook of language and intercultural communication* (pp. 559–573). Routledge.

Mark, M. (2019). *More people are moving from the US to Mexico than the other way around.* Business Insider. www.businessinsider.com/number-of-people-moving-from-us-to-mexico-2019-5?r=MX&IR=T

Masferrer, C., Hamilton, E. R., & Denier, N. (2019). Immigrants in their parental homeland: Half a million US-born minors settle throughout Mexico. *Demography, 56*(4), 1453–1461.

Menchaca, M. (1993). Chicano Indianism: A historical account of racial repression in the United States. *American Ethnologist, 20*(3), 583–603.

Miller, K. (2016). Education across borders: The relationship between age at migration and educational attainment for Mexico-US child migrants. *Teachers College Record, 118*(1), 1–48.

Montaño, A. M. P., & Cervantes, C. A. D. (2017). Población extranjera residente en México. Caracterización socio-demográfica y laboral 1990–2010. *Entorno Geográfico,* (14), 8–32.

Montoya Zavala, E. C., Herrera García, M. C., & Jiménez Díaz, I. D. (2020). Retorno de jóvenes transnacionales. Experiencias migratorias y fondos de identidad. *Relaciones. Estudios de historia y sociedad, 41*(161), 66–90.

Mora Vázquez, A., Trejo Guzmán, N. P., & Mora-Pablo, I. (2018). 'I was lucky to be a bilingual kid, and that makes me who I am:" The role of transnationalism in identity issues. *International Journal of Bilingual Education and Bilingualism.* https://doi.org/10.1080/13670050.2018.1510893

Moustakas, C. (1994). *Phenomenological research methods.* Sage.

Norton, B. (2013). *Identity and language learning: Extending the conversation.* Multilingual Matters.

Ortiz, V., & Telles, E. (2012). Racial identity and racial treatment of Mexican Americans. *Race and Social Problems, 4*(1), 41–56.

Provine, D. M. (2013). Institutional racism in enforcing immigration law. *Norteamérica, 8*(suplement), 31–53.

Rojas, A. G. (2019). Estadounidenses en México: por qué cada vez más deciden mudarse pese a la campaña de Trump contra el país. *BBC News.* www.bbc.com/mundo/noticias-america-latina-48998509

Schmelkes, S. (2006). La interculturalidad en la educación básica. *Revista Prelac, 3,* 120–127.

Sheridan, M. B. (2019). The little-noticed surge across the US-Mexico border: It's Americans, heading south. *The Washington Post.* www.washingtonpost.com/world/the_americas/the-little-noticed-surge-across-the-us-mexico-border-its-americans-heading-south/2019/05/18/7988421e-6c28-11e9-bbe7-1c798fb80536_story.html

Tuirán, R., & Ávila, J. L. (2013). Migración calificada entre México-Estados Unidos: Desafíos y opciones de política. *Migración y Desarrollo, 11*(21), 43–63.

Wise, R. D. (2015). Unravelling highly skilled migration from Mexico in the context of neoliberal globalization. In S. Castles, D. Ozkul, & M. Cubas (Eds.), *Social transformation and migration* (pp. 201–217). Palgrave Macmillan.

Chapter 2

Nepantla as Resistance for Transnational Youth in Northern Mexico

Sandra Candel

Introduction

There are more than 600,000 transnational, U.S. citizen youth currently living in Mexico due to return migration (Jarvis, 2019), oftentimes through deportation. This is in addition to other youth who may have returned without U.S. citizenship. After a deportation, many families move to border cities in northern Mexico hoping to return to the U.S. (e.g., de León, 2015). This relocation has detrimental consequences for children who, despite being U.S. citizens, are forced to leave with their parents. These children experience an unfamiliar language, a foreign culture, and unsupportive educational policies (Sierra & López, 2013). For purposes of this study, children with life experiences in the U.S. and Mexico will be referred to as transnational youth. Noticing this trend of return migration but to a foreign-to-them town, this chapter follows the trajectory of Hans and Peter, two brothers who moved to a city located south of the U.S.–Mexico border after the deportation of their mother Elsa in 2014. Theirs is a story of *nepantla* as resistance, where *nepantla* is understood as "a strategy for adapting, accepting, and rejecting, as a way of cultural survival, as a way of resisting the mainstream" (Posada, n.d.). This also draws from Anzaldúa's notion of *nepantla* as inhabiting the in-between, even when such work is complicated and at times requires resistance (Anzaldúa, 1987).

Gathering Transnational Youth's Narratives

The author examined the educational trajectories of U.S.-born children who were forced to attend schools in Mexico due to parental deportation in a study that took place between March and October of 2017 (Candel, 2017). This chapter focuses on two participants, brothers Hans,[1] age 12,[2] and Peter, age 10, who moved to Tijuana, located three miles south from the U.S.–Mexico border, after the deportation of their mother. The study took place at the *Programa Binacional de Educación*

DOI: 10.4324/9781003191575-4

Migrante (PROBEM), a government organization that is part of the state educational system. PROBEM's main objective is to identify transnational students statewide in order to provide them with educational and psychological support so that they can keep a record of transnational students and their needs.

Before continuing, the author invokes her positionality to help guide the reader in understanding both the author's motivations and points of entry into this work. As a Mexican immigrant and feminist scholar, the author's identity influenced the development of this chapter, the interpretation of findings, and the framing of this work within Anzalduan thought. The author, born in Guadalajara, Mexico, is a mother scholar (e.g., Lapayese, 2012) of color who came to the United States as a young adult to obtain a college degree. She has ample knowledge of the Mexican K-12 and the U.S. higher education systems and can understand firsthand the transnational experience.

The author and participants engaged in testimonios in recognition of the depths of confianza she developed with the participants. The author felt that testimonios were more appropriate for this project for two reasons: first, "testimonio differs from oral history . . . in that it involves the critical reflection of their personal experience within particular sociopolitical realities" (Delgado Bernal et al., 2012, p. 364), aligning with earlier definitions of testimonio which recognize that the teller speaks on behalf of a group who has survived (or not) forms of systemic oppression (e.g., Beverly, 2000). Second, the uprooting of U.S.-born students is a form of social trauma; therefore, testimonios can have a healing effect. Anzaldúa (2015) "identifies storytelling with healing and associates it with progressive and sociopolitical change" (p. xxxii). Furthermore, in the re-telling of events, people often reshape their narratives (Davis & Craven, 2016). Thematic analysis was used to analyze data. In the step-by-step guide developed by Braun and Clarke (2006), thematic analysis patterns are identified through a rigorous process that begins with data familiarization, continues with the development of codes, and is followed by the development, revision, and definition of themes. The process ends with a narrative that contextualizes the themes.

Anzaldúa embedded the concept of *nepantla* as part of her seven stages of *conocimiento* (2000a). *Conocimiento* literally means "knowledge and skill" (Anzaldúa, 2000b, p. 206) and "ways of knowing" (Anzaldúa, 2000b, p. 266). Anzaldúa drew from her experience of having lived in several borderlands, from those of sexuality to racial identification to physical borders of growing up Chicana in South Texas. One of her clearest definitions of *conocimiento* is:

> My term for an overarching theory of consciousness, of how the mind works. It's an epistemology that tries to encompass all the dimensions of life, both inner—mental, emotional, instinctive, imaginal,

> spiritual, bodily realms—and outer—social, political, lived experiences . . . you could say that conocimiento is basically an awareness, the awareness of facultad that sees through all human acts whether of the individual mind and spirit or of the collective, social body. The work of conocimiento—consciousness work—connects the inner life of the mind and spirit to the outer worlds of action.
> (Hérnández-Ávila & Anzaldúa, 2000, p. 177)

Anzaldúa shows that knowing is not only about what can be ascertained from only the five senses, but also other forms of perception. She highlights a collective way of knowing, demonstrating that forms of knowledge are contextually and culturally influenced. Anzaldúa explains that her theory is one that ruptures the subject/object divide which has been the pervasive and colonizing result of enlightenment thinking (Anzaldúa, 2002, p. 541). Anzaldúa wrote we are experiencing a "personal, global identity crisis in a disintegrating social order that possesses little heart and functions to oppress people by organizing them in hierarchies of power" (Ibid, p. 541). Her theory of *conocimiento* highlights ways of working toward healing this crisis through knowing, imagining, and acting (Keating, 2006), drawing from her own *conocimiento*, rooted in seven stages (Anzaldúa, 2002), *nepantla* being in among the middle stages, ending in spiritual and social transformation when one cycle might have engaged all seven stages.

With this sense of Anzaldúa's work on *nepantla* and *conocimiento* in mind, the author of this chapter explained to youth participants that this would be a very personal narrative about their migration to Mexico and that they would have freedom in their choice of topics and methods. They were given the choice to write a journal, make a video, tell their story through pictures, or meet with me. Since they said they were not sure what to write about, they chose to meet with me for a more guided session. Data obtained from testimonios helped to capture the complexity of transnational youth's educational experiences, the expectations and negative stereotypes put on them for being perceived as outsiders in a monocultural monolinguistic society, and the creative ways in which they picked and chose strategic aspects of their identity, choosing to be American in some instances, and Mexican in others according to the situation, and language, speaking English to his peers when requested to help them gain acceptance. Negotiating and resisting through *nepantla* allowed them to not only adapt, but to find a new sense of normalcy and happiness brought about by family reunification in their new Tijuana home.

Our Collective Learning

Despite a growing number of families being deported, there is surprisingly little research focusing on deportation. The fact that almost no one is paying attention to this population was the motivation to conduct this study in hopes that this research would give participants the opportunity to share their experiences in Mexico. While most research has focused on the experiences of undocumented immigrants in the U.S., the findings in this study examine how language, nationality, and identity are used to navigate and negotiate their in-between spaces as those who engage *nepantla*. While identity restricts their access to academic spaces due to negative stereotypes, language gives them access to a reserved status available only to native English-speakers. Findings also revealed that being "*del norte*" carried a set of expectations and assumptions, for example, that their choice of clothes revealed their allegiance to gangs because that's what they do in "*el otro lado.*"

Hans and Peter's Story of Migration: The Harsh Realities of Deportation

Hans and Peter were born in Southern California. They lived with their mother, their older sister, and their older brother. Although the children had a difficult life in California, they reported being "happy" despite their limited resources. Elsa was a single mother who had to hold several jobs in order to support her two young and two teenage children, and they lived a modest life in terms of material wealth together until they were forced to return to Mexico in 2014. With no family members able to care for the children in California after the deportation of their mother, Hans, then nine years old, and Peter, then seven years old, along with their older sister had no choice but to move to Mexico while their oldest brother managed to stay in California. This separation from their oldest brother was very painful for them.

Elsa's deportation story (Candel & Marrun, 2020) is so dramatic and heartbreaking that it deserves special attention so that we can contextualize the degree of resilience required on the part of Hans and Peter, and the influence this traumatic event had in how they made sense of their world after deportation. Elsa, a 35-year-old mother of four, ages 10 to 18,[3] was born in Tijuana but migrated north with the father of her then two small children when she was only 19. She eventually separated from her husband, who did not provide any type of financial support for their children. Being an undocumented single mother, she was unable to provide for her family even after working 12–14 hours cleaning houses and waitressing tables at a local restaurant. A decline in her health due to the long hours she worked forced her to quit her jobs and put food on the table by all means possible. That included accepting a proposition by a friend to deliver small amounts of drugs to local clients. She admits that the money was easy to earn, and she never saw the contents of the small packages they delivered. However, after a few months, she decided to get out of this illegal work, but it was too late. One December morning, she was caught by the authorities. Elsa remembers:

> When I get out of the car, I look back and I see a fleet of police cars, FBI, with guns. They did not let me speak, they threw me to the floor, they handcuffed me, and [told me] that I did not have the right to speak until I had an attorney, and they did not let me get my belongings, they took away my cell phone, they took away my purse, and they destroyed the car. When my children knew where I was, my mom tells me that my oldest woke up at night and he banged all the walls [participant starts weeping heavily]. My daughter began to cut her hands, the two youngest, Hans and Peter, cried a lot, they'd say that they wanted to see me, that they missed their home.

Elsa received a deportation order and was banned from entering the United States for life with the threat of years in prison if she were apprehended trying to re-renter. She moved to Tijuana in 2014, and after a few months, her children followed, except for the oldest, who was already 18 and decided to remain in the U.S. by himself.

Hans and Peter have vivid memories about the moment they learned they had to move to Mexico. Peter explains:

> They deported my mom to Mexico. I got a letter when I was in school that they got me out of there and when I went home, I had all my things and they said I was going to Mexico with my mom. I didn't like the feel of it 'cause I knew that something was going to change.

Hans also shared the moment he learned they were moving to Mexico, and his first impressions once they got to their destination. Hans remembered:

> I was coming out of school and they told me, "Your mom's in jail." I thought it was a prank or something . . . trying to scare me, so I didn't believe them. When I got to the house where we used to live everything, the bed and everything was broken . . . I started crying at first but then at one point I realized, why cry if one of these days I'm going to see her, or I'm going to see her again. I was seven, six years old when I barely came [to Mexico], my grandma came for us, we stayed in a garage, my aunt's garage, for a couple months, then she told us to pack, I didn't know what for, I didn't ask, I just came. When I first got here, I cried because I saw my mom. That was the first time I came. When they told me that we're here, the streets were kind of different and the words were in Spanish and

back then, I didn't know how to write or talk in Spanish. That was the first time I came. I didn't really like it though, because I left a lot of friends.

For Hans, this can be considered Anzaldúa's first stage of *conocimiento*, *el arrebato*, the rupture of what was once known (Anzaldúa, 2000a), and we see how he shifts into *nepantla* of the in-between of not knowing language toward learning more Spanish.

Life in Mexico was hard at first for both siblings. Aside from the trauma caused from the sudden uprooting from their birthplace and the traumatic circumstances under which it took place, the brothers had to adapt to a new country, a new city, a new neighborhood, a new home, a new school, and a new extended family. In addition, they also struggled with the language, since they were unable to speak fluent Spanish. Hans and Peter's journey of learning Spanish and adapting to Mexican culture led them to using the state of *nepantla* as resistance, as evidenced in their testimonios.

Nepantla as Resistance: Negotiating the "In-Between"

Hans and Peter use language and nationality to navigate a space in which they have to adapt to their new reality in Mexico, accepting and rejecting aspects of their identity to help them find a sense of belonging and acceptance, while at the same time using identity as a way of cultural survival. They are perceived as being "*del norte*" and, as such, they are expected to display certain attributes while at the same time being excused for certain behaviors. Their "otherness" is a *nepantla* state that is at the same time restricting and liberating, and school is the site where this *nepantlismo* takes place.

Being From "*El Otro Lado*"

In Mexico, being from "*el otro lado*" came with a set of expectations, stereotypical views, and negative connotations for Hans, as is often the case for returnees going back to Mexico (e.g., Kasun & Mora-Pablo, this volume). Unfortunately, far from being a safe haven for him, school became a place of contention. Some teachers showed a great degree of insensitivity toward him, refusing to offer any additional help or differentiated instruction. Elsa remembered her experience with Hans's teachers as follows:

> [Hans's] teacher scolded him all the time, she did not allow him to go to recess.

He did not finish the work they had him do. That was his first day of school. The teacher knew the situation. She knew that he did not speak Spanish well, she was well aware that he did not write absolutely any Spanish. Then Hans would cry every day when he had to go to school.

Hans' mother tried to remedy the situation by switching him to a different school, but the issue persisted, and Hans had to experience this humiliation over again. As a result, his self-esteem was visibly damaged. It was obvious that he was cautious not to speak too much during his participation in this research. Once he warmed up during our interactions, the author understood why when he shared: "[The teacher] would make fun of me 'cause I don't know Spanish, and he laughed at me in front of everyone and embarrassed me . . . in front of everybody in class." This was corroborated by his mother, who shared that many times Hans complained that if the teacher asked him something and he was unable to pronounce it or he did not know to answer, everybody made fun of him. Hans said, "I'd rather get a zero than to answer because the teacher always sends me to the principal's office, and everybody makes fun of me."

Once Hans entered *secundaria* [middle school], the expectations of what he could and could not do because he was a foreigner became another obstacle to overcome. His teacher complained that Hans was too arrogant, that he talked back, and that he made fun of classmates when they were in class. His mother tried to explain that Hans' behavior was in part because of his attention-deficit hyperactivity disorder (ADHD); however, she was dismissed, and Hans' teacher simply stated, "But here he's not supposed to do that, you're used to something else because *él es del otro lado* [he's from the other side, meaning, he was born in the U.S.]" Even the way Hans dressed was cause for his teachers to make stereotypical remarks. For example, a teacher once told his mother that Hans resembled a U.S. gang member because of the clothes he wore, adding contemptuously, "because in the U.S. it's the only thing that you see, gang members." To which Elsa, replied:

> Well, that's your point of view, what can I say? I can say the same thing about Mexico but I did not come to criticize others, I came here against my will, but we're here and that does not mean I'm here to criticize other people's children or your children. I'm not here to criticize anybody, but if that is your perspective about my son, *ni modo* [too bad].

The teachers in Mexico, like the one mentioned earlier, often were unwilling to see how and why Hans might have been different, expecting him to readily fit into a cultural performance that was premade prior to his arrival. Unlike Anzaldúa's *conocimiento*, these teachers were not willing to engage difficult stages of growth and knowing.

Language and Nationality as Currency

Language and nationality for Hans and Peter acted as some kind of currency. Speaking fluent English and being "Americans" gave them a competitive advantage over their Mexico-born, Spanish-speaking peers and positioned them in a somewhat privileged position. With their knowledge of English and their being born in the U.S. came some respect and recognition.

Hans described when and how he had to negotiate the in-betweens of his new context and reality while at school, saying:

> When I first got into the elementary school and when the people around me knew I was from the U.S. they were kind of excited. They would normally talk to me but there were also some kids from sixth grade, firth, that were trying to step up on me. They would call me "gringo," they would call me "stupid," they would call me a lot of bad words that I didn't even understand because I came from the other side and they were making fun of me. Some kids were trying to protect me but not much of a hope, so yeah. I honestly don't know why, I never asked them. I don't really care; I just ignored them. I don't really care what other people think about me.

Despite this seeming rejection, Hans' classmates were also fascinated with his persona. Hans's appearance was different from the local kids in that he apparently looked like a U.S. "*cholo*" [gang member] as described by his teachers. However, Hans was popular among his peers, as commented by a teacher who said, "Wherever he goes, all the other children try to imitate him, and what he does." Hans was aware of this popularity but did not necessarily welcome it, as indicated by his remarks:

> Honestly, I don't want to be like others'cause the other kids they're trying to be like little gangsters. I make fun of them because it's kind of stupid when they do gangs because they're little kids, they don't even know what they want. I don't even know what I want! It's just kind of stupid because they think they're all that, and I mean it's all right if they're gangster but when something happens or if happens to them what are people going to know what they risk their life for? What's their purpose for being a gang member if when you die what are you going to be recognized for? for being a drug addict or for being someone hopeful in life?

Then, Hans made a chilling revelation as he started his own reflection, saying:

> Sometimes I imagine myself, what would happen if I did drugs? A lot of people would try to find me, cops would be following me, there would be other people trying to kill me too, and I think about, so, what happens if I die too, so I get kind of scared when I think about that. If there's another life, if everything just goes white, I just think about that and sometimes I tell myself, "**I'm not going to last that long.**" [Emphasis added].

When I asked Hans what he would like to be recognized and remembered for, he replied:

> The things that I have been doing, or the good things that I've done; not the bad things that I didn't do. The good things, like, I can't see someone crying because it gets me kind of sad or sometimes I try to hold them or when I see a person that's hungry and if I have food, I would honestly just give it to them 'cause I know I can get more 'cause I have everything I need already, so if I see someone in the streets I would honestly I would give them what they would need, I would give them money if I had to.

Language for Hans came at a price. Speaking English afforded him attention, often unwanted. Hans shares how his peers used to seek him with requests such as, "How do you say bad words [in English]?" But Hans would refuse to comply, finding creative ways to get kids off his back, as he shared, "I don't tell them how to say that. I tell them weird things, random stuff, I don't really tell them bad words." Hans made fascinating revelations about language and identity in our conversation in the following:

Author: It was really interesting to me that you said when you speak Spanish . . .
Hans: I don't feel like myself.
Author: You don't feel like yourself. Wow! What does that mean?
Hans: That when I talk in Spanish I don't know why but I feel like a different person because I'm really used to talking English. I had, I think I had like five, seven years over there talking in English and when I talk in Spanish I feel like a different person because it's a different language and sometimes I ask myself "why do people talk different languages? Why can't we all just talk in one single language?"
Author: And what language would that be?
Hans: English. [Laughs effusively] Because for me English is easier.

Author: If you don't feel like yourself in Spanish, if I were to ask you What are you? Are you American? Are you Mexican? How do you feel? What do you feel you are?

Hans: Actually, I ask myself the same question, if I'm Mexican, if I'm American, and I don't really know. My mom normally says I'm Mexican, my sister says I'm American, and my brother says I'm just a weirdo [Chuckles].

Author: But what do YOU say?

Hans: Sometimes I feel like if I'm Mexican, sometimes I feel like I'm American so honestly I would like to be a Mexican because my whole family is Mexican too, all of them. It's only me, my brother and a little bit of cousins that are Americans, but. I don't really think, I don't have nothing against Americans, I think it's kind of better to be Mexican. Honestly.

Author: Do you know the word identity?

Hans: I've been through a lot, so, identity is a big word.

Author: Well, you know? That kind of is an identity too! You've been through a lot, and yet you're still doing well, you're here, like you're a pretty decent kid, you already told me you don't want the kind of future that other people have because they're not going to do well, so I think part of your identity is being a strong person. Wouldn't you say?

Hans: I . . . think you can say that.

Peter, Hans' younger brother, also had to negotiate the in-betweenness of being "American" in Mexico. Peter, who is attending fifth grade in Tijuana faced different challenges in elementary school than his brother Hans faces in middle school; yet there are common threads, among them violence in school. Peter, at 10 years old, is acutely aware of the different lifestyles he had while living in Mexico as opposed to when he was living in the U.S. Peter shared, "I changed a little bit of my lifestyle, um, I used to run a lot but not that much now. I used to go outside a lot but not anymore. I would say that it's not the same anymore." When asked to offer clarification, Peter elaborated, "It's not the same 'cause they cuss a lot in my school and I say to stop because I don't like listening and they fight way more over here, I don't like it."

Violence at school was not the only thing Peter found different from what he had experienced in the U.S. He also considered his education was negatively affected by being forced to move to Mexico. When asked if his education in Tijuana was better or worse than it was in the U.S. Peter answered. "Worse." Without hesitation. He then commented on how his teachers in Mexico were less supportive, saying,

> Some teachers here in Mexico don't treat the kids the same than in the U.S. Some teachers in the U.S. would help you a lot, like if you're

a new one, and right here they just say, "write that number there" and that's all.

Peter continued:

> Because over here [in Tijuana] some teachers don't work that hard. They say, "Put this on your notebook and close it up and now you can talk," and all that. In the United States the teacher wouldn't get distracted by their phone.

While much research points to how immigrant youth and transnational youth inside the U.S. suffer discrimination and racism (e.g., Valenzuela, 1999; Vallencia, 2010; Kasun, 2016) in this case, the student felt his educational experience was far worse in Mexico.

One of the most interesting ways Peter negotiates the in-betweens is through strategically negotiating his identity, as evidenced in our conversation, shared in the following:

Author: Do you consider yourself to be Mexican, do you consider yourself to be American, or do you consider yourself to be Mexican-American?
Peter: American.
Author: American. All right. Is it because you were born in the United States or is it because you like more being American than Mexican?
Peter: American.
Author: Yeah? Why?
Peter: Because, well, if I consider myself Mexican the other kids would be fighting with me and all that. Throwing rocks and all that. When I say that I'm American, that I don't like fighting a lot, they're all like, 'OK' then they're not going to fight with me that much.
Author: OK, so in some ways saying that you're American protects you?
Peter: When I say that I was American, and in the United States I used to go boxing and I told them, "In the United States I would . . . fight," that's why I don't want to fight them that much. I don't like fighting.

Much complicated work was at play. Like Anzaldúa stated in Borderlands, his home language was the one which he used as "home" language with his siblings (1987, p. 78). Just as Peter's identity as an "American" shielded him from some of the violence at school, it also helped him to adapt better by making friends more easily, as he explained, "The best part is that I make friends faster here that in the United States." Similar to the case with his brother Hans, Peter enjoyed a certain popularity for being "American" and for being a newcomer. Peter shared, "Because kids talk to me. A friend of mine told me that he doesn't like to see new kids without any friends and that's why they hang out with me a lot. That's why I like it here too." Here we see an integration of making sense of new forms of knowing, such as Anzaldúa's stage of putting the new identity together after all the resistance, *nepantla*, and painful growth that occurs in the recursive process of knowing (2000a).

Conclusion: The Transformative Power of *Conocimiento*

For Anzaldúa, *conocimiento* refers to a heightened consciousness or awareness that puts us in a deeper connection with ourselves and calls us to rewrite our own story. Anzaldúa (2015) believed that "this self-creation persists through a series of traumatic dislocations and is recorded by words and images—that is, by language" (p. 40). For Hans and Peter, life after the deportation of their mother forced them into *conocimiento*. They could no longer afford not being aware and critically conscious about themselves, their circumstances, and the world around them, unlike peers whose parents and family members have documentation privilege to reside in their countries. Their *conocimiento* allowed them to find creative ways to use language, identity, and nationality to negotiate their way through an unfamiliar and often hostile environment in Mexico, particularly at school.

Throughout their testimonios, we are able to perceive several of the stages of *conocimiento* as described by Anzaldúa. El *arrebato*, referring to the fragmentation, the rupture, the initial shock, was represented by Peter's premonition, "I knew that something was going to change" upon learning of the deportation of his mother and subsequent family move to Mexico. The initial shock was followed by a state of *nepantla*, of being torn between two identities, two realities, and two countries. It was at this stage that Hans and Peter negotiated the in-betweens to resist the expectations imposed on them by their teachers and their classmates for being "*del otro lado*," as well as to use their language, identity, and nationality as currency for acceptance among peers, even though at times their language use felt complicated and even at odds with their identity—true markers of the complexity of the *nepantla* state, including their resistances evidences in their testimonios. Then came the stage of *Coatlicue* (an Aztec creation and destruction goddess), in which we make meaning out of "our greatest disappointments and painful experiences" (Anzaldúa, 1987, p. 68). It was characterized by Hans' deep reflection about what could happen to him in the violent world in which he has lived not only in Mexico, but also in the U.S. with his older brother, a world filled with drugs and street violence due to Hans' exposure to gangs with his older brother in the U.S. and violence in Mexico due to the constant fights in his school, which ultimately lead him to come up with the realization, "I'm not going to last that long."

In the stage *Putting Coyolxauhqui Together*, we can see how Hans and Peter reinvent themselves adopting a multifaceted identity in which they rescue those aspects of their Mexican-American identity that afford them a sense of belonging in their new context. For Peter, it is clinging to his American identity, which protects him from the fights at school when he is left alone by his peers after declaring that he used to do boxing when he was in the United States, and therefore, he does not like fighting anymore. However, for his brother Hans, he reinvents himself by choosing his Mexican identity over his American identity because he sees value in the family legacy, in the *mexicanidad* of his mother, his sister, and extended family, asserting, "I think it's kind of better to be Mexican."

Although they achieve the stage of spiritual activism, the last stage in the path to *conocimiento* remains to be seen. What is clear is that Hans and Peter used their in-between place, the stage of *nepantla*, to resist the stiff expectations imposed on them by their Mexican society, while at the same time reinventing themselves and rewriting their stories by surviving, adapting, and even thriving in their new city of Tijuana. With a change in paradigm, *conocimiento* has the potential to turn defiance into personal and social transformation.

For the author, it was painful, difficult, and complex to bear witness to these testimonios. I could relate to them on personal levels as a Mexican transnational mother-scholar. It is both personal and political to thus make recommendations from these data. First, educators in any country need to allow space for young people to have their identities and to shift into identities when they go into formal education spaces (or informal ones, for that matter). Next, educators and policy makers need to consider how space can be allowed for multiple languages to be engaged so that young people, especially, feel welcome and validated in their identities while also embracing understanding the newer cultures to which they are arriving. Finally, we can all learn from the ways these brave young people in the research navigated *nepantla* and *conocimiento* toward adapting while managing multiple understandings. That is the world for which Anzaldúa advocated, and these participants showed in a way that world can be possible, even if in short glimpses.

Notes

1. All names of people and places are pseudonyms.
2. Ages at the time of the interview in 2014.
3. Ages are as of the time of this study in 2017.

References

Anzaldúa, G. E. (1987). *Borderlands/La frontera: The new mestiza*. Spinsters/Aunt Lute Book Company.

Anzaldúa, G. E. (2000a). Last words: Spirit journeys, an interview with AnaLouise Keating. In A. Keating (Ed.), *Interviews/Entrevistas/Gloria E. Anzaldúa* (pp. 281–291). Routledge.

Anzaldúa, G. E. (2000b). Making alliances, queerness, and bridging conocimientos: An interview with Jamie Lee Evans (1993). In A. Keating (Ed.), *Interviews/Entrevistas/Gloria Anzaldúa* (pp. 195–210). Routledge.

Anzaldúa, G. E. (2002). Now let us shift . . . the paths of conocimiento . . . inner work, public acts. In G. E. Anzaldúa & A. Keating (Eds.), *This bridge we call home: Radical visions for transformation* (pp. 540–579). Routledge.

Anzaldúa, G. E. (2015). *Light in the dark/Luz en lo oscuro: Rewriting identity, spirituality, reality*. Duke University Press.

Beverly, J. (2000). Testimonio, subalternality, and narrative authority. In N. K. Denzin & Y. S. Lincoln (Eds.), *Handbook of qualitative research* (pp. 555–565). Sage.

Braun, V., & Clarke, V. (2006). Using thematic analysis in psychology. *Qualitative Research in Psychology, 3*(2), 77–101.

Candel, S. L. (2017). Reverse migration: Documenting how the educational experiences of transnational youth in Mexican schools are shaped by parental deportation. *UNLV Theses, Dissertations, Professional Papers, and Capstones*. 3117. http://dx.doi.org/10.34917/11889674

Candel, S. L., & Marrun, N. A. (2020). US immigration policy and its impact on immigrants: Reassembling the stories of deported mothers and their transnational children through the healing spirit of Coatlicue and Coyolxauhqui. *Handbook on Promoting Social Justice in Education*, 2223–2242.

Davis, D., & Craven, C. (2016). *Feminist ethnography: Thinking through methodologies, challenges, and possibilities*. Rowman & Littlefield Publishing.

De León, J. (2015). *The land of open graves: Living and dying on the migrant trail*. University of California Press.

Delgado Bernal, D., Burciaga, R., & Flores Carmona, J. (2012). Chicana/Latina testimonios: Mapping the methodological, pedagogical, and political. *Equity & Excellence in Education, 45*(3), 363–372.

Hérnandez-Ávila, I., & Anzaldúa, G. E. (2000). Quincentennial: From victimhood to active resistance. *Interviews/Entrevistas/Gloria E. Anzaldúa. AnaLouise Keating*, ed, 177–194.

Jarvis, B. (2019). *The Deported Americans: More than 600,000 US-born children of undocumented parents live in Mexico. What happens when you return to a country you've never known?* https://story.californiasunday.com/deported-americans

Kasun, G. S. (2016). Transnational Mexican-origin families' ways of knowing: A framework toward bridging Understandings in US schools. *Equity & Excellence in Education, 49*(2), 129–142. https://doi.org/10.1080/10665684.2015.1086243

Keating, A. (2006). From borderlands and new mestizas to nepantlas and nepantleras: Anzalduan theories for social change. *Human Architecture: Journal of the Sociology of Self-Knowledge, 4*(Special Issue, Summer 2006), 5–16.

Lapayese, Y. V. (2012). *Mother-scholar: (Re)imagining K-12 education*. Sense Publishers.
Posada, G. (n.d.). [Project *Nepantla Pattern: Decolonizing History*]. www.gilda posada.com/nepantla-pattern-decolonizing-hxstory
Sierra, S. E., & López, Y. A. (2013). Infancia migrante y educación transnacional en la frontera Mexico-Estados Unidos [Child migrants and transnational education at the Mexico-US border]. *Revista Sobre La Infancia y La Adolescencia, 4*, 28–54.
Valenzuela, A. (1999). *Subtractive schooling: US Mexican youth and the politics of caring*. State University of New York Press.
Vallencia, R. R. (2010). *Dismantling contemporary deficit thinking: Educational thought and practice*. Routledge.

Chapter 3

Nations Within Nations

The Heterogeneity of Mexican Transnationals of Indigenous Descent From Anzalduan Lenses

David Martínez-Prieto

Prelude: My Initial Rejection of Anzaldúa's Framework

Due to the characteristics and goals of this book, I believe it is of paramount importance to reveal my own positionality and initial rejection of Anzaldúa's framework in past years. To clarify, as a Mexican (trans) national, I am convinced that revealing my initial rejection of Anzaldúa's work can help explain why many scholars in Mexico have simply ignored her concepts and framework. By explaining my own experience, I hope that other scholars, mainly those situated in Mexico, can use my experience to allow more space for Mexican-American epistemologies in their research.

It was in 2016 when I read Gloria Anzaldúa for the first time. I was a first-year doctoral student at the University of Texas at San Antonio. Most of my postgraduate education took place in the United States and Australia; I had attended public educational institutions in Mexico during my K-12 education. As I have stated previously (see Martínez-Prieto, 2020), the ideologies embedded in Mexican education influenced my identity significantly, especially those promoted during my *preparatoria* (which roughly equals to high school in the U.S. system). After being educated in Mexico for several years, I found it somehow difficult to accept the ideas of a pocha (a pejorative noun to refer to a Mexican-American woman) scholar, even while completing my doctoral degree.

My initial rejection of Anzaldúa's framework was based on prejudice and misinterpretations of her work, as well as my academic journey as a Mexican (trans)national scholar. During most of my schooling in Mexico, I was taught to reject *any* imperial intrusion of the United States. While *Mexicana*, Gloria Anzaldúa's national origin (she was born in Rio Grande Valley, in Texas) made me *a priori* question her knowledge of the Mexican cultures and history. This is because Mexican public education, at least before the broad adaptation of neoliberal market practices at the end of the 20th century (Torres, 2009), was a counter reaction to U.S.

DOI: 10.4324/9781003191575-5

imperialism—which has affected Mexican nations[1] since independence from the Spanish Crown until today.

Similar to what Anzaldúa experienced when she attended U.S. schools—see chapter 3 of Anzaldúa's "La Frontera" (1987), I initially rejected, despite her popularity among my classmates and professors, Anzaldúa's framework and work. That is, my first reaction toward Anzaldúa's work was similar to the one she described when she was taught to make fun of "Mexican superstitions" in Anglo schools. Even when my grandparents from my father's side were Indigenous Tlaxcalans and spoke Nahuatl as heritage speakers, Mexican education (based on positivist and Western perspectives) taught me to idealize European knowledge as superior compared with Indigenous ancestral knowledge.

It was not until I started doing pilot studies toward the completion of my doctoral studies when I understood the meaningfulness of Anzaldúa's concepts. My dissertation research concentrated on the ideological impact of U.S. ideologies among Mexican transnationals who came (back) to Mexico to pursue an English Teaching degree. While the scope of my dissertation operated from binary national conceptions (U.S. vs. Mexico), some of my participants during my pilot studies and doctoral investigation allowed me to realize that many of the participants navigated more than two transnational spaces. That is, because of their Mesoamerican origin, many Mexican transnational participants experienced challenges to (re)adapt into the Mestizo Mexican public educational system, but also into the cosmovision and customs of their Indigenous communities within Mexican geographical borders. Based on the Indigenous heterogeneity among the former participants, in this chapter, I use data from different studies to analyze the relevance and limitations of Anzaldúa's work when exploring the identity of Mexican transnationals who, after having lived and studied in the United States, returned to Mexico and enrolled in English language teaching degrees.

Mexican Indigenous Transnationals and Their Return Journeys

When located in the U.S., the identities of Mexican transnational Indigenous communities have been addressed by academia, especially during the last decade (i.e., Martínez & Mesinas, 2019; Saldaña-Portillo, 2016; Sánchez, 2018). Different from their mestizo counterparts, whose transnational return migration journeys have also been widely examined by academia (i.e. Hidalgo Aviles & Kasun, 2019; Mora-Pablo et al., 2014; Petrón, 2009; Sánchez & Kasun, 2012), the identities of Indigenous transnationals who return to Mexico from the United States have received scant scholarly exploration. As I have explained previously (see Martínez-Prieto, 2020), one of the main reasons for which transnational

Indigenous have not been broadly considered in former studies relates to the fact that most investigations about return migration have taken place in northern Mexico where, historically, there is less Indigenous influence.[2]

In general terms, scholars have analyzed the stories of Indigenous returnees not by studying indigeneity *per se*, but because researchers aimed to examine the *Mexican* transnational journeys of individuals (meaning, mainly, mestizo transnationals) who live in locations with a large Indigenous population in Mexico. That is, participants in most former research *happened* to be Indigenous returnees (i.e., Sayer, 2012). Despite this phenomenon, former research has pointed out that Indigenous transnationals who (come) back to Mexico usually prioritize their Indigenous affiliation instead of their belonging to the Mexican national state (Smith, 2006).

Unfortunately, like most previous studies, the present chapter did not originally focus exclusively on examining the identity of Mexican Indigenous transnationals. Yet, it exemplifies the heterogeneity of Indigenous pre-service teachers in their reincorporation into Mexico by analyzing participants from three different Mexican locations: Donají, a Zapotecan-origin person who returned to Oaxaca from Illinois; Cecy, a Mixtecan-origin woman who returned to Puebla from California; and Helena, a Nahuatl-origin woman who returned to Tlaxcala from New York.

Anzaldúa's Framework to Understand Transnational Indigenous Identities

Gloria Anzaldúa's (1987) concepts have been highly influential to understanding the complexity of the borderlands. By acknowledging hybrid identities, the impact of Spanish and U.S. colonialism, and the linguistic and home *conocimientos* (knowledge) of border communities, Anzaldúa's framework provided theoretical and practical tools to promote social justice among Mexican and Mexican-American communities in the United States. Anzaldúa's work, in this regard, celebrated the diversity of the hybrid heritage of Mexican-American and Chicana populations and, simultaneously, described the challenges that this hybridity implies, "the conflict of not belonging entirely to the cultures on either side of the border" (de Veritch Woodside, 2012, p. 8).

Besides describing the complexities of Chicana identity, Anzaldúa's framework has served to promote social emancipation and alliances among scholars and communities on both sides of the Río Grande/Río Grande Bravo. The following quote, taken from an email dialogue that Louse Keating (2009) had with Anzaldúa, exemplifies her desire for un *frente común* (common front) among oppressed groups, especially among Chicana and Indigenous populations:

> Raza [Chicana] and American Indians share many cultural, creative, historical, political, economic, and spiritual concerns. Both groups

are mestizos, although most Native people would reject this terminology. Both lead hybrid lives. Our historical lives have intersected in numerous places. We have many issues in common; we fight against similar oppressions. Both struggle against subordination, racism, etc. Both struggle against internal colonialism.

(p. 290)

Due to Anzaldúa's ultimate goal of fighting oppression (meaning racism, imperialism, and machismo), Anzaldúa's contributions to scholarship have impacted different areas of study in terms of the recognition of marginalized communities in the United States (see Cantú, 2011). Due to the transnational trajectories among oppressed groups, as explained by G. Sue Kasun and Irasema Mora-Pablo in this book, Anzaldúa's epistemologies promote an intersectional approach to recognizing the impact of colonial and patriarchal narratives in different contexts of identity hybridity. That is, Anzaldúa advocated for the acknowledgment of the trajectories, spiritualities, and knowledge of the borderlands.

One of the most salient contributions of Anzaldúa is her understanding of multinational colonialism and segregation. To this aim, she acknowledged that her identity was impacted by colonialism in Mexico, the United States, and Mesoamerican nations (Medina, 2009; Orozco-Mendoza, 2008). To explain, Anzaldúa understood that her trajectory was impacted by abuse and repression of Spaniards over the Indigenous in Mexico during and after the fall of Mexico-Tenochtitlan (1521), and of the discrimination that Mexicans experienced after Texas, California, New Mexico, Arizona, Utah, Nevada, and Wyoming were incorporated into the United States. In this regard, Anzaldúa looked for social justice for those who have been systematically disposed and discriminated against, especially those whose identities do not fit patriarchal and colonial patterns.

Pertinent to this chapter is the recognition of Anzaldúa to the patriarchal and colonial power of the Aztec empire toward other Indigenous cultures in Mesoamerica. To this end, Anzaldúa (1987) recognized the subjugation that Mesoamerican women experienced under colonial power (meaning Aztec, Spanish, Mexican, and Anglo): "During 300 years, she has been a slave, cheap labor forced, colonized by the Anglo, the Spanish, by my own people . . . in Mesoamerica, under the Indian patriarchy" (p. 64). While briefly, Anzaldúa mentioned the belligerent and economic domination of Aztecs toward other Mesoamerican communities which, ultimately, contributed to the fall of the Aztec empire. Unfortunately, besides briefly mentioning some Mesoamerican cultures (i.e., Tolteca, Cochise, and Tlaxcalteca), Anzaldúa's reference to pre-Hispanic nations is rather short.

Regardless of this brief recognition of Mesoamerican history, Anzaludua's work has been used as a framework to explain the subjugation of Indigenous (women) populations of *Lacandones* in Chiapas, Mexico (Adamson, 2012; Saldaña-Portillo, 2001), Bolivia (Prada, 2014), and even Bedouin communities in the Middle East (Marey-Sarwan et al., 2020). Indeed, this framing can be productive if at times somewhat limited. In the following, I explain how I collected and analyzed data for this chapter, as well as the characteristics of the participants' Indigenous nations before engaging an Anzalduan analysis.

Data Collection and Analysis

I turn to the work I did in three different sites in Southern and Central Mexico: Oaxaca, Tlaxcala, and Puebla during 2017–2018. I collected data using in-depth interviews. Because all of the participants were proficient in Spanish and English, the interviews took place in both languages, depending on the comfort levels of the participants. The purpose of the interviews was to understand the impact of curricular ideologies promoted in U.S. education on the identities of transnational pre-service teachers pursuing a language teaching degree in a Mexican public university. I did not plan to focus on the impact of indigeneity among transnationals who returned to Mexico. However, due to the strong presence of Indigenous communities in my sites of research, I found that some of my participants made sense of their transnational trajectory regarding Mexican, Indigenous, and the Anglo (meaning, to them, U.S. white) culture.

Initially, data were coded at three different moments because data belongs to three independent investigations. In all three investigations, as suggested by Saldaña (2009), I interviewed participants in a series of three interviews. As these interviews were part of different investigations, the participants' answers were coded in two coding cycles at three different momentums in 2017 and 2018. Later, for this chapter, I re-examined data in an iterative process—which Srivastava and Hopwood (2009) defined as the development of reflexivity and meaning making—to re-understand the data I collected three and four years ago. As part of this process, I found commonalities between the participants' answers, which allowed to identify three main themes that guided my data analysis: "Indigeneity and Contentions of National Origin," and "Lack of Acknowledgment of Indigenous Contributions by the Mestizo Nation."

Participants

Helena

I met Helena [this and all the other participants' names are pseudonyms] when I was doing pilot research in Tlaxcala, Tlaxcala, in 2017. She was pursuing a degree in English language teaching at the main public university of this Mexican state. She moved from Tlaxcala to New York when she was 10 years old. Helena's family decided to return to Mexico in 2015 so she and her sister could go to college. Once they returned to Mexico, they lived at their grandma's house. Her father and her grandma spoke a Tlaxcalan variation of Nahuatl. Helena told me that she understood some Nahuatl too, but that she preferred English to communicate with her sister and Spanish with her friends.

Donají

Donají had recently finished her degree in English language teaching when I interviewed her (2018), and was working on completing her social service,[3] so she could graduate. Donají's physical appearance did not match my expectations of an Indigenous student: she was *güera* (light skinned) and had green eyes. While studying in the capital city of Oaxaca, Donají was from Tehuantepec, in the Oaxacan isthmian region. Donají lived in Urbana, Illinois, and returned to Mexico because she wanted to pursue a university degree. Some of her family members were still in the U.S. Donají spoke some Zapotecan but she said she was not as fluent as she wanted to be.

Cecy

Cecy was from Izúcar de Matamoros, Puebla, and decided to drop out of the degree of English Language Teaching the week I met her. She had found a well-paid job in a private institution in Mexico and she was working on an online certification offered by a U.S. institution. Cecy moved to California when she was a baby and returned to Mexico when she was about to finish high school. When Cecy's family returned to Mexico, they lived with the grandparents, who were Indigenous. Cecy mentioned she spoke no Nahuatl and little Spanish when she arrived in Mexico, so it was hard for her to communicate with them.

Indigenous Communities of Participants

To understand the ideological orientation of Mexican transnationals from Indigenous communities, I provide some contexts demonstrating the heterogeneity of Mexico and the historical particularities of their Indigenous communities.

La Madgalena Tlaltemulco, Tlaxcala (Helena's Hometown)

Like the Aztecs, Tlaxcalans migrated from northern Mexico to Mesoamerica. They settled in the valley of Puebla-Tlaxcala around 1800 BC.

Before the Spanish conquest, Tlaxcaltecas and Aztecs had continuous tensions and wars. In spite of the militaristic power of the Aztec empire, the Tlaxcalan communities were not conquered by the Aztecs. Instead, Tlaxcalans and Aztecs had continuous battles during the "Flower wars." Some scholars have pointed out that the Aztec empire did not aim to conquer Tlaxcalans but, instead, the Aztec empire used Flower wars to obtain war prisoners and to keep their warriors in continuous war-like practice (Martínez Contreras, 1995).

Because of their rivalry with Aztecs, Tlaxcalans helped Hernán Cortés' army when attacking Tenochtitlan, the main city of the Aztec empire. In fact, it was in the Acuitlapilco's lagoon, in the current Madgalena Tlaltemulco, where Cortés designed and tested the ships that helped him to assault Tenochtitlan. After the fall of the Aztec empire, Tlaxcalans were given privileges and their territory was given the title of "*Ciudad de Indios*" (Indian city), in which Tlaxcalans were able to keep their original dress and government during the Spanish colonial times (1521–1821). The alliances between the Spaniards and Tlaxcalans impacted the *mestizaje*—or intermarriage of European men and Indigenous women—of the New Spain, as 400 Tlaxcalan families were given the encomienda of colonizing the current territories of Aguascalientes, Zacatecas, Nuevo León, San Luis Potosí, Guanajuato, Sinaloa, Jalisco, Texas, and New Mexico (Martínez Baracs, 1993). Currently, the Indigenous influence in La Madgalena Tlaltemulco is salient and can be noticed in the number of Indigenous public schools in the region.

Juchitán, Oaxaca (Donají's Hometown)

Juchitán, Oaxaca is located in the Tehuantepec Isthmian region of the state of Oaxaca. The so-called Binnizá people, or the communities of Zapotecan origin who live in the *Istmo de Tehuantepec*, are probably among the Indigenous communities who have preserved their traditions and culture more persistently despite the Spanish and mestizo influence (Marcus et al., 2001).

Before the Spanish conquest, Zapotecans lived in constant war with a different culture of the state of Oaxaca, the Mixtecs. During the hegemony of the Aztec empire, the Zapotecs also lived under the subjugation of the Aztecs due to the geographical location of Zapotecan communities and their trade with Central American communities (Medrano, 2011). While Zapotecans initially welcomed the Spanish conquerors, they quickly realized that the Spanish colonization would relegate them to oppression and subjugation. For this reason, Zapotecans revolted against the Spaniards several times, for which they acquired a reputation as violent communities. It is probably because of this constant fight against foreign cultures that the Zapotecans have been able to preserve their cosmovision through centuries through literature, visual art (Brígido-Corachán, 2016) and matriarchal social hierarchy (Mirandé, 2011).

Izúcar de Matamoros, Puebla (Cecy's Hometown)

I found limited information about the Indigenous communities that populated the region of Izúcar de Matamoros, in the Mexican state of Puebla. However, scholars (Carpintero, 2002) have emphasized that the Coatlalpan, the original name of Izúcar de Matamoros, was populated by communities that migrated from Northern regions of Mexico. Like most Mesoamerican civilizations, it was conquered by the Aztec alliance during the 15th century. For the Aztec empire, Coatlalpan represented a strategic geographical area to limit the expansion of other city-states that were still independent of the Aztec empire, such as Cholula, Huejotzingo, and Tlaxcala (Martínez, 1991). During the Aztec empire, the people of Coatlalpan were requested to pay a periodical tribute to the empire.

After the Fall of Mexico-Tenochtitlan, capital of the Aztec empire, Izúcar de Matamoros depended on the agricultural production of sugar cane, which motivated the Spaniards to bring African-origin slaves to the region. Currently, compared with other regions of Puebla, Izúcar de Matamoros has a small population of Indigenous origin people.

The Heterogeneity of Indigeneity and Identity of Transnational Returnees

Helena, Cecy, and Donají were aware that their Mexican origin was related to their Indigenous ancestry. In this way, the three of them made sense of their Mexicaness based on her Indigenous origin. However, due to the historical development of their Indigenous communities, their conceptions of indigeneity were heterogeneous. For example, when I asked participants if they considered themselves Mexicans, Donají mentioned:

> *Soy mexicana, pero a lo mejor me identifico más como oaxaqueña, como zapoteca . . . También en Estados Unidos, siento que entre mexicanos no había tanto apoyo, pero sí había más apoyo entre nosotros [los zapotecas] . . . Hay mucha gente [mexicana] que se lleva esas ideas para allá, que si los indios, que si los del norte, que si los de Oaxaca. De por sí ya nos discriminan allá por ser mexicanos, y entre nosotros mismos nos discriminamos. Ahora que regresé, veo que es lo mismo aquí [en Oaxaca], los indígenas sólo son buenos dentro de los libros de texto.*
>
> (June 28, 2018)

> I'm Mexican, but I probably identify as Oaxacan better, as Zapotecan . . . Also in the U.S., I feel that Mexicans don't support each other much, but we [Zapotecans] did support each other . . . Many Mexicans carry ideas [from Mexico to the U.S.], that [we are labeled] as Indigenous, from the north, from Oaxaca. We are already discriminated there [in the U.S.] because we are Mexican, and we discriminate among us. Now that I'm back [in Oaxaca], I see the same here, Indigenous are only good when reading about them in textbooks.
>
> (June 28, 2018)

In her answer, Donají explained that, before identifying herself as Mexican, she considers herself Oaxacan and Zapotecan. This is because she felt that the Zapotecan community was more supportive of each other when she lived in the U.S., where Mexicans experience discrimination. For her, Mexicans do not support each other while they are in the United States because they carry ideologies that discriminate against other Mexicans, such as those who are Indigenous. In a similar vein, she was explicit that Indigenous people in Mexico are only respected in textbooks, but not in real life.

Cecy, as Donají, mentioned that her Indigenous heritage was essential to understand her Mexican origin:

> *Claro que soy mexicana. Mira, en los Estados Unidos casi no hablan de los indígenas, de su papel. Pero yo veo a mis abuelos, y yo veo a México. En Estados Unidos no se ve tanto que uno tenga la oportunidad de vivir con sus abuelitos indígenas. Allá los discriminan . . . Bueno, aquí también, pero no tanto. Pero también pienso que mis abuelitos serían discriminados dos veces [en los Estados Unidos]: por ser viejos y por ser indígenas . . . Pero entonces, sí, soy mexicana y soy indígena y a mucha honra.*
>
> (March 18, 2018)

> Yes, of course I'm Mexican. Listen, in the United States, people don't talk much about Indigenous, of their role [of Indigenous]. But I see my grandparents and I see Mexico. In the United States, I don't see that people have the chance to live with their Indigenous grandparents. There [in the U.S.], Indigenous are discriminated . . . Well, here [in Mexico], they are discriminated, too, but not as much. But I also think that my grandparents would be discriminated twice [in the United States]: because they are Indigenous and because they are old . . . But yes, I'm Mexican, I'm Indigenous, and I'm proud of it.
>
> (March 18, 2018)

Cecy understands that she's Mexican and, different from Donají, she equates indigeneity to the Mexican nation. For her, she is Mexican because she has Indigenous grandparents. In her answer, Cecy is aware that Indigenous peoples in Mexico and in the U.S. are discriminated against. However, Cecy has a rather intersectional analysis of the prospective discriminatory situation her Indigenous grandparents would experience in the U.S. where, opposed to the integration of the *abuelitos* (grandparents) as functional members of Mexican families, the Indigenous and the elderly are segregated.

Helena was also critical of her transnational trajectory and her Indigenous ancestry:

> *Sí, soy mexicana. Pero la gran mayoría de mexicanos no entiende la importancia de Tlaxcala para México. Ellos nos ven como los traidores. Como aquellos que ayudaron a los españoles . . . Incluso hay gente se burla y dice "Tlaxcala no existe". En Estados Unidos igual, me tocó toparme con un par de paisanos que, cuando les dije que era de Tlaxcala, me decían, para burlarse, que éramos los traidores. La verdad es que ellos no entienden la importancia de Tlaxcala, sin Tlaxcala no hubiera México.*
> (May 2, 2017)

> Yes, I'm Mexican. But most Mexican don't understand the importance of Tlaxcala for the Mexican nation. They see us [Tlaxcalans] as traitors. [They see us] as those who helped the Spaniards . . . There are even people who make fun of us and say: Tlaxcala does not exist. In the U.S., I also found a couple of Mexican nationals that would make fun of me once I told them I was from Tlaxcala, they would say we [Tlaxcalans] are the traitors. They do not really understand the importance of Tlaxcala. Without Tlaxcala, Mexico would not exist.
> (May 2, 2017)

Different from Donají, who seems to identify herself as Zapotecan rather than Mexican, Helena understood her Tlaxcalan indigeneity as crucial in the construction of the Mexican nation. To explain that, for Helena, the Tlaxcalan civilization was pivotal in the construction of the Mexican mestizo nation. Because of the relevance of Tlaxcalans in the development of *mestizaje* and Spaniard colonialism, she rejects the ideologies that place Tlaxcala as traitors. In this vein, Helena is aware that Mexican transnationals carry these discriminatory ideologies when in the United States as well.

When analyzed from an Anzalduan framework, the Indigenous transnationals' answers represent an opportunity to deepen in the repercussions of the Aztec empire—even 500 years after its fall—among subjugated nations. In addition, Anzaldúa's concepts provide a meaningful approach to understand how Spanish, Mexican (meaning mestizo), and Anglo discourses tend to silence Indigenous nations' history. In contrast, Anzaldúa's work does not provide approaches to understanding the diversity of Indigenous nations in Mesoamerica and their internal and external struggles.

Former studies about Indigenous transnationals in their return journey to Mexico (i.e., Smith, 2006) have analyzed Mexican identity Indigenous communities of returnees. However, the complex differences in the conceptions of Mexican nationality and Indigenous nations' histories among Donají, Helena, and Cecy challenge monolithic representations of Indigenous nations. Because different Indigenous nations experienced and adapted differently to Aztec, Spanish, and U.S. processes of colonization, the historical development of their communities has influenced their own conceptualization of indigeneity.

The "Aztec-Only" Recognition of Being Indigenous in the United States

A monolithic conceptualization of Mexican indigeneity also permeated the academic trajectories of Donají and Helena in U.S. institutions. For example, Donají explained that:

> *La gente allá [en Estados Unidos] no entiende, no sabe que somos diferentes pueblos. [Para ellos] Todo es azteca. Todo. Incluso yo tuve una maestra en el high school, ella era México-americana, y ella estaba muy metida en la onda de los chicanos y todo eso. Ella nos hablaba en clase de Aztlán, de los aztecas, de cosas en Náhuatl, y esperaba que yo le ayudara en las clases, que participara más, que la secundara ¡Pero pues yo no tengo nada que ver con eso!*
>
> (June 28, 2018)

> People over there [in the United States] don't understand, they don't know that we are different nations. [For them] everything is related to Aztecs. Everything. I even had a teacher in high school, she was Mexican-American, and she was into the Chicano culture and all that. She would talk about Aztlan in the class, about the Nahuatl language, and she was expecting that I would help her in class, that I participated more, that I'd support her. But I don't have any relationship with this!
>
> (June 28, 2018)

Donají's answer reflects the history of the Zapotecan nation—which is different from the Aztec empire. In this sense, she explained that, even among Mexican-American teachers who are willing to learn about their Indigenous background, the diversity of Mesoamerican nations is ignored in U.S. schools.

In a similar vein, Helena emphasized that the Mexican-American society in the United States completely ignores the relevance of Tlaxcalan nation:

> *Antes de regresar [a México], yo pensaba en meterme a una carrera allá [en los Estados Unidos], a algo de Mexican-American Studies . . . Pero cuando me metí a ver su plan de estudios, cuando me involucré más acerca del programa, me di cuenta que todo era sobre los aztecas, puro azteca, sobre Aztlán, sobre los México-americanos . . . pero nada sobre mi cultura, de las 400 familias que incluso llegaron hasta allá [a los Estados Unidos].*
> (May 2, 2018)

> Before coming back [to Mexico], I considered doing a degree there [in the U.S.], something about Mexican American Studies . . . But when I researched more about their classes, when I looked more deeply at the program, I realized that everything was about the Aztecs, only Aztecs, about Aztlán, about the Mexican-Americans . . . but [they offered] nothing related to my culture, nothing related to the 400 families who arrived there [to the United States].
> (May 2, 2018)

Similar to Donaji's experience, Helena's answer shows that some U.S. educators, even those with an understanding of Indigenous nations, perpetuate discourses of Aztec hegemony. That is, by countering discourses of Spanish and Anglo colonialism, other Mesoamerican Indigenous civilizations are erased from academic emancipatory discourses. For Helena, the relevance of the Tlaxcalteca nation, which helped Spaniards in the colonization of several territories in the United States and Mexico, is also not recognized by Mexican-Americans in the United States.

Anzaldúa's framework, mainly based on the history of the Aztec empire and Aridoamerican nations, seems to unintentionally disregard the complexity of Indigenous nations in Mesoamerica. Some scholars (i.e., Alberto, 2016) have criticized that Chicano emancipatory practices are based on western-based conceptions of Indigenous created during the Mexican revolution. To an extent, I believe this is the case of Anzaldúa's work. As expressed by Donají and Helena, the negotiations, history, agencies, and identities of Mesoamerican nations are, unwillingly, silenced by many U.S. scholars who have mainly followed Anzaldúa's liberation practices.

Discussion: Anzaldúa's Framework to Understand Transnational Indigenous Nations

In this chapter, I related the perspectives of Indigenous transnational returnees to Anzalduan notions of colonial subordination at three different levels: Aztec, Spaniard, and U.S. hegemonies. To this end, I emphasized the diversity in the history of the Zapotecan, Nahua, and Tlaxcalan nations. Anzaldúa's framework provided a meaningful point of departure to examine the systemic subjugation which influenced participants' notions of Mexican national origin. In this sense, Anzaldúa (1987) explained that Mexican-origin populations in the United States are subjugated by various colonial and patriarchal powers. For this reason, Anzaldúa claimed that her identity was permeated by the systemic discrimination that Indigenous people received during the Spanish conquest. This discrimination continued during the postrevolutionary creation of the Mexican state, in which the concept of *La Raza Cósmica* (or Cosmic Race) placed Mexican mestizos as the ideal model for *Mexicanidad*[4] (or Mexicaness).

The conceptions of the national origins of Donají, Cecy, and Helena were related to the discrimination that Indigenous communities experience in the United States. Such discrimination, on top of the systemic relegation of Mexicans to second-class citizenship, takes place because of the ideologies that Mexican nationals carry with them when they migrate to the United States. In other words, the mestizo ideal affects Indigenous communities beyond Mexican borders.

However, Anzaldúa's notions of transnational colonialism were not sufficient to explain the heterogeneity in the intersection of *Mexicanidad* and indigeneity of the participants of this chapter. In other words, a monolithic depiction of Indigenous transnationals can cause simplistic explanations of their individual and nations' trajectories. In a way, the historical development of their communities influenced the acceptance, rejection, or accommodation of Mexican national identities, as evidenced in these three women's stories.

The Zapotecan history of resistance toward colonial powers—Aztecs, Spanish—can explain Donaji's conceptions of national origin. In contrast, the historical contributions of Tlaxcalans in the creation of the Mexican state, especially by contributing to mestizaje and colonization of Northern territory, are the results of their alliance with the Spanish Crown. This alliance, which ultimately helped Tlaxcalans keep some sovereignty and privileges during the Spanish colonization of Mexico, supports Helena's claims that Indigenous Tlaxcalans should be recognized as essential in the creation of the Mexican nation. In Cecy's case, the Coatlalpan's nation was not relevant for her to make sense of her Indigenous ancestry. Instead, she has adopted the mainstream mestizo notion of Mexicanness and only relates her Indigenous background to her family. As discussed by Aquino (2003), the historical memory of Indigenous nations has been reformulated in terms of local powers and the oppression—or privileges, in this case—that these nations have experienced during the hegemony of Spanish and mestizo institutions.

The transnational returnee journey of the participants of this chapter has allowed them to confront monolithic perspectives of *Mexican* indigeneity perpetuated in U.S. society, including some U.S. educators and scholars. As a Mexican (trans)national from Central Mexico, I align with Donaji's and Helena's statements. While Anzaldúa (1987) did recognize the colonial practices and consequences of the Aztec empire, some U.S. scholars who use Anzaldúa's theory tend to idealize the Aztec civilization (Martínez-Prieto, 2018), to the point of misinterpreting its cosmovision, history, and culture (Antuna, 2018).

Unwittingly, by only focusing on Nahuatl terminology and the Aztec cosmovision, Anzalduan scholars are (ironically) perpetuating colonial powers in some ways. Based on the answers of Donají and Helena, I found that the conception and notions of transnational indigeneity and colonialism proposed by Anzaldúa should be reformulated in four interrelated areas: 1) to demystify the Aztec empire and the power relations of Indigenous nations, 2) to understand that some Indigenous nations adopted and supported Spanish colonialism, as this was to the best interests of their nations, 3) to legitimize the history and current context of transnational Indigenous communities, which have been silenced because of mainstream conceptions of indigeneity, and 4) to emphasize the historical and current social agency of Indigenous communities in Mexico and the United States (as proposed by Urrieta & Calderón, 2019).

The first paragraph of this chapter aimed to acknowledge my personal initial bias toward Anzaldúa's work. Throughout the chapter, I aimed to analytically examine the breadth and scope of Gloria Anzaldúa's concepts when analyzing Indigenous transnationals who have returned to Mexico after living in the United States. By examining the history of three different Indigenous nations, I analyzed the meaningfulness of Anzaldúa's ideas when analyzing populations who have experienced colonial oppression from different hegemonic powers. Understanding the transnational experience of my participants, as well as the historical agency of their nations, allowed me to propose some areas in future research regarding Indigenous transnationals and Anzaldúa's concepts.

Throughout this chapter, I also aimed to balance citations from Mexican national and Mexican-American scholars based on both sides of the border. With some exceptions (i.e., Magallanes, 2018), Anzaldúa's work is barely used in Mexico. As Anzaldúa, I believe that one of our ultimate goals as scholars is to deconstruct ideologies that have separated Mexican (academic) communities on both sides of the Rio Grande/Rio Bravo. I hope that the present chapter analysis can motivate other scholars located in Mexico to adopt Mexican-American frameworks in their research because, as explained by Anzaldúa (1987), our common academic efforts can help fight the systemic repression not only of Mexican (transnational and Indigenous) communities, but of segregated nations and peoples in Latin American and the world.

Notes

1. In this chapter, the author claims that Mexico, because of its Indigenous multicultural origin, is a country in which different nations that have survived Aztec, Spanish, and Mexican mestizo oppression. While the imposition of "la Raza Cósmica" (or Cosmic Race) of José Vásconcelos (1923/2021), which promoted the mixture of races (or mestizaje) as the ideal one, has shadowed Mexican Indigenous nations to a secondary role, Mesoamerican and Aridoamerican Indigenous nations are still present within the Mexican State.
2. Different from Central Mexico, Spanish colonizers in northern Mexico did not "mix" with local Indigenous nations. Instead, when Spanish needed labor, they "imported" Indigenous populations from Central Mexico, especially from the State of Tlaxcala (see the description of Acuitlapilco, Tlaxcala, later in this chapter). Due to the constant belligerent encounters between Indigenous nations and Spaniards in Northern Mexico during colonial and postcolonial times, and the later genocide and disenfranchisement of entire Indigenous nations (i.e., the forced migration of the Yaquis to the Yucatán peninsula), the discrimination against Indigenous cultures is even more salient in this region of the Mexican Republic.
3. In Mexico, students who attend public institutions of higher education are required to reciprocate the support they have received from the Mexican society (in most universities, higher education is almost entirely free). Students need to work without remuneration from 6–12 months in some public or private institutions before graduation.
4. In spite of Anzaldúa's criticism toward José Vasconcelos, the creator of the "Raza Cósmica concept," some scholars (i.e., Pitts, 2014) have pointed out that both, Anzaldúa and Vasconcelos, shared common ground in terms of the rejection of (Yankee) imperialism.

References

Adamson, J. (2012). "¡Todos Somos Indios!" Revolutionary imagination, alternative modernity, and transnational organizing in the work of Silko, Tamez, and Anzaldúa. *Journal of Transnational American Studies, 4*(1).

Alberto, L. (2016). Nations, nationalisms, and indígenas: The "Indian" in the Chicano revolutionary imaginary. *Critical Ethnic Studies, 2*(1), 107–127.

Antuna, M. D. R. (2018). What we talk about when we talk about Nepantla: Gloria Anzaldúa and the queer fruit of Aztec philosophy. *Journal of Latinos and Education, 17*(2), 159–163.

Anzaldúa, G. (1987). *Borderlands/La frontera. The new mestiza.* Spinsters/Aunt Lute.

Aquino, S. (2003). Cultura, identidad y poder en las representaciones del pasado: El caso de los zapotecos serranos del norte de Oaxaca, México. *Estudios Atacameños*, (26), 71–80.

Brígido-Corachán, A. M. (2016). Una aproximación a la obra de Javier Castellanos Martínez en el marco de la literatura zapoteca contemporánea: Reflexiones, inquietudes y pláticas. *Diálogo, 19*(1), 175–183.

Cantú, N. E. (2011). Trabajando esta cuestión: el impacto de" Borderlands/la frontera: The new mestiza" de Gloria Anzaldúa. *Brocar. Cuadernos de Investigación Histórica*, (35), 109–116.

Carpintero, F. J. G. (2002). Costumbres comunes, derechos individuales. Barrios y agua en Izúcar, Puebla. *Relaciones. Estudios de historia y sociedad, 23*(89).

de Veritch Woodside, V. (2012). *Forging Alliances across Fronteras: Transnational narratives of female migration and the family.* Doctoral dissertation. https://digitalrepository.unm.edu/cgi/viewcontent.cgi?article=1012&context=span_etds

Hidalgo Aviles, H., & Kasun, G. S. (2019). Imperial language educators in these times: Transnational voices from Mexico on nationalisms and returnee transnationals. *Educational Studies*, 1–9.

Keating, A. L. (2009). Speaking across the divine. In A. L. Keating (Ed.), *The Gloria Anzaldúa reader* (pp. 282–294). Duke University Press.

Magallanes, M. D. S. G. (2018). Gloria Anzaldúa y el giro descolonial desde la frontera para el mundo. *Camino Real: Estudios de las Hispanidades Norteamericanas*, (13), 79–89.

Marcus, J., Flannery, K. V., & Santana, J. F. (2001). *La civilización zapoteca: Cómo evolucionó la sociedad urbana en el Valle de Oaxaca.* Fondo de Cultura Económica.

Marey-Sarwan, I., Roer-Strier, D., & Strier, R. (2020). Blurring the borders with Anzaldúa in context-informed, anti-oppressive research: The case of Bedouin women. *The British Journal of Social Work*, (0), 1–18.

Martínez, C. S. P. (1991). *El impacto de la conquista y colonización española en la antigua Coatlalpan (Izúcar, Puebla) en el primer siglo colonial.* Centro de Investigaciones y Estudios Superiores en Antropología Social, SEP.

Martínez, R. A., & Mesinas, M. (2019). Linguistic motherwork in the Zapotec diaspora: Zapoteca mothers' perspectives on Indigenous language maintenance. *Association of Mexican American Educators Journal, 13*(2), 122–144.

Martínez Baracs, A. (1993). Colonizaciones tlaxcaltecas. *Historia Mexicana, 43*(2), 195–250.

Martínez Contreras, J. E. (1995). En torno al concepto de guerra florida entre tlaxcaltecas y mexicas. *Dimensión Antropológica, 3*, 7–26.

Martínez-Prieto, D. (2018). Indexation and ideologies: Latinx and Nahuatl terms in our identity journey. *Journal of Latinos and Education.* https://doi.org/10.1080/15348431.2018.1432486

Martínez-Prieto, D. (2020). *The ideological impact of US curricula on Mexican transnational pre-service language teachers* [Doctoral dissertation, The University of Texas at San Antonio].

Medina, R. (2009). El mestizaje a travéés de la frontera: Vasconcelos y Anzaldúúa. *Mexican Studies/Estudios Mexicanos, 25*(1), 101–123.

Medrano, E. R. (2011). Un breve recorrido bibliográfico por la historia de los pueblos zapotecos de Oaxaca. *Dimensión Antropológica, 52,* 57–80.

Mirandé, A. (2011). The Muxes of Juchitan: A preliminary look at transgender identity and acceptance. *California Western International Law Journal, 42,* 509.

Mora-Pablo, I., Lengeling, M., & Crawford Lewis, T. (2014). Formación de identidad en migrantes de retorno y el impacto en su desarrollo profesional como docentes de inglés. *Academia Journals, 6*(5), 3199–3204.

Orozco-Mendoza, E. F. (2008). *Borderlands theory: Producing border epistemologies with Gloria Anzaldúa* [Doctoral dissertation, Virginia Tech].

Petrón, M. (2009). Transnational teachers of English in Mexico. *The High School Journal, 92*(4), 115–128.

Pitts, A. J. (2014). Toward an aesthetics of race: Bridging the writings of Gloria Anzaldúa and José Vasconcelos. *Inter-American Journal of Philosophy, 1,* 80–100.

Prada, A. R. (2014). Chapter two. Is Anzaldúa translatable in Bolivia? In S. E. Alvarez, C. de Lima Costa, V. Feliu, R. Hester, N. Klahn, & M. Thayer. (Eds.), *Translocalities/translocalidades: Feminist politics of translation in the Latin/a Americas* (pp. 57–77). Duke University Press.

Saldaña, J. (2009). *The coding manual for qualitative research methods.* Sage.

Saldaña-Portillo, M. J. (2001). Who's the Indian in Aztlan? Re-writing mestizaje, Indianism, and Chicanismo from the Lacandon. *The Latin American Subaltern Studies Reader,* 402–423.

Saldaña-Portillo, M. J. (2016). *Indian given: Racial geographies across Mexico and the United States.* Duke University Press.

Sánchez, D. (2018). Racial and structural discrimination toward the children of indigenous Mexican immigrants. *Race and Social Problems, 10*(4), 306–319.

Sánchez, P., & Kasun, G. S. (2012). Connecting transnationalism to the classroom and to theories of immigrant student adaptation. *Berkeley Review of Education, 3*(1), 71–93.

Sayer, P. (2012). *Ambiguities and Tensions in English Language Teaching: Portraits of EFL Teachers as Legitimate Speakers.* Routledge.

Smith, P. (2006). Transnacionalismo, bilingüísmo y planificación del lenguaje en contextos educativos mexicanos. In R. Terborg & L. G. Landa (Eds.), *Los Retos de la planificación del lenguaje en el siglo XXI* (pp. 419–444). UNAM.

Srivastava, P., & Hopwood, N. (2009). A practical iterative framework for qualitative data analysis. *International Journal of Qualitative Methods, 8*(1), 76–84.

Torres, C. A. (2009). *Globalizations and education: Collected essays on class, race, gender, and the state.* Teachers College Press.

Urrieta Jr, L., & Calderón, D. (2019). Critical Latinx indigeneities: Unpacking indigeneity from within and outside of Latinized entanglements. *Association of Mexican American Educators Journal, 13*(2), 145–174.

Vásconcelos, J. (2021). *La raza cósmica: misión de la raza iberoamericana. Argentina y Brasil* (Vol. 1). Editorial Verbum.

Part 2

Formal Schooling and Transnationalism From an Anzalduan Lens

Chapter 4

Navigating Multiple *Fronteras*

The Transnational Experiences of Latina Second-Generation Immigrant College Students

Janeth Martinez-Cortes

Introduction

Second-generation immigrants comprise 12% of the U.S. population (Krogstad, 2020). By 2050, immigrants and their children could account for 19% and 18% of the population, respectively (Krogstad, 2020). Reports further indicate that a majority of Latinx/a/o[1] students enrolled in higher education are second-generation immigrants (47%)—that is, U.S.-born children with at least one immigrant parent (Excelencia in Education, 2019). Scholars argue that Latinx/a/o second-generation immigrant educational experiences may be uniquely shaped by their bilingual and bicultural identities, and their immigrant and transnational experiences (Sánchez & Kasun, 2012). In addition, Latinx/a/o students' multiple identities and experiences may shape how they navigate and negotiate the complexities and challenges of higher education to successful college completion (Hurtado et al., 2018; Espino, 2020; Rendon et al., 2014).

Though much has been written about Latinx/a/o students in higher education, scholars acknowledge that Latinx/a/o students' transnational histories and cultures are often overlooked in the literature (Pérez et al., 2018). Latinas, in particular, make up a significant number of Latinx/a/o students attending colleges/universities and completing bachelor's degrees (Gándara & Mordechay, 2017). Therefore, it is important to validate Latinas' unique experiences, knowledge, and voices within higher education and educational research. For as Anzaldúa (2009) writes, "we [women of color and working-class people] want our histories, our knowledge, our perspectives to be accepted and validated" (p. 204). This chapter brings to the forefront the experiences and voices of young Latina women in college.

In this chapter, I examine the importance of transnationalism in Latina second-generation immigrant college students' experiences at a Hispanic-Serving Institution (HSI) in South Central Texas. In this study, I use Anzaldúa's concept of the *mestiza* consciousness, wherein Latinx/a/o students reject either/or duality and reconcile multiple cultural identities

DOI: 10.4324/9781003191575-7

(Anzaldúa, 2007) while navigating cultural, linguistic, and academic borders. Furthermore, the analysis uncovers students' understandings of education in the United States rooted through their second-generation immigrant and transnational experience. In this chapter, I examine the following research questions: 1) How have the transnational experiences of Latina second-generation immigrant college students shaped their cultural identities? 2) How has engaging in transnational practices influenced Latina second-generation immigrant college students' understandings of higher education?

Second-Generation Immigrant Students

In this chapter, I define a second-generation immigrant as a U.S.-born citizen with one or two foreign born parents. The children of immigrants comprise the fastest-growing segment of the U.S. population and make up a growing number of children attending public schools and higher education (Excelencia in Education, 2019; Mordechay et al., 2019; Krogstad, 2020). Many of these U.S.-born children are growing up in households with one or two undocumented immigrant parents (Leach et al., 2011) and more likely to live in working-class households in which neither parent attended college (Gándara & Mordechay, 2017). That is, many second-generation immigrants are the first in their families to attend and complete college (Excelencia in Education, 2019). Studies suggest that as first-generation college students, Latinx/a/os may encounter significant challenges in completing their degrees in a timely manner, and are more likely to enroll in community college due to finances, to stay close to home or live at home while attending college, and to provide financial support to their families while in college (Crisp et al., 2015; Hurtado et al., 2018; Forrest Cataldi et al., 2018).

Despite these challenges, the literature on the educational attainment of second-generation immigrants suggests that they tend to fare better in educational attainment compared with the first and/or third and later generations of immigration (Portes & Rumbaut, 2001; Telles & Ortiz, 2008; Kirui & Kao, 2018). Scholars have also documented higher educational aspirations among the children of immigrants (Feliciano & Rumbaut, 2005) and an increased sense of obligation to repay their parents for their sacrifice, in particular among females (Feliciano & Lanuza, 2017; Louie, 2012). Stronger cultural values and educational expectations instilled in the second-generation to succeed in the host country may motivate the children of immigrants to do well in school.

Unlike previous waves of immigrants and their children, Latinx/a/o immigrants and their children differ in that they are more likely to maintain closer ties to their cultural roots and form cultural identities that promote bilingualism and biculturalism as a result of Spanish language maintenance, maintenance of links with their parents' origin country, and preservation of cultural traditions in the home (e.g., music, religious events, food) (Delgado Bernal, 2006; Márquez & Romo, 2008; Sánchez & Machado-Casas, 2009). According to Gonzalez-Barrera (2020), 45% of Latinos in the United States believe that speaking Spanish is an essential part of their sense of cultural identity. Jiménez (2017), the daughter of Mexican immigrants, recalls her parents teaching her to embrace her Mexican culture by encouraging her to preserve the Spanish language and learning to value her bilingual and bicultural identities (p. 66). In maintaining one's culture and language, scholars suggest that these can be viewed as subtle and powerful acts of resistance to challenge deficit perceptions of Latinx/a/os' culture and language (Delgado Bernal, 2006).

Transnational Second-Generation Immigrant Students

Much of what is known in the field of education about transnational students and their lived experiences has been produced from research within the K-12 school context (Compton-Lilly et al., 2019; Orellana et al., 2001; Sánchez & Machado-Casas, 2009; Skerrett, 2020). The concept of transnationalism is often used to "describe immigrants' long-term maintenance of cross-border ties to their communities of origin" (The National Academies of Science, 2017, p. 87). Scholars note that transnational second-generation immigrant students may attend most of their schooling in the United States while spending school breaks (holidays and summers) in their parents' home country. For immigrant families, engaging in transnational practices may provide ways of knowing to persist in fulfilling their aspirations in the United States, despite the obstacles they may face as immigrants living in the United States (Kasun, 2015). In her ethnographic study of four transnational, Mexican-origin families, Kasun (2015) finds that families' "return visits became a form of substance as restorative pilgrimages that grounded their sobrevivencia knowing" (p. 278). Other scholars have documented how return visit to a families' country of origin deviates from tourist practices and rather revolves around "specific family celebrations and maintenance of kinship ties as well as for attendance at religious holidays and festivals" (Sánchez, 2008, pp. 191–192). Sánchez (2008) finds that family plays a key role in her three participant youths' continued participation in transnationalism.

Sánchez and Machado-Casas (2009) note that "as transnationals, such students are either immigrants themselves or have one or two immigrant parents and as a family remain attached to both their new country of settlement and their country of origin" (pp. 5–6). For some children of immigrants, they may never physically visit their parents' home country but rather engage in what is termed "emotional transnationalism" that maintain them connected to their family's homeland, culture, and language through the exchange of goods, people, or practices that exist in their daily lives (Sánchez & Machado-Casas, 2009; Viruell-Fuentes, 2006).

Scholars note that "maintaining connections with a country of origin is a central component of the Latino immigrant experience" (Waldinger, 2007). The transnational practices and activities of immigrants may keep them firmly connected to their native land, language, relatives, peers, and community and religious events (Sánchez, 2008; Romo, 2008). Scholars note, however, that the transnational participation of the children of immigrants, although not always visible or recognized by educators in U.S. schools, has the power to shape students' sense of identity, learning, and sense of belonging as documented by transnational scholars (Ek, 2009; Sánchez & Kasun, 2012; Villenas, 2009). For example, Ek's (2009) longitudinal study of a transnational Central American female college student demonstrates the role transnationalism played in helping her maintain her Guatemalan language, culture, and various identities. Ek (2009) points to the "pushes and pulls of schooling" as a factor contributing to the diminished trips to Guatemala and the shift in identity and belonging of her participant, especially as her academic obligations increased while in college (p. 79).

Levitt (2009) suggests that though "the children of immigrant are less likely to engage in their ancestral homes with the same intensity and frequency as their parents," nevertheless, "the strong potential effect of being raised in a transnational social field" should not be dismissed (Levitt, 2009, p. 1126). Second-generation immigrants "may acquire several cultural repertoires that they can selectively deploy in response to the opportunities and the challenges they face" (Levitt, 2009, p. 1226). Given the increase in academic obligations and responsibilities a student may experience while in college, including employment, participation in student organizations, and family obligations, these may limit second-generation immigrants' ability to engage in transnational practices. However, a continued dismissal of the transnational practices of students not only in the K-12 setting but within the context of higher education limits our understanding of the role transnationalism plays in their lives, in forming their multiple identities, and in navigating educational institutions.

Transnationalism and the *Mestiza* Consciousness

In conceptualizing transnationalism for second-generation immigrants living in the United States, in particular Latinas, one must consider the various identities, lived, and embodied experiences of women of color that shape their cultural identities and offer the skills to navigate, negotiate, and survive the physical and symbolic borderlands which they inhabit daily. Espino (2020) notes that "amid dominant ideologies that stereotype Latinx/as/os, educational institutions that are not designed to sustain Latina-identified students, and institutionalized oppression, Latina-identified students can lose their sense of self and cultural identities" (p. 141). This chapter draws upon the conceptual framework of a *mestiza* consciousness (Anzaldúa, 2007) to center the lived experiences of Latina second-generation immigrant college students and uncover the ways their transnational experiences shaped their cultural identities and understandings of higher education.

The concept of the *mestiza* consciousness has been used as a theoretical lens to examine the lives of Latina students by Chicana feminist scholars. Chicana feminist scholars have written about the *mestiza* consciousness as "a constant state of transition within lived experience where knowledge is produced, meaning-making occurs, and a sense of self is retained" (Espino, 2020, p. 142). The *mestiza* consciousness is thus born out of oppression, out of the contradictory messages, and inner struggles *la mestiza* (a woman of mixed ancestry) experiences as she "juggles cultures" and navigates the borderlands (Anzaldúa, 2007, p. 101). Anzaldúa (2007) writes that "the new mestiza copes by developing a tolerance for contradictions, a tolerance for ambiguity" and works to break down dualistic thinking (p. 101). This "new mestiza" is a third element or "category that threatens the hegemony of the neo-conservatives because it breaks down the labels and theories used to manipulate and control" women of color (Anzaldúa, 2009, p. 205).

In developing a *mestiza* consciousness, Latinas "are able to navigate and reconcile multiple identities and oppressions deftly" (Hernandez, 2020, p. 307). Scholars have pointed to community memory and familial knowledge in the development of a *mestiza* consciousness that help Latina students survive and navigate (Delgado Bernal, 2006; Espino, 2020). For transnational Latinas who engage in a back-and-forth movement, they may carry with them the pains and struggles of their immigrant parents, the pressures of succeeding in the United States, and the oppressive educational structures of their educational experiences (Sánchez, 2001), while also drawing on the hope of a better future for their parents and their families. Developing a *mestiza* consciousness would allow Latina students "to bridge the complexities, ambiguities, and contradictions" of their everyday experiences (Espino, 2020, p. 142) in ways that other women of color do not. That is, Latina college students may hold various cultural identities that may contradict and clash as they shift from the familiar space of home/transnational community to the unfamiliar space of a university campus. However, in drawing from their *mestiza* consciousness, Latina students can negotiate and navigate different worlds and overcome the challenges and struggles of higher education.

Methodology

This chapter is based on a larger qualitative study of Latina second-generation immigrants attending a Hispanic-Serving Institution (HSI)[2] in South Central Texas. For this chapter, I focus on eight Latina participants whom I recruited at various campus events, student organizations, and university courses. During the interviews, participants shared that they frequently visited their parents' home country growing up and/or continued to make visits on a regular basis and participated in transnational practices. In this study, transnational practices are defined as maintaining close familial, social, and cultural ties to the parents' origin country through the exchange of cultural practices, goods, and emotional support. All eight Latina participants were either in their junior or senior year of college and all identified as first-generation college students, or the first in their families to attend and complete a four-year degree. Participants were the U.S.-born children of immigrants. Six of the participants' parents were from Mexico, one from El Salvador, and one from Guatemala (see Table 4.1). All eight of the participants spoke both Spanish and English.

Table 4.1 Participants' pseudonym and demographic information

Pseudonym	Age	Classification	Degree/Major	Parents' Country of Origin	Self-Identification
Esmeralda	22	Senior	Art & Art History	Mexico	Mexican-American
Claudette	20	Junior	EC-6 Bilingual Generalist	Mexico	Hispanic
Diana	21	Junior	Interdisciplinary Studies	Mexico	Mexican-American
Mariana	22	Senior	Interdisciplinary Studies	El Salvador	Hispanic/Latina
Raquel	27	Senior	Interdisciplinary Studies	Mexico	Hispanic
Patricia	27	Senior	Education	Mexico	Hispanic
Valentina	22	Senior	Interdisciplinary Studies	Guatemala	Hispanic
Olga	28	Senior	History	Mexico	Mexican-American

Note: All participants are first-generation college students and second-generation immigrants.

Data Collection

This chapter draws on semi-structured interviews and *pláticas* with young women attending a Hispanic-Serving Institution. Latina students were recruited through purposeful and snowball techniques. Interviews were conducted over the course of two semesters (Spring 2018 and Fall 2019). Semi-structured interviews lasted between 30 and 60 minutes and were guided using an interview protocol with a list of open-ended questions with a range of queries about their family's history, their second-generation immigrant experience, their schooling experiences, and navigating college. After the initial interview, participants were asked to meet for a follow-up interview. Follow-up interviews were approached as *pláticas* (conversations), a Chicana feminist method for engaging in conversations that take place one-on-one in which the sharing of stories gives way to the theorizing of participants own experiences (Fierros & Delgado Bernal, 2016). Individual *pláticas* took place on campus or in participants' homes after the initial interview. Before our second meeting, participants had been sent a transcribed copy of their first interview and were asked to read it before our second meeting to verify accuracy. *Pláticas* lasted on average 30 to 40 minutes.

Data Analysis

Participant interviews from the larger study were transcribed for coding and analysis. Using both Dedoose (a qualitative analysis software program) and Saldaña's (2015) first cycle and second cycle coding scheme, I first coded transcripts and field notes, line by line, to develop codes using an open coding scheme (Saldaña, 2015). I then organized codes, grouping codes into categories and included sub-codes. For this chapter, I focus on the transcripts that included the code "transnationalism" and conducted an additional analysis that utilized a Chicana feminist perspective to understand the transnational experiences of Latina students. From the analysis, three themes emerged to offer a deeper understanding of the coping strategies Latinas with transnational histories used to survive and succeed in higher education.

Positionality

I am a second-generation immigrant Latina who was born to two immigrant parents from Mexico. Growing up, I engaged in transnational practices with my family, making visits to both my mother's home state of Zacatecas and my father's home state of Durango. All of our trips to Mexico were planned during the summer and usually lasted about two weeks. Our time there was completely consumed by family time and connections. Though my trips to Mexico were not frequent, I grew up surrounded by family members who traveled to Mexico every year and family members who made frequent trips to visit us from Mexico, in particular for special family occasions in which they would bring back goodies, like sweets, breads, and *quesos* (cheese). I recognize that my experiences, though they may be similar to some of my participants' experiences, are still different in other ways as several of my participants continued to engage in transnational practices throughout college, and two of my participants' families are from Central American countries. Therefore, I recognize the responsibility that I have to carefully and critically interpret the narratives of my participants.

Findings

For the Latinas in this study, transnationalism was fundamentally a familial practice. All of the Latinas recalled memories of visits to their parents' home country, visiting grandparents or extended family members and/or attending family celebrations. While some recalled longer and more frequent visits to their parents' home country, other participants recalled fewer visits either due to finances, parents' legal status, or the growing demands of school obligations over time. In the following, I present three themes that emerged from the analysis: 1) navigating identity, language, and belonging, 2) maintaining familial ties across borders, and 3) forming cross-border understandings about education.

Navigating Identity, Language, and Belonging

Anzaldúa states "the mestiza faces the dilemma of the mixed breed" (p. 100). The *mestiza* finds herself "cradled in culture, sandwiched between two cultures, straddling all three cultures . . . la mestiza undergoes a struggle of the flesh, a struggle of borders, an inner war" (p. 100). In the case of the women I interviewed, some described this "inner war" they faced as second-generation immigrants. Being second-generation meant juggling multiple cultures and identities and struggling with their sense of belonging. For example, Esmeralda, a senior in college, described the tensions and struggles with her second-generation immigrant identity. She shared, "It means 'ni de aquí, de de allá' [neither here, nor there].[3] You're just in this kind of limbo. Like I feel that I'm not completely American, at the same time I'm not completely Mexican." In this quote, Esmeralda shared her inner struggle with her sense of identity and belonging. To further exemplify, Esmeralda shared an image (see Figure 4.1) of an art piece she created where she illustrates this inner struggle of identities and of the liminal space she inhabits in her daily life.

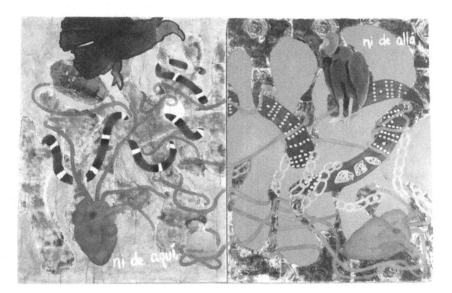

Figure 4.1 Ni de aquí, ni de allá (neither here, nor there) © Janeth Martínez
Source: Image of the painting also appears in the participant's personal website

Esmeralda drew creatively from her *mestiza* consciousness to reconcile the complexities of "having or living in more than one culture" (Anzaldúa, 2007, p. 100). She explained that the painting included elements from both the United States and Mexico to bridge her two cultures and identities. The painting illustrates the formation of a hybrid identity for Esmeralda that was closely connected to her immigrant and ethnic identity. She grew up in an immigrant household with emotional and physical ties to family members living in Mexico. However, because of her parents' undocumented status, she pointed out a single visit to Mexico with her parents. She has since then only traveled to Mexico accompanying extended family members and receiving visits from her grandparents on a regular basis who often shared stories about life in Mexico.

Similarly, Raquel (27, senior), who had just recently arrived from a visit to Mexico before our first interview, shared a similar idea. She explained:

> I go to Mexico, and then my people over there make me feel like I'm not Mexican enough for them. Like they're, "like you have a heavy accent," but people here tell me I have an accent. So, I don't understand where I belong.

Raquel expressed struggling with the tensions and contradictions of her language and identity. Raquel shared being shamed for speaking Spanish with an accent on her visits to Mexico while also being shamed for speaking English with an accent, complicating her sense of self. Anzaldúa (2007) argued strongly against "linguistic terrorism," writing, "So if you want to really hurt me, talk badly about my language . . . I am my language" (p. 81). In the case of the U.S. children of immigrants, many are often classified as English language learners and experience a push to assimilate to English-only (Valencia, 2011). Raquel recalled being punished by teachers for speaking Spanish in class in early elementary, and as a way of resisting deficit perceptions of her home language, she shared that she would only speak Spanish at school and would only make friends with other Spanish-speaking students. Raquel shared:

> So, I remember Spanish was my first language and I hated school as a little girl . . . I had a terrible kinder teacher. She wouldn't let us go to the restroom unless we asked her in English. I didn't speak English . . . because of [this] whole experience, initially I did surround myself around people that spoke Spanish in school too. Growing up all my friends were Spanish speakers, and I would speak 100% [Spanish], like I didn't care.

Similar to Delgado Bernal's (2006) findings, the Latina women in my study used Spanish and English in both academic and social settings, which could be seen as a form of resistance given commonly held English-only sentiments that exist in Southwestern states like Texas (Delgado Bernal, 2006; Valencia, 2011). Raquel and other participants embraced their cultures and Spanish language which was often replenished by their transnational experiences (Jiménez, 2010). Despite often feeling at a "crossroads" with her ethnic and cultural identity, Raquel drew on her *mestiza* consciousness by developing a sense of self that encompassed all her cultural identities, traditions, Mexican culture, food, language, and transnational life.

Finally, for Diana, an aspiring bilingual teacher, Spanish was an important aspect of her sense of identity and connection to her ethnic and transnational community. Diana grew up making frequent visits to Zacatecas, Mexico. She stated:

> When we were in elementary [school], we would go like as soon as school ended, and we would come back the first day of school. So, we would stay there for three months. And then in December, we take the two weeks, but now that we're a little bit older and we are involved in more school or camps, our vacations got a little bit shorter, but we still go.

For Diana and her family, visits to Mexico were frequent and often planned around their school schedules, but as they got older, trips to Mexico became shorter. Like Esmeralda and Raquel, Diana described being at a crossroads, struggling with her sense of identity. Though she felt connected to her parents' country of origin through her regular visits to Mexico, Diana shared feeling a sense of disconnect and miseducation of her cultural and historical origins. She explained that while taking a college course on Mexican-American studies, she became aware of the lack of knowledge she had of her ancestral histories and practices. She stated, "even though I consider myself Mexican-American, there's many things that I didn't know. Just because I live here, I kind of feel like there's a disconnect with my Mexican roots." She realized that there were celebrations such as patron saint festivals and *Dia de los Muertos* (Day of the Dead) that she did not get to participate in and did not know the history of until taking that college course. Scholars have found that for many Latinx/a/o students' ethnic studies, courses at the college level may be their first experience with learning about their histories and cultures (Marrum, 2018). It is courses like ethnic studies courses that may provide spaces of belonging for Latinx/a/o students on college campuses (Marrum, 2018), but it may also be a site that produces intense pain like for Diana who experienced feeling alienated from her Mexican origins despite her close ties to Mexico.

Maintaining Familial Ties Across Borders

Having family across borders was mentioned as the primary reason participants continued to engage in transnational practices. For many students, family was also a key source of support in navigating their educational journeys and forming aspirations for higher education. Families across borders were often sources of motivation for students to succeed academically and overcome academic challenges. For example, Valentina, a junior in college, who had not traveled to Guatemala in over 10 years, maintained close familial ties to her family living in Guatemala through her father and brother who frequently made visits to Guatemala. Though she had not physically been to Guatemala in years, she maintained a sense of connection to extended family members through frequent phone conversations and the exchange of pictures and videos, especially those of special family occasions like her older brother's college graduation.

> Like if [my older brother] ever had like a ceremony, we send videos or you know how like for graduation, they have those links, so we sent it to them over there [in Guatemala]. So hopefully, it's just something even for them over there, like they'll be able to go to los colegios de all [the universities over there].

The sharing of special family accomplishments, such as a college graduation, with extended family members living across borders was significant for participants as all students were first-generation college students. As the literature suggests, for first-generation college students and children of immigrants, college can be challenging territory to navigate, as students may be unfamiliar with the college application process, financial aid process, and culture of college (Espino, 2020; Rendon et al., 2014). Valentina, for example, shared how she struggled academically in her first year of college. However, with the support of family, she overcame the struggles she encountered and was on track to graduating with her bachelor's degree in education. The struggles Valentina and other participants encountered as first-generation, working-class students of color are not new but the result of the "walls and gates around fields of study and around the actual building . . . designed to keep us out . . . The mestiza is asked somehow or other to scale thick and tall walls" (Anzaldúa, 2009, p. 208).

Scholars have found that first-generation college students may struggle in their transition to college, as many may not feel academically prepared for college level work (Rendon et al., 2014). Patricia, a junior majoring in education, shared an academic learning experience in which she had to complete a small research project for an undergraduate research course. She explained that this was the first time she had conducted any type of research and "it was the hardest research class ever in [her] life." She shared how other students had dropped out of the course earlier that semester because of the level of difficulty. Despite Patricia's own worries with the course, she stayed enrolled. While in the course, she explained how having ties with cousins in Mexico helped her complete the required research project for the course.

> I was doing my research [survey on university student experiences, I was able to not just do my little research based on like just here and whoever answered it, but I sent it to my cousin in Mexico, and she sent it to her university people out there. They have a really nice education department in Mexico. And then she sent me back all the surveys that they did. And I was like, "Can I use these?" And he [my professor] was like, "Technically you can, they signed off."

In this excerpt, Patricia explains how useful it was to tap into her familial connection with her cousin who was currently attending a university in Mexico. Her cousin was able to help her by sharing her survey with peers at her university. Patricia was not confined to the borders of the U. S. but was able to extend her research project across borders because of the familial ties she maintained with family in Mexico who attended university.

For the women in my study, part of their *mestiza* consciousness involved learning how to negotiate and navigate unfamiliar contexts like the university drawing on their familial ties and strength to overcome educational obstacles. Latina first-generation college students may be perceived as lacking knowledge or support from a deficit standpoint (Espino, 2020); however, participants resisted negative stereotypes and embraced their familial knowledge and transnational ties to enable their success.

Forming Cross-Border Understandings of Education

One common theme across the data was students' perceptions of education. Although students enjoyed making visits to their parents' home country and spending time with family, many were reminded of their parents' struggles and reasons for leaving their home country due to economic hardship and the desire for better opportunities. Hearing stories about life in the home country and *consejos* that were rooted in their parents' lived experience motivated students to want to aspire to higher education and take advantage of the educational opportunities offered to them in the United States even though many had faced educational inequalities in their own educational journeys. Students took their family's history, struggles, and often conflicting messages and turned all the contradictions and ambivalence (Anzaldúa, 2007) into strength that inspired and motivated them to persist in their education.

For example, Mariana shared the following about her experiences growing up in an immigrant household.

> It made me more passionate about my roots and where I come from. And having these experiences that my peers didn't have, or that they didn't grow up with because their parents weren't immigrant parents, and I never saw it as a deficit or a problem, like it just made me happier to be brought up the way that I was brought up.

Mariana felt a sense of pride in having been raised in an immigrant/transnational household. Having experienced life on both sides (life in the U.S. and in El Salvador) gave her a different perspective and understanding of what life as an immigrant and daughter of immigrants in the U.S. was like.

In our interview, Mariana described her K-12 schooling experiences and her experiences in navigating higher education; she recognized the challenges, inequalities, and lack of access to academic resources she experienced as a first-generation college student. Despite the challenges, Mariana perceived education as a privilege, as she has seen first-hand the challenges her parents' home country experienced. She explained that her parents were from a remote area in El Salvador or *"la selva"* (the jungle) as she called it and that many people must leave the town due to limited job opportunities to find employment or attend schools in bigger cities. Visits to El Salvador made her aware of the reasons her parents immigrated to the United States and shaped her aspirations to succeed and give back to her parents and her community.

For Olga, a 28-year-old Mexican-American (self-identification), her educational pursuits were highly motivated by her parents. She explained how her mother and father both came to the U.S. from Mexico at a very young age and neither completed high school. Olga recalled her parents' advice about education, sharing they would tell her, "Your education comes first because that is the most important thing." This idea ultimately shaped her aspirations for higher education. Olga shared that her family had been making trips to Mexico every year since she could remember.

Now as an adult with her own children and husband, she continues to make visits to Coahuila, Mexico with relatives. She shared the following about her visits with family in Mexico, "They think highly of us because we are from over here. We are just fortunate we have free education, that's it . . . If you want to go far you have to have an education." However, this idea of Olga was complicated by her family's sarcastic comments, like, "Oh, *es que tu sí fuiste a la escuela*" (Oh, it's because you did go to school), or "*Hay perdón, tú eres de los Estados Unidos. Tú sí estudiaste*" (Oh, excuse me, you are from the United States, you did study). Olga's educational positioning often placed her at contradictory odds with her family members, as the aforementioned quotes suggest. For Olga, this was a struggle of the flesh, since she felt a strong sense of pride in her educational accomplishments, she noted "*es un orgullo ser una estudiante de colegio* [It is a sense of pride to be a college student] because not everyone gets that opportunity." She recognized the educational opportunities in the U.S. she had access to in comparison with the educational opportunities her family and friends living in Mexico had.

While Olga held strong educational aspirations and beliefs, these were often complicated by her family's messages about her schooling and education in the U.S. Her family's comments placed Olga at a crossroads, as her family did not fully comprehend the struggles she had endured throughout her educational journey. As Anzaldúa (2009) writes "being true to and maintaining ties with ethnic communities is sometimes at odds with developing her intellectual identities, especially if this intellectualism denies any notion of difference" (p. 208). Students like Olga were often left having to learn how to deal with the tensions and complexities of living between worlds (family and school) and crossing in and out of academic and familial spaces that include transnational spaces.

Discussion and Implications

Analysis of the participating Latina students' interviews provides insights into the complexities of their cultural identities and lived experiences. As Latina women of working-class and immigrant backgrounds, they often found themselves navigating multiple worlds. Though many of the women in this study felt a sense of pride of being the daughters of immigrants, some shared the tensions and struggles they experienced with their identities as the U.S.-born children of immigrants. Anzaldúa (2009) writes about this "crisis of identity" that *mestizas* "who inhabit so many world's" experience (p. 206). This identity crisis is spurred by hegemonic thinking that makes Latinas, like the participants in my study, feel like they did not belong (Anzaldúa, 2009, p. 206). The findings demonstrate how Latina students embraced a *mestiza* consciousness to navigate and negotiate the contradictions and ambiguities of their lived experience as transnational Latina second-generation immigrants attending college. Findings suggest that students' transnational experiences often complicated their sense of identity and belonging as second-generation immigrants. Latina students described living in between worlds and confronting the opposing messages and perceptions of their immigrant generation, culture, language, and education. Latina students' identities were constantly in flux as students crossed over into different worlds—university and home/transnational community—sometimes resulting in a struggle of identities. However, the work of the *mestiza* consciousness allowed students to balance multiple identities, cultures, and languages. Participants reconciled the tension and contradictions they experienced by maintaining their Spanish language, attempting to learn about their histories, and continuing to engage in transnational practices that now involved even their spouses and their children.

Like what other scholars have found, Latina students in this study drew on their cultural and linguistic resources and knowledge to form a *mestiza* consciousness that helped them persevere and persist (Delgado Bernal, 2006; Espino, 2020; Hernandez, 2020). The findings revealed the ways that Latina students tapped into their transnational familial connections for emotional and motivational support and in some cases for academic support to navigate higher education. Findings show how students bridged their transnational experiences with their academic commitments. Many of the participants in my study were aware that they were the first in their families both in the U.S. and in their parents' home countries to attend college which both inspired and placed a burden on them to complete college. For these students, moving toward a *mestiza* consciousness meant drawing on their family for inspiration, hope, and strength, as many of the students had to overcome challenges experienced as first-generation college students.

Finally, though visits and interactions with family abroad inspired Latina students to succeed and overcome their educational journeys, in some cases, visits to their parents' home countries also complicated their understandings of education in the U.S. Many of the participants considered having an education in the U.S. a privilege, as many were aware of the economic and educational hardships their parents and family members faced in their countries of origin, which was often the reasons for migration to the U.S. While scholars have noted the challenges that Latinx/a/o students may face—for example, low college expectations or a lack of support or resources provided to them to succeed in college as first-generation college students (Hurtado et al., 2018; Rendon et al., 2014)—the participants in this study often reconciled those challenges with their sense of responsibility to succeed for their parents. Many of the students in this study perceived education as a form of success, as many of the students viewed higher education as a means of upward social mobility and a way of repaying their parents for their sacrifice.

For the women in this study, pursuing higher education was a balancing act of their multiple identities, languages, and cultures. Embracing their *mestiza* consciousness meant reconciling opposing dualities that arose from their second-generation immigrant position, their transnational experiences, and first-generation college student identity. In this study, students confronted the obstacles of belonging to two nations and cultures and of having two languages, and of the obligations toward to their families (both here in the U.S. and abroad) to succeed educationally, as they were the first in their families to attend college. Implications for universities include recognizing that Latinx/a/o students come to college/university spaces with a wealth of knowledge and resources (Yosso, 2005) that are shaped by their various identities and lived experiences, including transnationalism. Therefore, it is important to continue to examine the extent of the impact transnationalism has on Latina students' identities and educational outcomes among those who continue to engage in transnational practices through college. While scholars note that the second-generation may not engage in the same transnational practices as their parents (Levitt, 2009), in this study, I found that Latina college students continued to make visits to their parents' home country during their semester breaks or maintained connections with family members abroad, sharing updates on their schooling or successes (e.g., upcoming college graduations). It is important that educators recognize and incorporate the knowledge and skills that can contribute to their educational success that derive from the children of immigrants' experiences and their *mestiza* consciousness.

Notes

1. The term Latinx/a/os will be used in this chapter as a more gender inclusive term and refer to people and communities of Mexican, Central American, and Latin American origin and live in the United States.
2. A Hispanic-Serving Institution is one that serves at least 25% of Latino/Hispanic students on campus. This particular HSI has a significant number Latino/Hispanic students, 56% of undergraduate students were Hispanic/Latino.
3. The phrase *"ni de aquí, ni de allá,"* is a phrase commonly used to describe the liminal experiences of the 1 or 1.5 immigrant generation (1.5 generation immigrants are those who were born abroad and brought to the U.S. at an early age) (Gonzales et al., 2016).

References

Anzaldúa, G. (2007). *Borderlands/La Frontera: The new mestiza*. Aunt Lute Books.

Anzaldúa, G. (2009). The new mestiza nation: A multicultural movement. In A. Keating (Ed.), *The Gloria Anzaldúa reader* (pp. 203–216). Duke University Press.

Compton-Lilly, C., Kim, J., Quast, E., Tran, S., & Shedrow, S. (2019). The emergence of transnational awareness among children in immigrant families. *Journal of Early Childhood Literacy, 19*(1), 3–33.

Crisp, G., Taggart, A., & Nora, A. (2015). Undergraduate Latina/o students: A systemic review of research identifying factors contributing to academic success outcomes. *Review of Educational Research, 85*(2), 249–274.

Delgado Bernal, D. (2006). Learning and living pedagogies of the home: The mestiza consciousness of Chicana students. In D. Delgado Bernal, C. A. Elenes, F. E. Godinez, & S. Villenas (Eds.), *Chicana/Latina education in everyday life: Feminista perspectives on pedagogy and epistemology* (pp. 113–132). State University of New York Press.

Ek, L. D. (2009). *"Allá en Guatemala"*: Transnationalism, language, and identity of a Pentecostal Guatemalan-American young woman. *The High School Journal, 92*(4), 67–81. https://doi.org/10.1353/hsj.0.0033

Espino, M. M. (2020). "I'm the one who pieces back together what was broken": Uncovering mestiza consciousness in Latina-identified first-generation college student narratives of stress and coping in higher education. *Journal of Women and Gender in Higher Education, 13*(2), 138–156. https://doi.org/10.1080/26379112.2020.1784752

Excelencia in Education. (2019). *Latinos in higher education: Compilation of facts*. Author.

Feliciano, C., & Lanuza, Y. R. (2017). An immigrant paradox? Contextual attainment and intergenerational educational mobility. *American Sociological Review, 82*(1), 211–241.

Feliciano, C., & Rumbaut, R. G. (2005). Gendered paths: Educational and occupational expectations and outcomes among adult children of immigrants. *Ethnic and Racial Studies, 28*(6), 1087–1118. https://doi.org/10.1080/01419870500224406

Fierros, C. O., & Delgado Bernal, D. (2016). Vamos a pláticar: The countours of pláticas as Chicana/Latina feminist methodology. *Chicana/Latina Studies, 15*(2), 98–121.

Forrest Cataldi, E., Bennett, C. T., & Chen, X. (2018). *First-generation students: College access, persistence, and postbachelor's outcomes*. US Department of Education.

Gándara, P., & Mordechay, K. (2017). Demographic change and the new (and not so new) challenges for Latino education. *The Educational Forum, 81*(2), 148–159.

Gonzales, R. G., Perez, J. B., & Ruiz, A. G. (2016). "Ni de aquí, ni de allá": Undocumented immigrant youth and the challenges of identity formation amid conflicting contexts. In H. D. Romo & O. Mogollon-Lopez (Eds.), *Mexican migration to the United States: Perspectives from both sides of the border* (pp. 119–139). University of Texas Press.

Gonzalez-Barrera, A. (2020). *The ways Hispanics describe their identity vary across immigrant generations*. Pew Research Center. www.pewresearch.org/fact-tank/2020/09/24/the-ways-hispanics-describe-their-identity-vary-across-immigrant-generations/

Hernandez, A. D. (2020). Developing a mestiza consciousness theoretical framework. *Sociological Spectrum, 40*(5), 303–313.

Hurtado, S., Ramirez, J., & Cho, K. (2018). The current Latinx/a/o landscape of enrollment and success in higher education. In A. E. Batista, S. M. Collado, & D. Perez II (Eds.), *Latinx/a/os in higher education: Exploring identity, pathways, and success*. NASPA.

Jiménez, R. M. (2017). "Nuestro camino es más largo:" A testimonio from a daughter of Mexican immigrants turned profesor in the academy. In G. Cuádraz & Y. Flores (Eds.), *Claiming home, shaping community: Testimonios de los valles* (pp. 59–78). University of Arizona Press.

Jiménez, T. R. (2010). *Replenished ethnicity: Mexican Americans, immigration, and identity*. University of California Press.

Kasun, G. S. (2015). "The Only Mexican in the Room": *Sobrevivencia* as a Way of Knowing for Mexican Transnational Students and Families: *Sobrevivencia* Way of Knowing. *Anthropology & Education Quarterly, 46*(3), 277-294. https://doi.org/10.1111/aeq.12107

Kirui, D. K., & Kao, G. (2018). Does generational status matter in college? Expectations and academic performance among second-generation college students in the US. *Ethnicities, 18*(4), 571–602. https://doi.org/10.1177/1468796818777542

Krogstad, J. M. (2020). *Hispanics have accounted for more than half of total US population growth since 2010*. Pew Research Center. www.pewresearch.org/fact-tank/2020/07/10/hispanics-have-accounted-for-more-than-half-of-total-u-s-population-growth-since-2010/

Leach, M. A., Bean, F. D., Brown, S. K., & Van Hook, J. (2011). *Unauthorized immigrant parents: Do their migration histories limit their children's education?* US2010 Project.

Levitt, P. (2009). Roots and routes: Understanding the lives of the second generation transnationally. *Journal of Ethnic and Migration Studies, 35*(7), 1225–1242.

Louie, C. (2012). *Keeping the immigrant bargain: The costs and rewards of success in America*. Russell Sage.

Márquez, R. R., & Romo, H. (Eds.). (2008). *Transformations of la familia on the US-Mexico Border*. University of Notre Dame Press.

Marrum, N. A. (2018). The power of ethnic studies: Portraits of first-generation Latina/o students carving out un sitio and claiming una lengua. *International Journal of Qualitative Studies in Education, 31*(4), 272–292.

Mordechay, K., Gándara, P., & Orfield, G. (2019, April). The effects of demographic change. *Educational Leadership*, 34–40.

Orellana, M. F., Thorne, B., Chee, A., & Lam, W. S. E. (2001). Transnational childhoods: The participation of children in the process of family migration. *Social Problems, 48*(4), 572–591.

Pérez II, D., García-Louis, C., Arámbula Ballysingh, T., & Martinez Jr., E. (2018). Advancing an anti-deficit achievement framework for Latinx/a/o college students. In A. E. Batista, S. M. Collado, & D. Pérez II (Eds.), *Latinx/a/os in higher education: Exploring identity, pathways, and success*. NASPA-Student Affairs Administrators in Higher Education.

Portes, A., & Rumbaut, R. G. (2001). *Legacies: The story of the immigrant second generation*. University of California Press.

Rendon, L. I., Nora, A., & Kanagala, V. (2014). *Ventajas/assets y conocimiento/knowledge: Leveraging Latin@ strengths to foster student success*. Center for Research and Policy Education.

Romo, H. D. (2008). The extended border: A case study of San Antonio as a transnational city. In R. R. Márquez & H. D. Romo (Eds.), *Transformations of la familia on the US-Mexico border* (pp. 77–104). University of Notre Dame Press.

Saldaña, J. (2015). *The coding manual for qualitative researchers* (3rd ed.). Sage.

Sánchez, P. (2001). Adopting transnationalism theory and discourse: Making space for a transnational Chicana. *Discourse: Studies in Cultural Politics of Education, 22*(3), 375–380.

Sánchez, P. (2008). Coming of age across borders: Family, gender, and place in the lives of second-generation transnational Mexicanas. In R. R. Márquez & H. D. Romo (Eds.), *Transformations of la familia on the US-Mexico border* (pp. 185–208). University of Notre Dame Press.

Sánchez, P., & Kasun, S. G. (2012). Connecting transnationalism to the classroom and the theories of immigrant student adaptation. *Berkeley Review of Education, 3*(1), 71–93.

Sánchez, P., & Machado-Casas, M. (2009). At the intersection of transnationalism, Latina/o immigrants, and education. *The High School Journal, 92*(4), 3–15. https://doi.org/10.1353/hsj.0.0027

Skerrett, A. (2020). Social and cultural differences in reading development: Instructional processes, learning gains, and challenges. In E. B. Moje, P. P. Afflerbach, P. Enciso, & N. K. Lesaux (Eds.), *Handbook of reading research, Volume V* (pp. 328–344).

Telles, E. E., & Ortiz, V. (2008). *Generations of exclusion: Mexican Americans, assimilation, and race*. Russell Sage Foundation.

The National Academies of Sciences, Engineering, & Medicine. (2017). *Promoting the educational success of children and youth learning English*. The National Academies Press.

Valencia, R. R. (Ed.). (2011). *Chicano school failure and success: Past, present, and future* (3rd ed.). Routledge.

Villenas, S. A. (2009). Knowing and unknowing transnational Latino lives in teacher education: At the intersection of educational research and the Latino humanities. *The High School Journal, 92*(4), 129–136.

Viruell-Fuentes, E. A. (2006). "My heart is always there": The transnational practices of first-generation Mexican immigrant and second-generation Mexican American women. *Identities, 13*(3), 335–362. https://doi.org/10.1080/10702890600838076

Waldinger, R. (2007). *Between here and there: How attached are Latino immigrants to their native country?* Pew Research Center. www.pewresearch.org/hispanic/2007/10/25/ii-introduction-6/

Yosso, T. J. (2005). Whose culture has capital? A critical race theory discussion of community cultural wealth. *Race, Ethnicity, and Education, 8*(1), 69–91.

Chapter 5

Language as Boundary, Language as Bridge

The Linguistic Paths of Children of Return Migrants in Mexican Schools as Reported by Adults

Kathleen Tacelosky

Introduction

Gloria Anzaldúa's life, work, and theory invite an approach that goes beyond borders (1987), stretches the boundaries of categories (2002), disrupts binaries (2002), and finds "home" (2002, p. 548) in the liminal space she calls nepantla. In this application of Borderlands theory, I examine the life stories of three young women who, though unfamiliar with the writings of Anzaldúa, embody the adaptability and sensitivity required of those who, in Anzaldúa's words, "inhabit los intersticios, the spaces between the different worlds" in which they reside (1987, p. 42).

The observations and conclusions presented in this chapter are part of a large and long sociolinguistic research project in which I research students who have been wholly or partly educated in the United States and through familial return migration become part of the Mexican education system. Since 2010, I have been observing and interviewing transnational families in Mexico, mostly children and youth, but also school administrators and educators with experience with transnational students. In the course of the work, some of the participants have grown into adults. The focus here is on three young adult women, each of whom I have known for several years and who have generously shared their lives and their stories. Their adult reflections on their earlier experiences offer insights into the ways transnational children and youth maneuver bordered spaces, broadly defined. In particular, their stories serve as the basis for an understanding of transnational experiences in the U.S.–Mexico context of schools and with the education system. I follow their life stories, as they were told to me, and conclude that their experiences, particularly with language, have been both a boundary and a bridge that have allowed them to maneuver bordered, liminal spaces.

In what follows, I introduce Jimena, Kiara, and Wendy (names changed per wishes of each participant) and briefly trace each woman's migrant trajectory. Next, I summarize their linguistic transition to Mexico and

DOI: 10.4324/9781003191575-8

Mexican schooling from the United States including the particular challenge of English class. Then, I examine the transition in terms of other adaptations, namely differences in school culture, gaps in content area knowledge, and feelings of exclusion. I conclude the chapter with an analysis of how these women have traversed the spaces they inhabited, exhibited agency, overcome obstacles, and embraced their identities in adulthood.

Background

This research began in the Mexican state of Puebla in 2010 when I began to visit schools and interview elementary school children who had had experience with the U.S. education system. I found the students by talking to school administrators and then through snowball sampling where participants introduce researchers to family members and friends with similar experiences. I worked in Puebla, an interior state in east-central Mexico, for one academic year with a grant that afforded me the opportunity for this research as well as to teach one university class per semester. As described elsewhere (Tacelosky, 2013), I included a community-engaged learning component that required my university students to tutor the transnational students in English and/or Spanish, per the younger learners' requests. For six summers, I continued the interview-based research, following up with the same students when possible. In 2018, I was invited to the north-central state of Zacatecas for six months where my access to schools and students was facilitated and guided by the state Ministry of Education. The work continued for six months in 2019 and was to be for six more in 2020 but was cut four months short due to the COVID-19 pandemic. In all, open-ended interviews were conducted with 45 different students for a total of 67 student interviews. Additionally, I interviewed six parents and six teachers as well as three school administrators in Zacatecas.

Although child-centered studies in transnational migration are extremely valuable (Gardner, 2012; Tyrrell et al., 2013), I wanted to understand adults' perspectives on their childhood experiences. Thus, through purposive sampling (Tongco, 2007), I sought adult participants for whom the experience of transnational schooling was a significant part of their childhood in terms of both duration and self-identity. After seven years of exploring questions of transnational education with children and youth (Tacelosky, 2013; Tacelosky, 2017), I repurposed my open-ended guiding questions to be more appropriate for adult participants and interviewed two young adult transnational women in Zacatecas: Jimena, age 31 in 2018, and Wendy, age 29. Together with Kiara, a 20-year-old from Puebla who has been part of the study since she was 12, their responses are the focus of this chapter.

Participants

Jimena, Kiara, and Wendy are three of an estimated one to three million (García Zamora, 2017; Passel et al., 2012) Mexican-origin individuals who moved from the United States (back) to Mexico since the 21st century began, a phenomenon that has been called *La gran expulsión* (Zúñiga & Hamann, 2019). For some individuals, moving to the country of origin is a homegoing; thus, it has been labeled return migration. Some are circular migrants, who make not one return, but several. Due to changing migration patterns from Mexico to the United States in the 20th century that include family units, the movement from north to south in the 21st century has included an increasing number of school-aged children and youth born in the United States or taken to the U.S. at a young age. Recently estimated at 600,000 (Jensen & Jacobo-Suárez, 2019; Jensen et al., 2017), these children and youth have found themselves faced with the challenge of entering the Mexican school system. These individuals, known broadly in the literature as transnational students (Hamann et al., 2006; Smith & Martínez-León, 2003; Zúñiga & Hamann, 2006), usually have spoken Spanish at home from birth and have been wholly or partly schooled in English.

All students traverse a border of sorts when they leave home and start school. Students who speak a language or variety at home that is different from that of education cross a linguistic border as well (Cummins, 1979; Heath, 1983; Reiss, 2005). Although some research suggests that birth order may be a factor in bilingual individuals' language development, maintenance, and shift (Parada, 2013; Silva-Corvalán, 2014; Zentella, 1997), older children having more Spanish input than younger siblings, the transnational students that I have met over the years all began their young lives with Spanish as the primary or only language of the home. Starting school meant starting to learn English. The young women in this study fit this pattern. I introduce each one with a brief biography of the first years of their lives as they told it.

Jimena: Born in Los Angeles, 1987; Attended U.S. School Through Sixth Grade

In 1987, just one year after the U.S. Congress passed the most restrictive immigration legislation in decades (Immigration Reform and Control Act), Jimena was born in Martin Luther King Jr. Hospital in Los Angeles, California. Her parents had moved there five years earlier to work and save enough money to build a house in Mexico.

Jimena's education began at age three at a local Headstart, a federally funded program in the United States that prepares students for school. She transitioned to kindergarten and started elementary school in the

Unified Los Angeles Public School District, where during that time, 46.5% of students spoke a language other than English at home—42.9% of students spoke Spanish (data from 1995 to 1996 school year, California Department of Education, 2021a, 2021b). In first and second grades, she was one of about a dozen students who attended a special class to learn Spanish while other students were studying English/Language Arts. By the time she was in third grade, Jimena was identified as gifted and enrolled in the magnet program at her school. "I was a straight A student," she reported.

Throughout her young life, she and her family traveled to Mexico to visit relatives for short trips, three or four all told, but she never considered living there. Mexico was her parent's homeland, not hers. However, in March of 1999, when Jimena was in sixth grade, her dad started to talk seriously about moving back to Mexico. She had heard him share his dream of having his own business in Mexico, but she "didn't really believe it would happen." By August, just one month before her 12th birthday, in the middle of sixth grade, the family packed up and set out on what, for Jimena, would be a one-way journey to her parents' homeland, specifically, to a small town in the north-central state of Zacatecas. "I remember the last day that we were in my house in LA," she recalled almost 20 years later. "There was no furniture there. I remember crying; it was really sad for me."

Kiara: Born in Pasadena, 2000; Attended U.S. School Through Fifth Grade

One year after Jimena left southern California, Kiara was born there. Her parents, who had immigrated to the United States a few years before, took great care in decisions regarding her schooling and language use. Her father, who worried that Kiara might be confused when she started school in English, spoke to the teacher about his concerns. The teacher encouraged him to continue to communicate with his daughter in Spanish at home and assured him that she would learn English in school. This calmed him, and the family adopted the practice of language use by domain for Kiara. Kiara recalled how her parents read to her in Spanish from a young age and encouraged her to continue to read in Spanish at home.

One day in 2011, when she was 11, Kiara's parents told her that her maternal grandmother had advanced throat cancer. Kiara's mother wanted to see her dying mother and say goodbye. However, traveling to Mexico and returning was not possible for Kiara's mom. In 2005, a new law in the United States introduced ten-year prison sentences for those who entered the United States with false documentation. Kiara's mother did not have, and had no way to acquire, documentation for legal re-entry. The threat of being detained and imprisoned deterred any serious consideration of a return to the United States. Thus, the summer before her sixth grade, Kiara and her mother made the one-way trip to Kiara's parents' homeland.

Wendy: Born in Zacatecas, 1989; Moved to the U.S. at Age 5, Attended U.S. School K-2nd Grade; Attended Mexican School, Third and Start of Forth Grade; Attended U.S. School Fourth Through Ninth Grade

Wendy was born in the north central Mexican state of Zacatecas. When she was five years old, her parents moved the family to the United States so that she and her brothers "could go to school and learn English." Reflecting on her parents' explanation as an adult, she supposed that there were other reasons having to do with the family's economic status and her father's work, but at the time, she went along with the idea that it was for her education. But when the first day of kindergarten arrived, she stood frozen on that border between what she knew, her home life in Spanish, and a classroom full of English speakers. She did not want to walk through the classroom door. She recalled thinking how she would be unable to communicate with classmates. "*Todos van a hablar otro idioma y no voy a poder hablar con ellos.*" She mustered her courage and went in.

In the two years that she was in Denver, Wendy finished three years of schooling: kindergarten, first grade, and second grade. Then, the family moved back to Mexico for her third grade and the start of fourth. In October of her fourth-grade year, she moved with her family back to Denver where they stayed for six more years. At her school, only about 50 students of 3000 spoke Spanish. Wendy and a friend were called to the principal's office one day. They were told that another girl had reported feeling uncomfortable when she heard them chatting in Spanish. They were reminded that use of Spanish was prohibited, not just in class, but anywhere on school property. She told me that they had to be surreptitious about communicated in Spanish "*cuando coincidíamos [hablábamos] muy, muy bajito o, [con] papelitos.*" Wendy was about to finish her first year of high school when the family moved back to Mexico.

Language: The Linguistic Transition to Mexico and Mexican School

International migrants, like the women in this study, cross international borders and then academic ones for (at least) a second time as they make their way into Mexican schools. Almost immediately, transnational students are confronted with the reality that the Spanish they have been using at home and in the community in the United States is not the same as academic Spanish. Home language is marked by familiarity. The lexicon and even the syntax of daily life and familial interactions vary considerably from that of academic language. I recognize that the construction and propagation of the concept of "academic language" has served to marginalize certain students—indeed, possibly these very students while they were in school in the United States—and discriminate against them on the basis of language and race (Rosa & Flores, 2020; García & Solorza, 2020). Likewise in Mexican schools, discrimination through neglect and denial abound. Elsewhere, I have encouraged the Mexican system and educators to recognize transnational students' "funds of knowledge" (González et al., 2005), many of them linguistic (Tacelosky, 2018a, 2018c). In this chapter, academic language/Spanish refers to the linguistic variety used in Mexican schools, not on the playground, but by teachers and through texts. This is the language encountered by students whose school experience has been largely and/or recently in English. I distinguish this formal variety from the oral language of the home, which, for all of its intricacies and complexities, does not prepare students for the text-based experience they will encounter in Mexican school.

The transnational students who arrive in Mexican schools with little or no formal education in Spanish often have limited or nonexistent reading and writing skills in Spanish. Many transnational students learn to read in English first or only, making a smooth transition to Mexican schooling difficult, increasingly so the higher the grade level. A great deal of educational research and practice is dedicated to the teaching and learning of reading in early grades, with the goal of fostering independent reading, because school success depends on it (Lucero, 2013; Reinking & Watkins, 2000; Reiss, 2005). Each of the participants in this study experienced some difficulties with written and spoken Spanish. Wendy said that when she arrived in Mexico, in third grade, she was given a pile of books and wondered why if she did not know how to read Spanish. "¿Para qué si yo no sé leer? Leer español.... Sí batallaba." She felt much more comfortable in English, "*Me sentía más en mi onda en inglés, pero regresar de Estados Unidos a México, el sistema educativo en las escuelas cambia todo.*"

Likewise, Kiara expressed fear and shame at saying something wrong when she arrived in Mexico,

> *el miedo de hablar, y la pena y cómo el, "¿Qué pasa si lo estoy diciendo mal?", fue hasta que llegué aquí a México. Porque aquí, ya como que ... me mencionaban como "es que esto no se dice así, se dice así, o estás mal en esto", y allí yo decía... "mejor me quedo callada".*

In my research, I have heard Mexican teachers say that students who come from the U.S. are reserved or shy, but their inhibition may be due to the response they get when they speak. Kiara said both at school and among familia she *"mezclaba inglés y español, y la familia como que se reía, tal vez no por hacerme sentir mal, pero como que ay que chistoso habla esa niña, no. Entonces ya fue cuando me fui cohibiendo."*

At first glance, the transition from reading English to Spanish may not seem so difficult. The two languages share a common alphabet, some common history (Spanish and English are relatively close on the language family tree), and a good deal of borrowing due to contact. However, as many monolingual English speakers who have taken Spanish in school can attest that the similarities and cognates are an insufficient route to competent comprehension and proficient production.

An example from phonology is illustrative. The primary speech unit of Spanish is the intonational phrase; thus, the focus of pronunciation is more at the syllable level than the word level. Sounds may jump word boundaries to join with other sounds to make a syllable that becomes part of an intonational phrase. This characteristic of Spanish renders some common Mexican educational practices a challenge. The regular practice of dictation in Spanish class, in which students are required to write word for word exactly what the teacher is reading or saying, poses problems for Spanish speakers who have not yet learned to read. They find it difficult to distinguish where one word ends and the next one starts. Over the years, I have heard many sad stories from U.S.-educated children and youth regarding that first dictation experience in Mexican schools, one that has generally been difficult, to say the least.

Due to the focus on syllables rather than words or individual sounds, reading education in Spanish emphasizes the syllable as a basic unit (Quiroga et al., 2002). By contrast, in English, which has more variation in terms of association of pronunciation with spelling, reading education focuses on letter–sound correspondence or a whole word approach (National Reading Panel, 2000). Further comparison of the similarities and differences of English and Spanish is far beyond the scope of the chapter. Suffice it to say that one does not simply transfer skills and competencies learned over years in, through, and about one language to another. Thus, the age at which transnational students arrive in Mexico can have a tremendous effect on their academic transition.

Students who begin their Mexican schooling in late elementary or early secondary, as the women in this study, have progressed through the U.S. school system and thus have been developing style, skills, and vocabulary concomitant with their school grade level. Rare is the transnational student who would have developed Spanish to the same degree because rare are the dual-language bilingual education offerings in the United

States, despite compelling research that demonstrates high language proficiency in students who have attended well-implemented dual-language programs (Collier &Thomas, 2004). Jimena mentioned that she attended a pull-out Spanish class for a few years, which helped her attain some literacy in Spanish, but even she reported difficulties transitioning to academic Spanish after several years of English-only schooling. Early on she had an experience with the dictation exercises mentioned earlier.

> So I remember like the first day of school like *"saquen su cuaderno y empiecen a escribir"* and I just like couldn't keep up with the rest of the kids cause I wasn't used to that. They tell you what you're supposed to write, eh, for example, in history, . . . and you're supposed to be writing everything they're saying, *"en mil novecientos sesenta y cuatro se fundó* whatever." You're supposed to be learning, and I didn't even know how to write in, in Spanish. . . . I would use a *k* the same way I would use *c* and an *s* and a *z* and just everything all over the place.

Simply put, the Spanish learned at home is not readily transferable to a school context, and the English learned in U.S. schools is not easily translatable to Spanish. As a result, students with years of schooling in the United States likely will encounter significant challenges in Mexican schools. Combined with gaps in content—geography, history, etc.—this puts transnational students in a position of feeling like they are behind as soon as they arrive. Speaking in the second person plural, perhaps as a representative of other transnational students, Jimena said, "We don't know anything about Mexican history, and throughout all of elementary school these students took history. I had no idea of Mexican history, Mexican geography, Spanish, just about everything."

Another matter related to transition to Mexico is that of the maintenance of English. Transnational students often worry about and work at maintaining English, which in addition to all of its practical purposes for future employment and mobility is part of their identity. "Ethnic identity is twin skin to linguistic identity—I am my language," says Anzaldúa (1987, p. 80). She is referring to her particular code and that of other Chicanas in South Texas, but the observation applies here. Many transnational students identify with being bilingual (Hamann et al., 2017). Others associate themselves more with one language than the other. English, which used to be part of their everyday lives at school, with friends and in their communities, takes on new domains. Some transnational students speak English with their siblings or other local family members in Mexico. Others maintain contact with people and English through social media, online gaming, texting, or talking by phone. At school, English is relegated to a few hours a week.

English language education had not been a part of the public primary school curriculum in Mexico until recently. The *Secretaría de Educación Pública*/Ministry of Public Education established the Programa Nacional de Inglés en Educación Básica (PNIEB), or National English Program in Basic Education (NEPBE), the pilot of which was to take place in 2009–2010 (SEP, 2016). After that, English was to be taught in all schools for 2.5 hours per week at all levels of Basic Education (Ramírez Romero et al., 2014), which is primary and middle school (equivalent to ninth grade in the United States). In 2017, under President Peña Nieto, an ambitious initiative called *Estrategia Nacional de Fortalecimiento para el Aprendizaje del Inglés* was launched. This program had the lofty goal of a bilingual populace in 20 years. The programs began in 2018 at the level of teacher preparation and purportedly included six hours per week of classroom instruction (Nuño Mayer, 2017). The reality on the ground has been uneven. For example, Kiara confirmed that she had had English class every year from her arrival in Mexico in 2012: one hour per week in sixth grade (2012–2013); two hours a week in *secundaria* (2013–2016); and four hours a week in *preparatoria* (2016–2019).

English Class

English classrooms are fraught territories for transnational students. They can be places of burden and embarrassment (Tacelosky, 2018b; Kasun & Mora-Pablo, 2021) or sites of status and stardom (Bybee et al., 2020). The women in this study recounted their experience in English class with mixed emotions and experiences. For example, Jimena said that at first, English class was fun.

> It was like, it was easy; it's something you already know. . . . I didn't mind being in English class, but when I got to high school, my high school teacher told me, . . . he was like "don't come to English class if you don't want to."

Instead, the teacher gave her different, more advanced work, such as novels to read outside of class.

It is not uncommon for English teachers to ask U.S.-schooled students to serve as helpers of teachers (Hamann et al., 2006; Kasun & Mora-Pablo, 2021). When she was in sixth grade, 11 or 12 years old, Kiara was regularly told by her teacher to "take care of the class," while the teacher did something else. Kiara remembered that another English teacher said to her, "you already know [English]." Thus, the teacher told her she did not have to do the work or take exams. That was difficult on two levels for Kiara. First, she was embarrassed and concerned that others were thinking that she was the teacher's pet: "Everybody just looked at me like, oh my god, she's like the *consentida* or something." But at the same time, Kiara fought for her right to be taught and challenged her teacher saying, "I want to do it even just to prove myself or . . . learn a little bit more." Unfortunately, that teacher denied her.

For Wendy, English class offered a sense of belonging, where she "felt more American," and "more connected." But when the other students pleaded with her to teach them, Wendy, a middle-schooler at the time, declined. "*Yo sé inglés, pero yo no sé enseñarlo. Es más, todavía estoy aprendiendo inglés.*" She acknowledged the strengths she possessed due to her transnational experience. However, she let them know that even though she knew English, she was not a trained teacher and, furthermore, that she was still in the process of learning it herself.

Beyond Academic Language: Adapting to Mexican School

In addition to adapting to academic Spanish, transnational students have to deal with differences in school culture, gaps in content area knowledge, and subsequent feelings of exclusion.

Exclusion and Belonging

Kiara's initial experience in Mexican school, at age 11, was complicated by the fact that her grandfather had told her not to tell anyone that she had come from the United States, not to brag or show off, "*No presumas.*" For Kiara, the advice to remain quiet suited her as she had no intention of drawing extra attention to herself. However, on the very first day, her teacher asked her to stand, introduce herself, and say where she was from. She, like Wendy in the doorway of the kindergarten classroom, stood with uncertainty in that bordered space between honoring her grandfather and doing what her teacher demanded. She continued,

> When he said, "tell us where you are from," I was like, "do I say it?" and he was like, "Yeah, say it, go ahead." And I was like, "no!" and I got really nervous. So everybody just started staring at me, so I had to say it. . . . "I'm from Pasadena, California." And everybody started whispering.

The other students were curious and tried to get her to talk to them at recess. But she did not feel comfortable in her role as newcomer. "It was good to be welcomed, but . . . I wanted it to be a little normal. Like, ok, it's the new kid, but like not trying too hard or something like that."

While it may be that the arrival of any newcomer, even one from another Mexican state, would provoke a reaction from curious classmates, research suggests that for transnational students, there maybe be more consequential implications. Transnational youth in Mexican schools have to decide if and how to reveal their status, citizenship, and prior experience. (It is worth noting that sometimes their status is shared without their permission and sometimes it is exposed when researchers enter their school looking for them.) Sharing U.S. experience with classmates and teachers may invite praise and privilege or derision and disadvantage. Privilege may be included what Bybee et al. (2020) call "star-student" status (p. 135), perceptions on the part of teachers and others in authority that might confer advantages due to assumptions about academic preparation or acumen (2020). Derision may take the form of being mocked for Spanish-language ability or accused of being a show-off due to citizenship status, knowledge, or experience. Jimena recalled how "the other students would laugh at me, because of the way I spoke, because of the way I wrote, because I didn't understand."

School Differences and Expectations

Wendy's transition back to Mexico the second time was complicated first by the difference in size of the schools and cities of Denver and Valparaiso, and second by the way the two countries distribute the grade levels. In Mexico, the ninth year of school is the last year of Basic Compulsory Education, secundaria. Thus, that year, when she was 14, Wendy went from a 3000-person high school in a city of over a million people to a small middle school in a town of approximately 10,000 inhabitants. After about two months, the teacher called roll for the first time. When he asked, "Anyone whose name I did not call?" Wendy raised her hand and said her name. "You are not on the list." Shocked, she asked, "How can I not be on the list when that is the first thing you should have done when I arrived?" His response was to tell her to go clean the restroom. She grabbed the bucket, marched directly to the principal's office and said, "I'm not cleaning the restroom." And she didn't. Mismatches between acceptable behaviors (telling a teacher in Mexico what he should have done is not tolerated) and expectations (cleaning the restroom is not a form of disciplinary action in the United States) in the two schools systems confuse transnational students and complicate their acclimatization to the new environment. Wendy summarized her transition to Mexican school saying she felt like a fish out of water: "*Regresar de Estados Unidos a México, el sistema educativo . . . en las escuelas, cambia todo. Es como un pez fuera del agua en México, bueno yo así me sentía un pez fuera del agua.*"

Content-Area Gaps

After being in a gifted and talented program in the United States, thriving and achieving high marks, Jimena got mediocre grades in middle-school in Mexico. "I had no idea of Mexican history, Mexican geography, Spanish. Just about everything." When a teacher assigned the class to write the names of Mexico's Indigenous languages on a map in which the Mexican states were outlined but not labeled, Jimena was unable to do so, not because she did not know the languages of Mexico and the regions where they were spoken, but because she did not know which state was which. She had not studied Mexican geography in her prior schooling. Furthermore, all of her classmates had known each other since elementary school. "So I was like the weird one; I was the *bicho raro* there."

The course names—*matemáticas, ciencia, historia*—might be similar, but pedagogy, concepts and terminology for each course, vary considerably between the Mexican and the U.S. school systems. Assumptions on the part of teachers regarding what transnational students know and their ability to talk about and understand the material based on grade level or course completion can be cause for difficulty and confusion for transnational students. Mexican history and geography may not be covered in U.S. schools, especially in states not near the border. Mexican teachers may not be aware that content varies by state since Mexico's education system is very centralized. Because until very recently no part of teacher training included awareness of or teaching for transnationals, the burden has been on the students themselves to adjust, fill in the gaps, and overcome hurdles not only in content areas, but also, as mentioned earlier, linguistically. Furthermore, they must do these two simultaneously and with great urgency as their school success depends upon it.

Overcoming Obstacles and Constructing Identity in Adulthood

Jimena, Kiara, and Wendy have developed strategies to become adept at what Anzaldúa calls "switching modes" (1987, p. 59) and overcoming obstacles, at times by standing up to authoritative structures and at other times by seeking help within them. Both are means of exercising agency. Agency has been defined as the "socioculturally mediated capacity to act" (Ahearn, 2001, p. 112). None of the women reported any kind of systematic accommodations for students like them, who were unfamiliar with the educational system. However, each one was able to successfully finish not only required basic education (through grade 9), but complete high school and study at university. Lifelong sojourners, they have learned to construct bridges (Anzaldúa, 1987) from where they were to where they wanted to be, and, when needed, to seek support and help along the way.

Wendy recalled an interaction with a Mexican teacher who told the class to make "*un cuadro sinóptico.*" When he saw her bewilderment, he did not consider that the language he was using might be the root of the confusion. He questioned her ability to *do* the task: "*¿No sabes hacer un cuadro sinóptico?*" when he could have framed the question as language related "*¿No entiendes las palabras 'cuadro sinóptico'?*" In reply, she defended her knowledge, "*Yo sé muchas cosas, pero no sé que es eso.*" By entreating him to draw what he meant, she found her way to a solution and claimed in advance that she would understand. "*Si me lo dibuja, sí puedo entenderlo.*" The teacher obliged, sketching a classification chart that she recognized from her prior schooling experience in the United States. Thus, she was able to complete the assignment.

Wendy's discursive interaction with this authority figure, her teacher, is socioculturally situated. She carried her own history to the temporal and physical spaces of the Mexican education system and engaged the collective in her actions and reactions. This example from Wendy's life demonstrates "how microstructures of power in communicative events are indexical of larger ideological practices" (Norton & De Costa, 2018, p. 92). Teachers in Mexico, more so than in the United States, often exert an authority that is not to be questioned.

Likewise, Jimena and Kiara demonstrated agency by seeking the help they needed. Both women recognized their need for linguistic support, Jimena with Spanish and Kiara with English. In her early days in Mexican school, Jimena sought and got help from a Spanish teacher. Jimena attributed her exceptional grasp of Spanish grammar today to that teacher's kind and attentive assistance. Kiara and her mother decided that for Kiara to maintain her English, she would attend private English language classes after school. Though she was only able to afford that luxury for a short time, she continued to identify as bilingual.

A poststructuralist view (Davies, 2000) recognizes that enacting agency is not in-the-moment autonomous decision-making. Rather, it is a social act that is informed by "a history of incorporating social realities" (Miller, 2014, p. 11). Jimena, Kiara, and Wendy have charted their courses by associating with identities that resist binaries of *aquí* OR *allá* and the notion that they need to identify with only one place. Words like bicultural and binational may be limiting. Such terms, insofar as they imply knowledge and experience of two cultures, may be misleading and inaccurate, leaving the impression of two entities, two identities, when the reality is something that is merged, fused as one (Arnett, 2002) or mestizaje to use Anzaldúa's terminology (1987). Transnationals incorporate into their self-perception not only the place where they were born and the place they are now, but also a "global culture, thus leading to a multicultural identity or a complex hybrid identity" (Arnett, 2002, p. 778).

When we talked about identity and how she identified, Jimena stated simply, "I'm both." By way of example of her deep affinity for both sides of herself, she said that when Mexico and the United States play soccer against one another she does not take a side. She smiled when she related that her boyfriend says that she is a part of La Raza Dorada: Mexico and the United States, the best of two worlds. After being utterly uninformed regarding Mexican geography in school, Jimena completed university and was employed by The Walt Disney World Resort in Florida to work as a Cultural Representative in the Mexico Pavilion. In other words, she crossed the border from Mexico to the United States to work. Her job was to be a Mexican. This same woman who as a teen could not put the names of the Mexican states in their place on an assignment was required to carry a map of Mexico around Disney World and indicate the state where she lived/is from and communicate to thousands of visitors a day that Mexico was "more than just Cancún and Cabo."

Growing up in Pasadena, the daughter of two Mexican parents, Kiara loved to tell people she was Mexican. "I was born in Mexico," she would assert, taking liberties with the facts. Adjusting her autobiography by moving boundaries, she claimed at once her heritage and her identity. "I don't usually say it, but I'm really proud because I have, like, two kinds of cultures. So, I'm really proud of both sides. The Mexican side and the U.S. side."

When she was 18, Kiara, by chance, or "destiny" as she calls it, found a book in which she saw the word Chicano for the first time, on the cover, as it is the title of a book from 1979 by Ettore Pierri. She picked up the book and started to read. She shared her reaction in an interview:

> *y me dije "wow" me impresionó mucho el término de Chicano por qué pues dije, por fin encontré una palabra que me puede identificar. Sí, soy mexicana por mis padres, pero pues nací del otro lado, digámoslo así. Entonces el libro en verdad me inspiró demasiado. Dije, "Ok. Ya. De aquí en adelante soy Chicana."*

Reading the book called to her mind a line from the movie about the life and death of Selena Quintanilla in which her father said to her, "*no eres suficientemente mexicana como para que los mexicanos te reconozcan como parte de ellos. Pero tampoco eres lo suficientemente estadounidense para que te reconozcan como estadounidense.*"

Kiara, like Quintanilla and Anzaldúa, has found herself in a liminal space: "*Entonces es como estar en el limbo.*" She recognized that the Chicano movement was from another place and time with a particular history and later, in the time of Selena, even a style all its own of big earrings and big hair. She admitted that she did not necessarily relate to that part, but "*el hecho de ser mexicoamericana me da el derecho de decir que soy Chicana.*" She completely embraced the term even though she knows no one else personally who uses it. She started an online presence, where, at first, she intended to sell trinkets, but she quickly admitted that really she was looking to connect with people who might identify like she did. She was waiting to see if that happened.

Wendy: "No Tengo una Identidad Definida en Cuanto a de Dónde Soy."

Wendy stated emphatically and without a trace of anguish that she did not have a clearly defined identity in terms of where she was from. This is not a deficiency or inadequacy. She did not lament her unbounded identity, she embraced it, recognizing that her experience was what has motivated her to engage with others and their cultures. She identified herself as a migrant. "*Soy migrante por naturaleza.*" Wendy summed up the advantages of her transient life by highlighting her adaptability and flexibility: "*Me ayuda como a discernir a poder adaptarme. Soy un poco más flexible.*" And through language, she found her way back to feeling at home, back to the water. At the time of our interview, she was enrolled in a course called ICELT (the In-service Certificate in English Language Teaching) a training program for practicing English language educators. "*Y cuando estoy en mis clases de inglés, ahora que estoy en el ICELT, siento que otra vez estoy como un pez en el agua.*"

Conclusion

"I am my language" declares Anzaldúa (1987, p. 80), and in so doing lays claim to an identity of hybridity, where a variety of languages and language varieties are spoken. She challenges notions of a single standard and scoffs at prescriptivist Spanish speakers, who attempt to throw their "bag of rules" at her (1987, p. 76). She speaks of "home tongues" rather than a mother tongue or a native tongue (1987, p. 78). Her dentist, perhaps standing in for all who intend to bridle and control, wants to tame her strong and stubborn wild tongue so that he can do his work on her. Her tongue angers and impedes him. In college, others wanted to control her tongue as well: she was forced to take accent-reduction classes.

Anzaldúa embraced her multi-faceted self-expression. She bristled at the insults and consequences her speech and language provoked in others. Like Wendy, she was punished by her teachers for speaking Spanish at school (recess) and making requests of teachers. Anzaldúa's mother was "mortified that [she] spoke English like a Mexican" (1987, p. 76) downgrading her daughter's education to nothing if she spoke accented English. As with the rest of Anzaldúa's Borderlands theory, language is not reduced to the duality of either/or but where a distinct (id)entity is formed when emulsifying one with another. More than a new linguistic amalgam, in Borderlands theory "[t]he third element is a new mestiza consciousness" (1987 p. 102), a hybrid space of resistance and activism.

The women presented in this chapter, for whom every day is a crossing of linguistic and cultural boundaries, have been, in Anzaldúa's words "forced to live in the interface between the two" realities (1987, p. 59). With no ready mediators or guides to escort them from one world to the other, no mentors, orientation or support group, they have become young *nepantleras*, "boundary-crossers, thresholders" (Anzaldúa, 2002, p. 571). Wendy is an English teacher. Jimena prepares others to teach. Kiara is studying psychology, in part, because when she struggled to find her footing not long after arrival in Mexico, she sought psychological help herself. She imagines a future supporting transnational students' mental and emotional well-being.

As adults, these women "initiate others in rites of passage, activistas who, . . . rise to their own visions and shift into acting them out, haciendo mundo nuevo (introducing change)" (Anzaldúa, 2002, p. 571). Perhaps among these "others," the ones who would listen to their voices, are those of us whose research and advocacy work has brought us into their stories and their lives. These young women have chosen to disassociate with a narrative of colonization and exclusion by gaining an awareness of and claiming their identity. As if taking a cue from Anzaldúa herself, they have responded to the call to "create a new narrative" (2002, p. 545). Will we join them?

References

Ahearn, L. M. (2001). Language and agency. *Annual Review of Anthropology, 30*, 109–137.

Anzaldúa, G. E. (1987). *La frontera: The new mestiza*. Spinsters/Aunt Lute Books.

Anzaldúa, G. E. (2002). Now let us shift . . . the paths of conocimiento . . . inner work, public acts. In G. E. Anzaldúa & A. Keating (Eds.), *This bridge we call home: Radical visions for transformation* (pp. 540–579). Routledge.

Arnett, J. J. (2002). The psychology of globalization. *American Psychologist, 57*(10), 774–783.

Bybee, E. R., Whiting, E. F., Jensen, B., Savage, V., Baker, A., & Holdway, E. (2020). "Estamos aquí pero no soy de aqui": American Mexican youth, belonging and schooling in rural, Central Mexico. *Anthropology and Education Quarterly, 51*(2), 123–145.

California Department of Education. (2021a). District enrollment by ethnicity and grade. [Data set].

California Department of Education. (2021b). English learners by language and grade. [Data set].

Collier, V. P., & Thomas, W. P. (2004). The astounding effectiveness of dual language education for all. *NABE Journal of Research and practice, 2*(1), 1–20.

Cummins, J. (1979). Cognitive/academic language proficiency, linguistic interdependence, the optimum age question and some other matters. *Working Papers on Bilingualism, 19*, 198–205.

Davies, B. (2000). *A body of writing, 1990–1999*. AltaMira Press.

García, O., & Solorza, C. R. (2020). Academic language and the minoritization of US bilingual Latinx students. *Language and Education*, 1–17.

García Zamora, R. (2017, March 10). Frente al retorno creciente. Una política de Estado de desarrollo, migración y derechos humanos. *La Jornada de Zacatecas*. http://ljz.mx/2017/03/10/frente-al-retorno-creciente-una-politica-desarrollo-migracion-derechos-humanos/

Gardner, K. (2012). Transnational migration and the study of children: An introduction. *Journal of Ethnic and Migration Studies, 38*(6), 889–912.

González, N., Moll, L. C., & Amanti, C. (Eds.). (2005). *Funds of knowledge: Theorizing practices in households, communities, and classrooms*. Routledge.

Hamann, E. T., Zúñiga, V., & García, J. S. (2006). Pensando en Cynthia y su hermana: Educational implication of United States-Mexico transnationalism for children. *Journal of Latinos and Education, 5*(4), 253–274.

Hamann, E. T., Zúñiga, V., & García, J. S. (2017). Identifying the anthropological in a mixed methods study of transnational students in Mexican schools. *Current Anthropology, 58*(1), 124–132.

Heath, S. B. (1983). *Ways with words: Language, life and work in communities and classrooms*. Cambridge University Press.

Jensen, B., & Jacobo-Suárez, M. (2019). Integrating American—Mexican students in Mexican classrooms. *Kappa Delta Pi Record, 55*(1), 36–41.

Jensen, B., Mejía Arauz, R., & Aguilar Zepeda, R. (2017). La enseñanza equitativa para los niños retornados a México. *Sinéctica, 48*, 1–22.

Kasun, G. S., & Mora-Pablo, I. (2021). El anti-malinchismo contra el mexicano-transnacional: Cómo se puede transformar esa frontera limitante. *Anales de Antropología, 55*(1), 39–48.

Lucero, A. (2013). Teachers' use of linguistic scaffolding to support the academic language development of first-grade emergent bilingual students. *Journal of Early Childhood Literacy, 14*(4), 534–561.

Miller, E. R. (2014). *The language of adult immigrants: Agency in the making* (Vol. 39). Multilingual Matters.

National Reading Panel. (2000). *Teaching children to read: An evidence-based assessment of the scientific research literature on reading and its implications for reading instruction*. www.nichd.nih.gov/sites/default/files/publications/pubs/nrp/Documents/reprep.pdf

Norton, B., & De Costa, P. I. (2018). Research tasks on identity in language learning and teaching. *Language Teaching, 51*(1), 90–112.

Nuño Mayer, A. (2017, June 17). *Comunicado 184.- Presenta Nuño Mayer la estrategia nacional de inglés, para que México sea bilingüe en 20 años*. www.gob.mx/sep/prensa/comunicado-184-presenta-nuno-mayer-la-estrategia-nacional-de-ingles-para-que-mexico-sea-bilingue-en-20-anos

Parada, M. (2013). Sibling variation and family language policy: The role of birth order in the Spanish proficiency and first names of second-generation Latinos. *Journal of Language, Identity & Education, 12*(5), 299–320.

Passel, J. S., Cohn, D., & Gonzalez-Barrera, A. (2012). *Net migration from Mexico falls to zero—and perhaps less.* Pew Research Center. www.pewresearch.org/hispanic/2012/04/23/net-migration-from-mexico-falls-to-zero-and-perhaps-less/

Pierri, E. (1979). *Chicanos: El poder mestizo.* Editores Mexicanos Unidos.

Quiroga, T., Lemos-Britton, Z., Mostafapour, E., Abbott, R. D., & Berninger, V. W. (2002). Phonological awareness and beginning reading in Spanish-speaking ESL first graders: Research into practice. *Journal of School Psychology, 40*(1), 85–111.

Ramírez Romero, J. L., Sayer, P., & Pamplón Irigoyen, E. N. (2014). English language teaching in public primary schools in Mexico: The practices and challenges of implementing a national language education program. *International Journal of Qualitative Studies in Education, 27*(8), 1020–1043.

Reinking, D., & Watkins, J. (2000). A formative experiment investigating the use of multimedia book reviews to increase elementary students' independent reading. *Reading Research Quarterly, 35*(3), 384–419.

Reiss, J. (2005). *Teaching content to English language learners: Strategies for secondary school success.* Longman.

Rosa, J., & Flores, N. (2020). Reimagining race and language: From raciolinguistic policies to raciolinguistic perspective. In H. S. Alim, A. Reyes, & P. V. Kroskrity (Eds.), *The Oxford handbook of language and race* (pp. 90–107). Oxford University Press.

SEP (Secretaría de Educación Pública). (2016). *Evaluación de Diseño Programa Nacional de Inglés.* SEP.

Silva-Corvalán, C. (2014). *Bilingual language acquisition: Spanish and English in the first six years.* Cambridge University Press.

Smith, P. H., & Martínez-León, N. (2003). Educating for bilinguals in Mexican transnational communities. *NABE Journal of Research and Practice, 1*(1), 138–148.

Tacelosky, K. (2013). Community-based service-learning as a way to meet the linguistic needs of transnational students in Mexico. *Hispania, 96*(2), 328–341.

Tacelosky, K. (2017). Transnational students in Mexico: A summer writing workshop as a way to improve English writing skills. *International Education Journal, 16*(4), 89–101.

Tacelosky, K. (2018a, June). Estudiantes transnacionales, retos y riquezas. [Video]. TED. www.ted.com/talks/kathleen_tacelosky_estudiantes_transnacionales_retos_y_riquezas

Tacelosky, K. (2018b). Teaching english to english speakers: The role of english teachers in the school experience of transnational students in Mexico. *Mextesol, 42*(3), 1–13.

Tacelosky, K. (2018c). Transnational education, language and identity: A case from Mexico. *Society Register, 2*(2), 63–84.

Tongco, M. D. C. (2007). Purposive sampling as a tool for informant selection. *Ethnobotany Research & Application, 5*, 147–158.

Tyrrell, N., White, A., Ni Laoire, C., & Carpena Mendez, F. (2013). *Transnational migration and childhood*. Routledge.

Zentella, A. C. (1997). *Growing up bilingual: Puerto Rican children in New York*. John Wiley and Sons, Inc.

Zúñiga, V., & Hamann, E. T. (2006). Going home? Schooling in Mexico of transnational children. *CONfines de relaciones internacionales y ciencia política*, 2(4), 41–57.

Zúñiga, V., & Hamann, E. T. (2019). De las escuelas de Estados Unidos a las escuelas de México: Desafíos de política educativa en el marco de la Gran Expulsión. In J. L. Calva (Ed.), *Migración de Mexicanos a Estados Unidos, derechos humanos y desarrollo* (pp. 221–239). Juan Pablos Editor/Consejo Nacional de Universitarios.

Part 3

Theorizing Transnationalism With Anzaldúa

Chapter 6

Double *Mestiza* Consciousness

Aquí y Allá

Colette Despagne and Mónica Jacobo-Suárez

Prelude

Following Gloria Anzaldúa's statement, "I cannot separate my writing from any part of my life. It is all one," we engaged with her framework and in this book because we also clearly identify as border women. Colette identifies as a transnational migrant after having grown up in two different European cultures and then settled in Mexico for over 25 years. And Monica underwent a profound transformation after having lived ten years in the United States and after having created a binational and bicultural family. Both of us had to become conscious of our Shadow-Beast and create our own *mundo zurdo* (back) in Mexico.

Introduction

The United States (U.S. henceforth) and Mexico are two countries deeply intertwined by a shared history. About one in every eight residents in the U.S. is foreign-born, representing approximately 44.7 million immigrants in the country, 25% of them being from Mexico (Budiman, 2020). Historically, Mexicans also account for a majority of the U.S. undocumented population. However, a dramatic change occurred in 2015 when more Mexicans left the U.S. than those who arrived, driving down the overall population of unauthorized immigrants. In 2017, there were 4.9 million undocumented Mexicans compared with 6.9 million in 2005 (Passel & Cohn, 2019). In other words, 2 million Mexicans were removed by the U.S. Department of Homeland Security (DHS) or voluntarily came back to Mexico, between 2005 and 2018.

From Mexico's perspective, this unprecedented amount of returning citizens implies multiple challenges, particularly in reference to young adults who belong to the 1.5 generation of undocumented immigrants. These young people arrived as children in the U.S., where they grew up, attended school, learned English, and adopted U.S. cultural values. Yet, their lack of a regular immigration status often caused them to live

DOI: 10.4324/9781003191575-10

in precarious conditions. Once back in Mexico, they become "return migrants" in the official discourse and oftentimes feel uprooted and unwelcome because their social, emotional, and cultural attachments are with the U.S. In other words, the conditions of these migrants raise questions about national loyalties, adaptation processes, multiple belongings, and social and linguistic allegiances.

A long debate has focused on the issues of integration, segregation, and discrimination of undocumented Mexicans in the U.S. (Pérez-Soria, 2017). Also, in the last two decades, research in Mexico began to make visible and analyze return migrants' educational and professional adaptation processes once in Mexico (e.g., Cortez Román & Hamann, 2014; Petron, 2003). However, research addressing migrants' trajectories and life experiences both, in the U.S. and in Mexico, is scarce (Silver, 2018; Petrone, 2020). This chapter contributes to advance this area of research and analysis by drawing on Anzaldúa's (1987) *mestiza* consciousness framework to present an in-depth analysis of two Mexican migrants' struggles and ambiguities on both sides of the border. We first show how migrants try to break down dualistic hegemonic paradigms that impose culturally determined roles that make them feel unaccepted (or rejected). Second, we observe how these individuals defy the pre-established norms by creating their own *mundo zurdo* (Anzaldúa, 1987) to produce their own definitions of what it means to be Mexican on both sides of the wall. To do so, this chapter will first present a brief overview of the migration context of the 1.5 generation. Second, it will focus on the concept of *mestizaje*, Coatlicue's state and the creation of a *mundo zurdo*. We then present our methodology and participants' stories prior to our analysis. Finally, we discuss our findings.

Belonging and Exclusion *Aquí y Allá*

Generation 1.5 is a concept coined by sociologist Rubén Rumbaut (2004) to make reference to undocumented immigrants who arrived in the U.S. in their early infancy, attended school, and were raised in the host country. Although these young people could pass as U.S. citizens due to the values they have internalized, their command of English, and their development in society, their unauthorized immigration status leads to a systematic exclusion once they come of age. Landmark U.S. Supreme Court case Plyler versus Doe allowed in 1982 educational access to basic and upper secondary education to all children regardless of their immigration status. Yet, this protection is lost as undocumented immigrants' transition into adulthood. That happens once they reach the age of 18 years old.

The spotlight and media coverage have focused on the DREAMer movement and the beneficiaries of the Deferred Action for Minor Arrivals (DACA), an executive order implemented by former U.S. President

Barack Obama in 2012 to provide a temporary and renewable work permit and protection from being deported. To qualify for DACA, enrollees must meet certain conditions, such as being enrolled in high school or having a high school diploma or GED equivalent and not being convicted of a felony, significant misdemeanor, or three or more other misdemeanors (López & Krostrad, 2017). To be eligible for DACA, the applicant must have arrived in the U.S. before reaching the age of 16, in addition to having lived in that country continuously since before June 15, 2007. Requirements to qualify for DACA are not an easy matter, neither to obtain the $475 U.S. dollars to pay the application fee. Even obtaining DACA, the future seems uncertain for recipients for whose lawful stay in the U.S. often mirror a roller-coaster. In 2017, President Donald Trump attempted to end the program, calling it unconstitutional. Three years later, a district judge reinstated the program, although no new applications were allowed. According to López and Krostrad (2017), two metro areas concentrate the highest numbers of DACA recipients as of September 2017: the Los Angeles-Long Beach-Anaheim metropolitan area (89,900 recipients) followed by New York-Newark-Jersey City metro area (47,200). The top areas of current DACA recipients are similar to those of the unauthorized immigrant population as a whole. In fact, both of the participants interviewed for our research have resided in these metro areas. One is still living in New York while the second one was raised in Los Angeles and now lives in Guadalajara.

Gonzáles (2016) untangles the great diversity of the 1.5 generation to show how their precarious status affects every aspect of their lives: educational, professional, personal, and economic, among others. Oftentimes, conditions are usually far from ideal to continue an educational and career path, which in turn may exclude them from immigration programs or policies such as DACA, even though this executive order does not mean legal residence. It is important to remember that undocumented youth usually experience family and community conditions different from those of their documented adolescent peers. Many of these youngsters are required to financially contribute to their families significantly and to take care of themselves (Gonzáles, 2011).

Transition to Mexico, either forcefully or voluntarily, is not easy either for the 1.5 generation immigrants after spending their formative years in the United States. Mexico's federal government has only recently started to look at the returning migrants' population, considering they may require some services and support in adapting to their old-new country. Yet, actions to support returnees are scarce, limited, short term, and mostly focused on the deported nationals. In other words, Mexico's government basically offers reception services (e.g., food, transportation, and phone calls in repatriation centers) instead of support for long-term reintegration, such as job training, certification of abilities, or even programs of educational continuity for young adults (Jacobo & Cárdenas, 2020). Even though they are citizens in Mexico, return migrants usually plan their strategies for reintegration (or re-emigration) on their own or with the support of other returnees and/or social organizations (Jacobo & Despagne, 2019). Belonging, attachments, and identities are thus crucial aspects experienced by the 1.5 generation in the U.S. and in Mexico that we analyze through Gloria Anzaldúa's framework, a woman who experienced many of these subjectivities in her own flesh.

Mestizaje and the New *Mestiza*: Two Opposing Concepts

In her first major autobiographical book, Anzaldúa (1987) writes from La Frontera, The Borderlands, and from nepantla, which means in-between in Náhuatl, a multi-bonded and liminal space through which she constructs a new hybrid subject, the new *mestiza*. The new *mestiza* not only negotiates and redefines the Chicana identity in the U.S., but also challenges the very idea of *mestizaje* in Mexico. This is important because Anzaldúa's perception of *mestizaje* is very different from the ideological foundation of *mestizaje* on which the Mexican nation-state was created as will be analyzed in the following.

Anzaldúa (1987) promotes the conception of the human being as an interdependent, hybrid subject in process, the new *mestiza* which means "a product of the transfer of the cultural and spiritual values of one group to another" (p. 78); a product that breaks down dualistic hegemonic paradigms which impose geographically, linguistically, culturally, racially, and sexually determined roles. Anzaldúa is a "border woman" (1987, preface) who has lived on the border between the U.S. and Mexico, between English, Spanish, and Náhuatl, between people of color and white people, between the feminine and the masculine. She is not only Indigenous, not only white, neither Mexican nor North American, she does not speak only Spanish or only English. She defines herself racially, culturally, linguistically, and sexually as a new *mestiza*, a subject built upon different fragments, like a collage. Anzaldúa is part of a minority, like the 1.5 generation participants of this study. Such individuals always have to cross the lines, transgress, and are considered aliens who intrude into the hegemonic U.S. culture and then into the mainstream Mexicaness. Individuals that are likely to be discriminated against and feel uprooted in their very own "home" country.

In opposition to Anzaldúa's new *mestiza*, *mestizaje* in Mexico represents the dominant culture. The ideology of *mestizaje*, which has been created in the 19th and 20th centuries, refers to a cultural mix between Indigenous people, Africans, and Europeans. José Vasconcelos, one of the main artifacts of this ideology and who wrote the essay "La raza cósmica"

(1925), aimed to disseminate the idea that all Mexicans are mestizos, that they are all equal, and that they all speak only one language, "Mexican Spanish." *Mestizaje* as ideology has aimed to homogenize the Indigenous culturally and linguistically different populations, leading to the belief that diversity is a problem that can jeopardize the homogeneity of the nation. The linguistic and educational policies that derive from this ideology are of social assimilation led through a Hispanization process in the school system since the creation of the Mexican Public Education System where social inclusion is carried out based on clearly pre-established norms of what it means to be a "real" Mexican. Hence, when the 1.5 generation (re)integrates the Mexican school system, they have to adapt to the *mestizaje* ideology. Their differences will therefore not be easily accepted, even though they are formal Mexican citizens.

Migrants "Inner War": From the Coatlicue State to the Creation of Their *Mundo Zurdo*

Like Anzaldúa, the 1.5 generation faces "the dilemma of mixed breed" (Anzaldúa, 1987, p. 78) on both sides of the border. They are "sandwiched" between cultures and value systems. In the U.S., they have to adapt to the culture of the United States, to new gender roles which do not correspond to their parents' beliefs, and speak American English "without an accent." They experience segregation and discrimination based on skin color, their migratory condition, and speaking English with an accent (Pérez-Soria, 2017) what Anzaldúa describes as "linguistic terrorism." (1987, p. 53). As mentioned by Anzaldúa (1987), "the dominant white culture is killing [them] slowly with its ignorance" (p. 86). In Mexico, the 1.5 generation has to speak and write "real," standard Mexican Spanish; not the Spanish they spoke at home with their family or with their friends in the U.S. Spanglish, the language which represents their border identities is often de-legitimized, perceived as a "mutilation of Spanish." They are told that they speak *raro* (weird) or pocho as a criticism of their "lack" of Spanish language efficiency.

Their fragmented social, professional, and linguistic life experiences can be related to Anzaldúa's Coatlicue state where she takes Coatlicue, the Aztec god of fertility, as a reference because she represents conflicting identities, of both, life-giver and life taker, compassionate yet all powerful. Anzaldúa uses this image to represent fragmented social, sexual, cultural, and linguistic identities and uses the shield-shaped stone of Coatlicue as a reference which depicts a dismembered Goddess to reflect the narrative of her defeat in Coatepec where she felt in pieces. Anzaldúa focuses on Coatlicue to analyze identities in constant process of (re)construction through the awareness of personal and social memories and (re)membering and to make sense out of "our greatest disappointments and painful experiences . . . [which] can lead us to becoming more who we are" (p. 68). This remembering of painful life experiences can allow, if the 1.5 generation can analyze and make meaning out of them, to lead to a *mestiza* consciousness that will help them to know who they really are. It could allow them to go deep into a reflective state of their identity, a very painful process, yet one which could also faciliate reconfiguring their fragmented identity.

Through conscious remembering, migrants on both sides of the border who "decide to act and not react" and who are able to develop a "tolerance for ambiguity" (Anzaldúa, 1987, p. 79), can create a third space, a liminal space as a counterstance from the imposition of unique identities on both sides of the border that Anzaldúa calls *mundo zurdo* (left-handed world). Anzaldúa's *mundo zurdo* refers to a world, a sort of interconnected community, which accepts diversity, a world where being different does not lead to social discrimination; it is a world where many different people can live together—each one with its own words and world visions—and where all together they can transform the planet. This transformation must not be based on homogeneity—like Mexico's idea of *mestizaje*—but from the respect of difference, from the experience of having been marginalized, of not having had a place in the world, of having lived in the shadows and having been invisibilized, of being excluded and of being sensitive to the alienation felt by others.

To be able to create this *mundo zurdo*, the new *mestiza* subject must get to a state of higher consciousness through which she becomes conscious of her perpetual transition from one collectivity and language to another and accepts that she lives in various in-between worlds. She must aim to break down the duality that is imposed on her from the social world that surrounds her and that keeps her a prisoner—to be American or Mexican, to speak only English, only Spanish, or only one of many Indigenous languages. Hence, the problem, for the 1.5 generation, lies in dismantling the dual world in which they live, to accept to be cultureless by defying "the collective cultural/religious male-derived beliefs of Indo-Hispanics and Anglos" (Anzaldúa, 1987, p. 80); and yet, to be cultured because the aim is to create another culture, the *mundo zurdo* which Anzaldúa (1987) defines as "a new story to explain the world and our participation in it, a new value system with images and symbols that connect us to each other and to the planet" (p. 81).

Participants and Methods

This research is part of a wider narrative inquiry (De Fina & Georgakopoulou, 2015) that aimed to delve into 20 participants' past, present, and future life stories as migrants and new mestizos. Ten participants currently live in New York, where 19% of the population is Hispanic

(Pew Research Center, 2014). The other ten participants live in Jalisco, the state with the highest percentage of return migrants during the period from 2005 to 2015, 9% (Unidad de Política Migratoria, 2017, p. 46).

For this chapter, we selected two representative participants to carry out an in-depth analysis of their personal narrative accounts of self and identity which were particularly instructive: Ana in New York and Javier in Jalisco. Qualitative data were obtained through fieldwork, interviews, surveys, and research diaries. Fieldwork in New York lasted two months in 2018 during which we accompanied Ana to different places and discussed her everyday life. We met several times for lunch and were also invited to a poetry workshop Ana organized with an Argentinian teacher for the domestic workers she worked with. The workshop allowed them to write about themselves and to accept themselves for who they are. In Jalisco, we met with Javier and other young adult returnees, all of them were part of a substance abuse rehabilitation group, in April 2019. We visited them at the rehabilitation facility, which is also Javier's house, on a day they were having a social gathering. We spent the day with them, barbecued, listened to their favorite rap music, and finally interviewed Javier. Interviews lasted about 2 to 3 hours and were then transcribed. Data were analyzed thematically through Anzaldúa's framework. We specifically looked at how they lived their *mestizaje* in New York and how they lived it in Mexico; how they faced ambiguities on both sides of the border and lived "the dilemma of mixed breed" to create their own *mundo zurdo*. We now present our participants. We used pseudonyms for both of them and for the places where they worked to protect their anonymity.

Ana is a young woman, single mother, full of energy. Originally from Atlixco, Puebla, Ana arrived in New York with her mom and sister when she was 11. She attended a bilingual school in New York but could not study further because she had no papers and no money. Today, she is one of the leaders of the Domestic Workers' Association (DWA), a non-profit organization for the defense of domestic workers of color in the U.S. After the beginning of #MeToo, Ana denounced the sexual abuse she suffered, along with 500 other domestic workers. However, to make ends meet, she still has to work three different jobs. In addition to DWA, she also works cleaning houses and as a teacher assistant in a kindergarten. Ana's mother died last year, but she still lives with her sister, her sister's son, and her own daughter. Ana has not returned to Mexico since she left. She identifies herself as a New York *mexicana* who doesn't know Mexico, and as a citizen of the world.

Javier was born in Sinaloa, Mexico. A few months after his birth, his mom took him to the U.S. with his older sister. He grew up and attended elementary and middle school in Los Angeles, California, where his two younger siblings were born. Raised in a violent neighborhood and being constantly exposed to, and later a member of gangs, Javier started a criminal record from a very young age. Thanks to the amnesty granted to undocumented immigrants by former U.S. President Ronald Reagan, Javier obtained a permanent residence green card. Yet, being involved with gangs took him in and out of prison until finally serving an eight-year conviction, after which his green card was taken away and he was deported to Mexico. In Mexico, Javier spent several years traveling from state to state in Mexico, trying to find a place where he could fit in. In addition to his prior gang and prison experience, Javier had a history of substance and drug abuse, which made it very difficult for him to reintegrate into society. He did not have any close relatives in Mexico; his mom and siblings are all in the U.S. After finding a 12-step rehab program and getting back on his feet, Javier decided to start his own rehab group, GDL 13, in Guadalajara, where he chose to stay.

Ana and Javier's Coatlicue state point to their ambiguities and painful life experiences from a very young age as shown next.

Ana's Coatlicue State: Linguistic, Educational and Labor Discrimination

When Ana arrived in New York, gangs tried to recruit her, but she decided instead to get involved in a religious Christian community which allowed her "to stay away from the streets." During her studies, she had to work after school and on weekends to help her mother. Ana worked in numerous factories, as a cashier, as a nanny and in a deli. Her immediate school and work environments were all Spanish speaking; none of them helped her to learn English.

Her dream was to study and to fulfill her mother's "American Dream," a discourse she still feels identified with today. However, at school, she felt discriminated against because she did not speak English: "*el idioma [inglés] me gustaba, pero me daba miedo porque no entendía ni una palabra . . . y sí hubo un par de veces en la escuela que varias niñas se burlaron de mí porque no sabía.*" Later, once she looked for study opportunities, she was told that "*mira, tú no sabes hablar inglés, eres indocumentada, la verdad no hay muchas opciones para ti.*" She felt that her whole world closed in front of her eyes: "*ya se cerró todo, o sea ¿dónde voy? No sé inglés. Soy indocumentada, no tengo dinero para poder aplicar* [to university]."

Ana also experienced labor discrimination. She recalled that once she was refused a hostess job in a restaurant because she looked "too" Mexican: "*me dijo el manager es que tú te ves muy mexicana y además no hablas mucho inglés.*" For the manager, a hostess had to be "*alta, rubia y con ojos claros.*" Moreover, payments are low because most undocumented migrants do not know their rights. Referring to domestic workers, Ana expressed that: "*muchas de ellas no saben, les pagan 10 dólares la hora o menos. Muchas trabajan días largos, de 12 a 14 horas, sin alimento o poder tomar agua.*" According to Ana, employers take advantage of migrants' disadvantageous legal situation to execute wage theft or pay less and to manipulate them "*si me acusas, te echo a migración y me aseguro que te deportan.*" They have to accept very low-income jobs, above all when they are heads of family, which is Ana's case.

In 2009, she was about to marry a Cuban American in California through whom she would have been able to access American citizenship. Ana said that her boyfriend "*me tuvo semi-secuestrada, no podía yo usar el teléfono; a cada ratito me cambiaba el número, me prohibía hablar, usar el internet y si yo quería ver a mis amigas, él venía conmigo.*" However, Ana thought he was taking care of her and got pregnant, but the father never acknowledged his daughter. Instead, he disappeared and robbed Ana's life savings: "*nos dejó en la calle a la bébé y a mí; sin comida, sin nada . . . cuando salí [del hospital], no tenía para comprar leche, no tenía para la renta . . . Fue desesperante*, you know." It was like a dream that collapsed: "*tenía esa idea genial que iba a ser una mujer casada y que mi situación legal iba a mejorar.*" After a while, Ana discovered that this man was an ex-convict and that police was looking for him for fraud.

When she got back to New York, she had no place to live, her sister got cancer, and then her mother got sick too. Over the years, Ana became the only one who financially supported all her family members. She had to pay all the medical expenses for her mother's and her sister's diseases.

Javier's Coatlicue State: A Long and Obscure Fight Before Acceptance

Javier's childhood and youth were even more turbulent than Ana's. He grew up in one of the most violent neighborhoods in Los Angeles, surrounded by constant fights between gangs, drugs, and youth going in and out of prison. Javier was surrounded by an environment that proved fatal for many of his friends and neighbors: "the gangs, many deaths, many shootings, this one overdose, this one jail for life." He himself started with prison experiences just as a teenager, about 20 years of going in and out of jail until the last time he was deported to Mexico. Interestingly, he thanks being alive to this long period of not being in the streets; prison was safer for him, he said. Inside the jail, he started his first transformation. He went from fighting other Mexican gang members in the streets to joining them as one unified group in prison, "*mi propia raza,*" realizing there was no point in fighting who he belongs to.

Javier was first deported to Mexico in his early adulthood. During these years, he traveled through Mexico for what he called "*los estados más bonitos, más mexicanos."* This experience helped to integrate the *mexicanidad* into his already Chicano identity. Yet, Javier did not stop consuming alcohol and drugs and started to affect his health with overdoses. He remembered these years as a wakeup call: *"despierta güey, ¿qué estás haciendo con tu vida? tienes 17 años, no tienes nada, no estás estudiando, eres un pinche drogadicto, eres un pandillero, eres deportado, o sea ¿qué tienes güey?"* Javier came back to the U.S. but could not keep out of the gangs nor from drugs. He returned to prison, this last time serving a conviction of eight years and deported again to Mexico.

While in Mexico, Javier hit rock bottom. He spent two years going from place to place, trying to feel at ease, feeling different, rejected. He went through Sinaloa, Guanajuato, and Michoacán until he finally arrived in Guadalajara. "I saw a valley with a huge metropolitan area, it reminded me of LA. So I decided to stay for some time, besides, I'm a *chiva* and wanted to see a game." It was Guadalajara where Javier would undergo his most important fight, an internal one, one against drugs, solitude, and lack of purpose.

Javier hit rock bottom in Guadalajara, after years of being homeless, and when one day, he tried to die crossing the street to be run over by a truck. When the truck stopped, Javier thought that if he was still alive it was because he had a life purpose. After that incident, he decided to clean himself from drugs, stay in Guadalajara, and create a home for other migrants with similar life stories. Ana hit rock bottom when she got back to New York. She had to work one week after giving birth, and had at the same time, to look after her sister who got cancer and her young child.

Consciousness Raising

Both Ana and Javier reacted after hitting rock bottom; they became conscious about their lack of access to rights and opportunities, and began to fight against all the injustices they experienced. Ana decided to learn English, to apply for DACA, and to work for DWA to defend the rights of domestic workers like herself. Javier decided to create his own association, GDL 13, to help ex-convicted deported migrants, just like him, to reintegrate into society in Mexico.

Ana was aware that learning English would allow her to partially leave the shadows in which she lived, and to access and better understand the dominant Anglophone world that surrounded and oppressed her. Ana recalled *"yo lo voy a aprender porque lo voy a aprender, pero bien. No va a haber acento, no va a haber esto."* She wanted to imitate native-like accent: *"cuando quería hablar, se burlaban de mi acento, entonces, eso me daba coraje y me impulsaba a mejorar."* However, Ana speaks only

Spanish at home: "*en el momento que entro a mi casa, sólo hablo español, no hay otra palabra, la música, la televisión, todo en español.*" Spanish at home, English at work, and Spanglish with her friends. By defining the context of the use of each of her languages, Ana clearly claimed the multiplicity of her *mestiza* consciousness. She constructed different hybrid spaces or communities for herself where she could use her unique linguistic and cultural profiles. As a *mestiza*, she resists being identified by the language of a single country.

Ana became even much more conscious about her rights when she applied for DACA in 2011, for which she had to borrow money to pay the fees, 475 U.S. dollars as mentioned earlier, and once she worked at DWA. Through DACA, she got a work permit, and therefore access to better paying jobs: "*Daca, la verdad, sí me ha abierto muchas puertas . . . para mí eran 8 dólares la hora y con DACA, 15, o sea la gloria.*" With a work permit, undocumented migrants are no longer as prone to scams from labor agencies or from people who offer jobs in the newspaper. Once she got DACA, Ana dreamt of to travel to Mexico, to get to know her own country. However, at the time of the interview, in May 2018 under the Trump government, she was not allowed to travel anymore:

> *Tenía planes de hacerlo [ir a México] pero justo cuando planeaba hacerlo en septiembre, octubre del año pasado, es cuando dicen que se acaba todo, no más. Y ya no pude viajar . . . no podemos salir del país, podemos trabajar y pagar impuestos, pero no podemos salir. Estamos aquí, encarcelados.*

Despite feeling imprisoned, Ana is grateful that DACA gave her the possibility to work at the DWA, which is what really changed her life and allowed her to become who she is today. Ana always felt that she could do more: "*yo siempre le decía a mi mamá ¿por qué yo tengo tanto talento y nadie se da cuenta? Yo sentía que, debido a mi situación legal, por no tener documentos, no podía sacar este brillo.*" Today, at DWA, Ana is the coordinator of the Latino office in New York where she informs undocumented Latino domestic workers about their rights (minimum wage, overtime pay, sick day pay, etc.). Hence, DACA partly allowed her to overcome the oppression she was experiencing which did not allow her to be creative and to empower herself. DWA became Ana's border space, a flexible and creative space of negotiation and contestation.

When Javier hit rock bottom in Guadalajara, he fell into a profound, long depression.

> I spent two years being a vagabond, I had nothing, the only thing I carried was some torn shoes, shitted and pissed pants and a shirt that was already a month old. Everything stinky, everything rotten

inside, disappointed, I crossed the streets regardless of whether there were trucks or not.

He thought that he was alive by a miracle, *"because God wants it that way."* As in Ana's case, it was hitting rock bottom that motivated him to rehab through a 12-step process and leave behind violence, alcohol, and drugs: *"llegó un momento en mi vida que yo dejé de tener sangre en mis manos."* After years of being in his own cleansing (detox) process, and finding in Guadalajara a place where he wanted to build a home, Javier decided to create his own group. Once he himself experienced a 12-step rehab program, and felt motivated and empowered about who he was and what capacities he had, Javier created various groups to help people like him to go through two main processes: drug and alcohol rehabilitation and reintegration to Mexico. The current group meets every other week to discuss the 12 steps of rehabilitation. Sometimes they have social gatherings with friends who spent some time in the group but are now recovered. While recovering from drug addictions is a main purpose, creating and maintaining a bicultural, bilingual, and "cholo" community is also at the heart of Javier's group.

At his current group, GDL 13, Javier provides a home to people who arrive in Mexico after having been deported from the U.S.; having completed a prison sentence and addiction problems to alcohol and drugs. The project is located in a winery that used to be a garbage dump and now is Javier's place: *"in this house, Chicano culture welcomes the community Western Mexico Region identity."* On many occasions, people who arrive at the GDL 13 have no family in the country; they do not have economic resources to pay rent; they lack identity documents that allow them to get a job; they speak little Spanish and do not know Mexico; or they feel they do not belong to the country.

> *Yo ya dejé de preguntarme ¿qué puede hacer el PRI, el PAN, los gobernantes por mí? Ahora me pregunto qué puedo hacer yo por mi país y eso es lo que he hecho. El GDL 13 es un servicio de recuperación. Yo salvo vidas, así de fácil y es un proceso integral . . . hay personas que llegan sin nada, como cuando yo estaba en las calles . . . lo mío no es un lucro, yo salvo vidas, esta es una casa de vida, nosotros grupo GDL Sur, somos los únicos en todo Jalisco, bilingual, que damos servicios gratuitos.*

Just like Ana, Javier decided to act, and not to react. GDL 13 became his third space, this liminal interconnected bilingual and bicultural community where he feels accepted, just like he is, and where he can help others, just like him. In addition, it is important to understand here that both, Ana and Javier, were able to create their own *mundo zurdo* based on their own lived experiences of having been marginalized and discriminated against, as shown next.

The New *Mestizas*' *Mundo Zurdo*: From Self-Acceptance to Self-Empowerment

Ana recalled: "*yo fui una de esas que no sabía mis derechos, que no sabía que tenía derechos, hasta que conocí la alianza.*" She feels that her job at DWA empowered her because "*por haberlo pasado en carne propia . . . yo puedo hacer ese cambio porque yo lo pasé y no quiero que más gente lo siga pasando.*" Something similar occurred to Javier, as mentioned earlier; after having survived the gangs, prison, drugs, and deportation, he decided to create GDL 13 to help people with similar life stories.

Ana does not rule out returning to Mexico because she would love to get to know her country, but she can also imagine herself migrating elsewhere where she could continue to grow. She perceives Mexico as her "patria" because she was born here and yet has no connection with her family anymore. Her family is in New York now: "*tengo más conexión con mis amistades aquí y como aquí dicen, tu familia son tus amistades mayormente.*" She identifies as a *mexicana* from New York, a *mexicana* who does not know Mexico. When people ask her about Mexico, she always feels bad and answers "*es que no sé nada . . . Atlixco, Puebla es lo único que conozco, pero si tú me preguntas de Nueva York, yo te puedo decir de todo.*" However, this internal conflict, to be a Mexican who does not know Mexico, makes Ana also identify as a "*citizen of the world*":

> *así me describo, o sea siento que soy de todo el mundo . . . y me gustaría cambiar el mundo . . . me gustaría que mi nombre, que cuando dijeran mi nombre, la gente supiera quién es Ana Rodríguez . . . no por el título, sino por lo que yo he hecho por otra gente, por la comunidad . . . no quiero que más gente siga pasando por lo que yo pasé.*

Through her professional participation at the DWA, Ana was able to dismantle at least one main duality, that is, the documented versus undocumented by showing undocumented workers that they also have rights in New York and that they have the right to claim them. Ana became who she is today "*por el empuje, por ver tanta injusticia durante mi adolescencia y la vida de inmigrante.*" Hence, Ana feels being a different person after obtaining DACA and working at the DWA: "*yo siento que era como ese diamante y que me han estado puliendo y que ahora estoy brillando con mi luz propia porque yo siento que tengo ese talento y gracias a la organización que me ha dado tanto.*"

Social rejection also forged Javier's identity, as he seemed to be very aware and proud of each of the elements that constitute his current identities. He showed pride in considering himself part of the U.S. and Mexico; of living in Guadalajara, a city that reminds him of Los Angeles, the place where he grew up; of his years in prison and his time of freedom; of his moments of substance addiction and his moments of sobriety. In other words, Javier has worked for years, and perhaps decades, to construct acceptance from many places and communities he belongs to, while fighting against what he's not.

Javier started our conversation by referring, first, to his identity as cholo while identifying the very early roots of this word: "*primeramente la palabra cholo, no es ni mexicana, ni americana, es de los Aztecas.*" He is very animated about history and aware of this knowledge he said, "*I know a lot about history, I'm very intelligent because I read a lot.*" Then, he narrates how the Aztecs used the word cholo to refer to the son of two races, the Azteca and the Spanish, what later was called Creole, mixed-race, "*what many of us call binational, two-bloods.*" Javier explained to us how, in its origins, the word cholo was not related to the "denigrating" meaning it has nowadays. In his youth, cholo was started to be used in the U.S. to describe low-income migrants and over time it was adopted to refer to gang members, particularly in Los Angeles where Javier grew up: "the third generation cholo becomes what we consider Mexican, the bicultural culture, being proud of who we are." He concluded with "I (as a cholo) am different, we (cholos) always wanted to be different, even from our own parents. We want to be part of (America) but distinguish ourselves from it."

Dominant in Javier's identity is the association as *homie*. Homie is an urban language term, used by the Mexican community in the U.S., which results from the abbreviation homeboy, amigo de casa (Arreguín et al., 2018). In Spanish, homie would be the equivalent of paisano. When referring to Mexico, Javier considered homies those who come from Culiacan, the city where he was born, even though he was taken to Los Angeles still as a baby. He used homie as a reference point during the several years he was in prison in the U.S.

> In jail it is not allowed to identify yourself by neighborhoods (gangs), because there we are already identifying ourselves as enemies. Instead, among Mexicans, we identify ourselves as homies to refer to those who are from our same area in California, for example one from San Diego, from LA, from South California.

Once he was deported to Mexico, Javier used homie to basically identify people like him, who grow up in the U.S., that have a previous gang or substance abuse history who speak English and dress like a cholo (very loose clothes). In fact, Javier assured that being a homie goes along some unmistakable traits he can identify right away when he sees one:

> we (homies) have a different way of walking, a different way of speaking, a different way of looking at people. We are very respectful; we are not rude to women. . . . They are internal rules of our culture and that is what distinguishes us, homies, from other cholos.

Being homie, deported and Chicano are the main identities that guide Javier's life nowadays. And these are also the people he aims to help in Mexico, through GDL 13, where he focuses his energies on people like him, because people like him, according to himself are difficult to understand, which he summarized as follows:

> I'm still a gang member, but well, I'm not fighting with anyone anymore. I'm still a drug addict, but I'm not using drugs anymore. I'm still an alcoholic, but I don't get drunk anymore. I'm still a person who was in prisons, a convicted, but I'm not in jail anymore. When I accept my reality, there is not so much internal resistance, there is one thing, is acceptance.

Acceptance is a fundamental move in the Coatlicue state that allowed Javier to become conscious about himself and to follow the path toward the new knowledge that would define him as a new *mestizo*.

Conclusions

Ana and Javier both clearly experienced the "Shadow-Beast" which represents a central figure informing the self-affirmed identity of marginalized people, like Anzaldúa (1987), but as generation 1.5 members. The Shadow-Beast is representative of counter hegemonic subjectivities posed against the dominant culture. The Shadow-Beast is a reactionary figure whose agency is derived from directly opposing the normative philosophies that surround her. While Ana and Javier's subversive figures of the Shadow-Beast work within the interior spaces of the world, they also learn to refigure their inner beast within their own social spheres by acting as facilitators of passage to their chosen community. In other words, they shifted their own realities. They are hybrid subjects in process who decided to act and not to react. They both experienced a long and difficult path that led them through cracks, places where Ana and Javier found their own dark sides, that is, their own Shadow-Beasts, but this also allowed them to create bridges that confronted the dominant cultures in which they lived.

Ana and Javier first seemed to avoid rejection from their peers and therefore did not "push the unacceptable parts [of themselves] into the shadows" (Anzaldúa, 1987, p. 20). They did what the culturally imposed determined roles of their immediate context expected them to do. Ana felt highly discriminated against for not speaking English, looking "too Mexican" and being undocumented. She thought that marrying would save her, because she would have a man that would protect her, and a father for her child. Her *"idea genial"* of being a submissive and conforming married woman suddenly collapsed by being abandoned with her newborn and defrauded by her Cuban American boyfriend. Javier was expected to become a gang member and to fight for his *"propia raza,"* which he did and which caused him many years of incarceration. He became addicted to drugs, had blood on his hands, and finally got deported to Mexico where he felt even more different and rejected.

By following what was expected of them, Ana and Javier hit rock bottom. They were both sandwiched between cultures and value systems: Ana, in New York, had to negotiate between the traditional Mexican patriarchal system and different North American gender roles, her social role as an undocumented Mexican worker in New York and her impetus of being herself in a country where she had nearly no rights. She felt defeated at times, especially when her boyfriend disappeared with her life savings. Javier, after losing his United States residency and being deported, had to negotiate a new Mexican identity. He was sandwiched between being a Mexican-American gang member in the United States and following the pre-established norms of the *mestizaje* ideology in Mexico to become a "real" Mexican. He also felt defeated, especially when he became a drug addict and a vagrant, fell into a profound depression and wandered the streets of various Mexican states. They both lived in the borderlands, torn between a failed dream and a life in the shadows, between a life in the United States and a life in Mexico. By feeling defeated and dismembered, just like Coatlicue in Coatepec, Ana and Javier felt in pieces and entered Nepantla, this "in-between, unstable, unpredictable, precarious, always-in-transition space" which lacks clear boundaries (Anzaldúa, 2002a, p. 1).

During their depression, they also "locked the door, kept the world out; . . . vegetated, hibernated, remained in stasis, idled" (Anzaldúa, 1987, p. 44). And suddenly, they saw the Shadow-Beast, the rebel in themselves, this part of themselves that "refuses to take orders from outside authorities" (Anzaldúa, 1987, p. 16). By making themselves conscious of their Shadow-Beast and their inner selves, they both began to make meaning out of their greatest disappointments. They realized that they did not want the patriarchal order, the gangs nor the pre-established Mexican norms to become a "real" Mexican to rule their lives. Javier woke up and chose to live in Guadalajara because "the city is in a valley," just like Los Angeles; he followed a 12-step rehabilitation program and fought against drugs, alcohol, and loneliness. Ana began to learn English. She did not want to belong to the 66% of Mexican-born nationals ages 5 and over who reported limited English proficiency in the U.S. (Israel & Batalova, 2020) and decided to learn it on her own. She wanted to imitate a native-like accent to fight English language terrorism in her own way. Because she belongs to generation 1.5 who arrived in the U.S. before 2007, before she was 16, and got a U.S. high school diploma, she qualified for DACA which allowed her to work at DWA where she learnt about her rights as a domestic worker in New York. At this stage, Ana and Javier no longer were the persons they were before. The Shadow-Beasts inside themselves woke up, and they confronted them. Even though Ana was convinced that she could use English as a cultural capital (Bourdieu, 1982), she was also clearly aware that she did not want to lose Spanish, her native language. Both still felt the inner fight but began to accept their painful experiences and, above all, forgive themselves. As stated by Anzaldúa (2002b), "forgiving yourself and others, you connect with more aspects of yourself and others" (p. 559). Thanks to this self-acceptance, they were able to heal their painful life experiences, become stronger, and shift their lives completely. This point seemed to be the moment of their own transformation through which they were able to negotiate their own conflicts and differences (Gutiérrez Magallanes, 2018). They did not let the Beast drag them underground again. Their sense of self was beginning to get reconfigured. Both, Ana and Javier, began to get passionate about defending the rights of people of their own communities. Ana strengthened alliances with undocumented domestic workers and Javier with former convicts, gang members, and drug addicts who were deported to Mexico and wanted a new life.

They reconstructed themselves by putting their pieces back together and by reinterpreting how they saw themselves. This conscious remembering allowed them to reach Anzaldúa's *mestiza* consciousness. This state of higher consciousness empowered them to act and to create their own *mundo zurdo*. In their own *mundo zurdo*, they became conscious of the perpetual transition between their different worlds, world views, and values. They broke down the duality between patriarchy and new gender roles, documented versus undocumented worlds, Mexican in Los Angeles and Mexican in Mexico, to speak English or Spanish, to be Mexican or white. They created their own culture by reclaiming their rights as cholos, homies, Chicanos, Mexican New Yorkers, and as citizens of the world. In their new world, their *mundo zurdo*, they created a liminal space of transformation that allowed Ana and Javier to move away from focusing on their painful life experiences on both sides of the border, from their victimhood, "to a more extensive level of agency" (Anzaldúa, 2002a, p. 2); they crossed the lines and created a shared space with people who live similar life experiences as they did, they created holistic alliances through which they fight, on one side for the rights of undocumented domestic workers, and on the other, for the adaptation to Mexico of deported, ex-convicts, gang members, and drug addicts. They became new *mestiza/o, aquí y allá*. Constituting themselves as 1.5 generation *New Mestizos* on both sides of the border is not an easy task as they constantly need to negotiate their belonging to their *mundo zurdo* with their immediate context.

This in-depth analysis of Ana and Javier uncovered their subjectivities and agencies as border woman and border man and shows that the enactment of borders can be both limiting, but also highly empowering. Javier's story also points to the emptiness of government programs to support deportees and return migrants during their reintegration process in Mexico's society. In fact, the scarce resources previously allocated by the Mexican federal government to this population were abruptly cancelled by Mexican President López Obrador in 2018, who as a presidential candidate had claimed to be close to the poorest and most disadvantaged. Ana, on the other hand, improved her economic situation thanks to DACA. Yet, her legal status continues to be precarious as this program does not equal a path to citizenship, and it depends on the political winds. Both Ana and Javier are not considered priority to the governments of the countries they live in. In response, they both have created their own support networks with others they feel similar to. And yet, as a society, we should not ignore our responsibility to coexist, respect, and support others who on behalf of difference may be systematically excluded and discriminated against.

These lived experiences should allow us to deconstruct ourselves and to question our governments, schools, educators, and ourselves as researchers how we impose these dominant paradigms, frameworks, and visions, and what we could, instead of perceiving diversity and difference as a problem, to see it as a highly valuable resource in today's knowledge society. The seal of biliteracy implemented in most of the United States, for example, is a recent initiative to promote recognition on linguistic diversity at schools. Associating value to diversity, instead of rejection, is a viable strategy to gradually change deeply ingrained prejudices. In Mexico, scholars have proposed welcoming protocols as a way to facilitate transition among immigrant students when they first arrive to school. Step by step, these few actions are oriented to highlight, normalize, and welcome diversity within school institutions, which are a primary site of possibility for cultural change.

References

Anzaldúa, G. (1987). *Borderlands. La frontera. The new mestiza.* Aunt lute books.

Anzaldúa, G. (2002a). Preface: (Un)natural bridges, (Un)safe spaces. In G. Anzaldúa & A. L. Keating (Eds.), *This bridge we call home. Radical vision for transformation* (pp. 1–5). Routledge.

Anzaldúa, G. (2002b). Now let us shift . . . the path of conocimiento . . . inner work, public acts. In G. Anzaldúa & A. L. Keating (Eds.), *This bridge we call home. Radical vision for transformation* (pp. 540–578). Routledge.

Arreguín, E., Martínez, I., Cariño, I., Wendelin, J., Silva, J., López, L., de la Pena, M., Zaragoza, M., Patlán, y Mino, S. (2018). *Empezar desde cero. Historias de vida y experiencias en el retorno a México*. Sistema Universitario Jesuita.

Bourdieu, P. (1982). *Language et pouvoir symbolique*. Éditions Fayards.

Budiman, A. (2020). *Key findings about US immigrants*. Pew Research Center: Factank News in the Numbers.

Cortez Román, N., & Hamann, E. (2014). College dreams à la mexicana . . . agency and strategy among American-Mexican transnational students. *Latino Studies, 12,* 237–258.

De Fina, A., & Georgakopoulou, A. (Eds.). (2015). *The handbook of narrative analysis*. Wiley-Blackwell.

Gonzáles, R. (2011). Learning to be illegal. *American Sociological Review, 76*(4), 602–619.

Gonzáles, R. (2016). *Lives in Limbo. Undocumented and coming of age in America*. University of California Press.

Gutiérrez Magallanes, M. S. (2018). Gloria Anzaldúa y el giro descolonial desde la frontera para el mundo. *Camino Real, 10*(13), 79–89.

Israel, E., & Batalova, J. (2020). *Mexican immigrants in the United States*. Migration Policy Institute. www.migrationpolicy.org/article/mexican-immigrants-united-states-2019

Jacobo, M., & Cárdenas, N. (2020). Back on your own: migración de retorno y la respuesta del gobierno federal en México. *Migraciones Internacionales, 11*(11), 1–22.

Jacobo, M., & Despagne, C. (2019). After the American Dream: Immigrants finding new opportunities in Mexico. *ReVista, 19*(1), 1–9.

López, G., & Krostrad, J. M. (2017). *Key facts about unauthorized immigrants enrolled in DACA*. Pew Research Center, Factank News in the Numbers.

Passel, J. S., & Cohn, D. (2019). *20 metro areas are home to six-in-ten unauthorized immigrants in US*. Pew Research Center: Factank News in the Numbers.

Pérez-Soria, J. (2017). Mexican immigrants in the United States: A review of the literature on integration, segregation and discrimination. *Estudios Fronterizos, 18*(37), 1–17.

Petron, M. A. (2003). I'm bien pocha: Transnational teachers of English in Mexico. [Doctoral dissertation, The University of Texas at Austin].

Petrone, E. A. (2020). A DREAMer's transnational pursuit for higher education and the impenetrable wall of neoliberalism. *Latino Studies, 18,* 558–580.

Pew Research Center. (2014). *Demographic and economic profiles of Hispanics by state and county*. www.pewresearch.org/hispanic/states/state/ny

Rumbaut, R. (2004). Ages, life stages, and generational cohorts: Decomposing the immigrant first and second generations in the United State. *International Migration Review, 38*(3), 1160–1205.

Silver, A. (2018). Displaced at "home": 1.5-Generation immigrants navigating membership after returning to Mexico. *Ethnicities, 4*(2), 208–224.

Unidad de Política Migratoria. (2017). *Prontuario sobre Migración Mexicana de Retorno*. Secretaría de Gobernación. http://portales.segob.gob.mx/work/models/PoliticaMigratoria/CEM/Investigacion/Prontuario_ret.pdf

Vasconcelos, J. (1925). *La raza cósmica*. Agencia Mundial de Librería.

Chapter 7

It's All Gone *South!* Applying Anzalduan Frameworks to Metonymy, Metaphor, and Mythologies to Understand the Language About Transnational Youth

Steve Daniel Przymus and José Omar Serna Gutiérrez

Introduction

"So, if you want to really hurt me, talk badly about my language... I am my language. Until I can take pride in my language, I cannot take pride in myself" (Anzaldúa, 1999, p. 81). Themes and lessons of unapologetic linguistic defiance, *rebelde*, glissade down Gloria Anzaldúa's writings like a "serpent's tongue" (p. 81) and leave *pistas* in the sands of the physical and psychological borderlands and spaces of the "in-between" for transnational youth to follow and take pride in their language practices and identities. Like "the border artist who constantly reinvents herself," transnational youth must be able to ponder "I wonder who I used to be, I wonder who I am" (Anzaldúa, 1993, p. 41).

Concepts of fluid yet contested identities link Anzaldúa's work to the lived experiences of today's transnational youth, who like Anzaldúa, occupy the physical and psychological U.S./Mexico borderlands. This chapter takes up how the identities of transnational youth are often invented through the conceptual language used by others but also puts forth ways in which these youths can reclaim that language and reinvent themselves with desired, positive identities. Like the snake metaphor mentioned earlier or Anzaldúa's (2002) bridge metaphor, conceptual metaphor has the power to humanize transnational youth through insurgent discourse and counterstories (Santa Ana, 2002). Anzaldúa (1993) explains, "Through the centuries a culture touches and influences another, passing on its metaphors and its gods before it dies. (Metaphors *are* gods)" (p. 39). Anzaldúa uses metaphors to both teach us how to live *and* to understand how life imposes upon some and keeps specific populations *down*.

DOI: 10.4324/9781003191575-11

Life is awash with metaphor, but what we take up here is that all metaphors are first built upon metonymy. Metonymies are hidden shortcuts in language, thought, and communication (Littlemore, 2015) and work to help individuals understand the world around them without having to truly think about it. One of the most common metonymies that Anzaldúa wields is the BORDER/*NEPANTLA* (BOTH PHYSICAL AND SPIRITUAL) BEING PART OF THE WHOLE BODY.[1] Just the one place metonymically (through synecdoche) stands in place for the whole being/person/nation/state/land, etc., no matter where that person resides. Anzaldúa's epigraph description of psychological, sexual, spiritual, and physical borderlands existing everywhere, concerning *under, lower, middle,* and *upper* classes are cognitively understood in a large part first through the STANDS FOR function of directional metonymy of WHAT'S FIRST, ABOVE, ON TOP STANDS FOR THE BEST (Przymus & Huddleston, 2021) and secondly through spatial metaphors of GOOD IS UP/BAD IS DOWN (Lakoff & Johnson, 1999). In turn, through these mental connections, humans discover their place in the world and perhaps how to resist and defy it. It is through the metonymy, metaphor, and mythologies (controlled, naturalized particular worldviews) of culture that "we perceive the version of reality that it communicates" (Anzaldúa, 1999, p. 38). In other words, "culture forms our beliefs" (p. 38), but conceptual language and discourses of internalized myths form our culture.

With this chapter, we place common idiomatic phrases, expressions, images, and words under a critical discourse analysis (CDA) lens and expose how unquestioned, normalized language can position transnational youth to become *othered*. CDA focuses on the "relations between discourse and other social elements (power relations, ideologies, institutions, social identities, and so forth)" (Fairclough, 2013, p. 9). Transnational students are those with academic and migratory experiences in the U.S. and Mexico. Like Anzaldúa, who left her *tierra*, her *gente*, so she could find herself, due to these migratory experiences, transnational youth can find their "own intrinsic nature buried under the personality" imposed on them (Anzaldúa, 1999, p. 38) by teachers and peers in their new communities. They live in blended worlds, they are multilingual and multicultural, yet these resources are often misunderstood and/or underrepresented in education. In Mexico, there are roughly 600,000 U.S.-born children (Jacobo & Jensen, 2018). However, the exact number of transnational students is unknown, in part, due to ambiguities in census information and the migratory patterns of transnational families. This is especially the case with Mexican-born students, also known as returnees, with academic experiences in the U.S. who are currently in Mexican schools (Gándara, 2020). It is estimated that over 500,000 Mexican-born and nearly seven million U.S.-born children of Mexican immigrant families are enrolled in U.S. schools (Gándara, 2020), and while not all of these students are transnational in their academic experience, they come from transnational families.

Anzaldúa recognized that individuals who occupy and are at the same time between two worlds can be socially ostracized, by falling outside of the "dualistic hegemonic paradigms . . . imposed on individuals and peoples from the outside" (Aigner-Varoz, 2000, p. 47). Anzaldúa understood that these dichotomous paradigms of acceptable/unacceptable, normal/abnormal, etc., are created, circulated, and recirculated through conceptual metaphors, and that these metaphors could be restructured through her writing for "both appropriation and resistance" (Aigner-Varoz, 2000, p 47). A resistance, agency, and re-appropriation of language, needed for transnational youth to bring about change and embrace both their differences and commonalities as strength in what Anzaldúa (1983) refers to as *el Mundo Zurdo*, a place where people from all disadvantaged backgrounds can forge alliances.

We fight the urge to deny and explain the inaccuracies of each idiomatic phrase, expression, image, and label used to position transnational youth negatively, and instead point out the implicit conceptual meaning and impact of these common ways of talking, in order to re-appropriate these through our own metonymies, metaphors, and myths. Using Anzaldúa's words as inspiration, we offer a semiotic bridge for shifting the consciousness on what transnationalism is and how it is that educators on both sides of the Mexico/U.S. border can recognize transnational youth as bridges. The act of rewriting conceptual language about transnational youth creates a bridge from the old way of talking about them to a new way that mirrors the lived experiences of transnational youth as transformers, who create new realities, and perspectives. They are, as Anzaldúa (2002) explains, bridges building upon unstable ground to connect two worlds.

> Bridges are thresholds to other realities, archetypal, primal symbols of shifting consciousness. They are passageways, conduits, and connectors that connote transitioning, crossing borders, and changing perspectives. Bridges span liminal (threshold) spaces between worlds, spaces I call *nepantla*, a Nahuatl word meaning *tierra entre medio*. Transformations occur in this in-between space, an unstable, unpredictable, precarious, always-in-transition space lacking clear boundaries.
>
> (p. 1)

If we are to learn from Anzaldúa's vast work, however, and extend it as a bridge to more equitable teaching and life experiences for transnational youth, we must first look at the conceptual thinking behind the ubiquitous language used to talk about these youths. We posit that both before the metaphor, metonymy exists, and after the metaphor, mythologies (Barthes, 1972) carry the meanings into the future. We have organized this chapter into two main parts: 1) a critical discourse analysis of deficit-based communication (idiomatic phrases, expressions, labels, etc.) that explains how these are perpetuated through metonymy, metaphor, and myth and 2) an exercise in how to dismantle this communication.

Throughout, we share pieces of the testimonios of four Mexican-born transnational individuals to both give insight into the pain and struggles faced by transnational youth and to relay examples of positive counterstories that highlight the funds of knowledge (Moll et al., 1992) and strengths of these individuals. *Testimonios* are "a nonfictional, popular-democratic form of epic narrative" (Beverley & Zimmerman, 1990, p. 175), where subjects are usually marginalized members of society who can give a human voice to the moral, political, educational, and economic struggles of those in that society. We weave these throughout the chapter, with the first two here, followed by Part 1: an explanation of how transnational youth are negatively positioned through conceptual metonymy, metaphor, and myth. *Testimonio* #3 is placed right before Part 2: an exercise in dismantling the mythologies of transnational youth. Finally, *Testimonio* #4 is shared at the end of the chapter, before the conclusion, as it leaves the reader with a concrete example of the topics taken up within.

Throughout the chapter, our analysis is filtered through Anzalduan themes of language and identity, as to both learn from her work and advance it. *Testimonio* #1 is the transnational story of Serna, who was born in Mexico, grew up in the U.S. He finished schooling in Mexico, where he studied a bachelor's in English language teaching (ELT) and master's in applied linguistics in ELT. He now lives and teaches English in the U.S.

Testimonio #1: Omar

For me, and many other transnationals, **language is a marker of our identity.** *Language(s) has always played an important role in my everyday life. At home, I was the official interpreter and translator. I recall interpreting for my grandparents during their doctor's appointments. It was extremely stressful and I had to remember everything because I would have to explain everything to my father later that evening. I was always* **happy to help** *because there was a candy shop and toy store next to the clinic and I usually got a small reward for helping. I also felt important because* **I was helping my family** *in a way that they couldn't.*

At school, I felt less confident. From elementary school in Southeast Idaho, I always knew that **something was different about my English.** *I remember* **being pulled out** *of class and taken to the mobile classrooms* with their rows of computers. *The entire ordeal always felt so secretive as I wouldn't discuss this with my teacher or other classmates. Of course, I wasn't the only child taking the 'language exams' in the trailer. Other children did too, but we never discussed it.*

Other instances when I felt "linguistically different" were when I returned from Mexico. My family and I would typically travel to Mexico around Thanksgiving and return mid-January. These were the months when my parents did not have as much work on the farm. I always looked forward to our trips to Mexico. The posadas (nine-day, traditional celebration leading up to December 25), playing with cousins who lived in Texas, but I only got to see in Mexico. The entire family would stay at my grandparents' house. However, **I always had a difficult time returning and was very anxious about this.** I knew that I had missed assignments and gossip. I also did not look forward to **people telling me that I sounded like a Mexican.** This happened several times and I recall **always trying to make a conscious decision to sound more American.**

These insecurities compelled me to try harder in my English classes to the point that I was taking AP English classes in High School. I remember during one class, we were discussing our papers on the novel we were reading in class, The Scarlet Letter (Hawthorn, 1850). The teacher questioned my use of the word castigate and had me look it up in front of the class to prove that it was a real word. *I felt upset.*

In Mexico, my insecurities shifted toward Spanish. People would say, "You don't speak like the others," meaning that I didn't sound like other transnationals in Mexico—or in their words "pochos" and "cholos." However, **when something would slip,** either in pronunciation or vocabulary, they would say, **"Es que eres de allá"** and **I'd be corrected amid** laughter.

Looking back, I grew up and lived in **places that did not embrace multiculturalism and multilingualism.** This resulted in me **feeling linguistic insecurity.** *I still feel this way,* but my background in applied linguistics (a field of study that includes second language acquisition, sociolinguistics, psycholinguistics, English language teaching, and other areas of study) *has helped me place some reason to these feelings.*

On the surface, this *testimonio* appears to be about living in two physical worlds, but beyond the physical, we have marked places in Serna's *testimonio* that highlight what it means to live *entre dos mundos psicológicos* of on the one hand feeling pride in being able to help the family through language and on the other hand being "othered," through language. Testimonio #2 tells the story of Isaiah (pseudonyms used for testimonios 2–4), who was born in Mexico, grew up in both the U.S. and Mexico, and now is working on his doctorate in the U.S. In Mexico, he studied both a bachelor's in ELT and a master's in applied linguistics in ELT. Isaiah provides a nuanced view into the metalinguistic processing (trying not to have an accent in either language, understanding how one is positioned as different due to an accent, and ultimately accepting this difference) and the trajectory of identity development that many transnational youths experience.

Testimonio #2: Isaiah

*I can say that Spanish was my first language and the language used at home. **At the age of 4,** my family decided to migrate to the US. We arrived to the state of Oregon. I soon began kindergarten with a full immersion approach. **There was little support from school** staff and administrators for ESL students. Thus, we were encouraged to gradually **learn the English language as quick as possible.***

*I have an older sister and an older brother. As they also enrolled into school, they were **faced with the same shock** that I was. I remember we relied on each other to keep learning any vocabulary and phrases that would help us develop along the English language.*

*At home, our parents had a strict Spanish only policy. My mom always encouraged us to **continue to use Spanish to not lose the language,** and to not develop that "accent" that Chicanos do while living in the US. She always highlighted how we would one day **go back** to our hometown in Guanajuato (either to visit or permanently), and she wanted **to avoid us from having that marked accent.***

*At the age of 10, we (my sister, my brother, and I) decided **to go down** to our hometown in Guanajuato for approximately a year under the supervision of our grandparents. We enrolled into school for a year while we were there. I can recall all of us **being signaled out for having an** "accent." In school, I was usually called on to read aloud or say something **in order for my teacher to highlight my accent.** I do not know how positive or negative this was, but **I did not refuse.***

After that year, we went back to Oregon, and I enrolled into middle school. School adaptation was rather natural. I believe that what helped this transition flow smoother was arriving to the same place and having the same friends and support from the same community.

*After a year and a half in Oregon, we (my sister, my brother, and I) decided to go back to Guanajuato again. I enrolled into school again (in middle school). In terms of the language, I did not have any issues adapting back as **I had certain pragmatic knowledge and knew about certain terms, idioms, and collocations** that were present throughout my hometown. I had the same friends who I was able to keep in touch with, and this was also key in adapting back home to Guanajuato.*

*After a year and a half **down in Guanajuato,** we (my sister, my brother and I) decided to migrate back to Oregon. This time, I enrolled into high school as a freshman. I had the same friends on this side of the border,* *and relied on the same community support. I did not have any issues with the English language.*

*After a year and a half in Oregon, I decided to migrate **back down to Guanajuato** with my mother. This was during my sophomore year (in winter break). The reason was due to an illness of one of my relatives **down in Guanajuato**, and I was uncertain about how much time we were **to be down in Guanajuato**. I enrolled into high school while **down in Guanajuato**. As I was near finishing my high school, I began looking for a university and felt fortunate to find the BA TESOL (Teaching English to Speakers of Other Languages)/ELT (English Language Teaching) at the Universidad de Guanajuato. I did not hesitate to go through the admission process as I felt confidence in the proficiency I had in the English language, and had hopes of doing something productive with the language **(in terms of sharing it and teaching others about it)**.*

*As I began the program, I immediately identified many classmates and peers with similar experiences as myself. We tended to gravitate toward each other, and we maintained close ties with one another. We also engaged in recalling our lived experiences while in the US, and we **switched from one language to another, mixing and blending elements of both languages**. I believe that **this helped me maintain my English language in a rather natural way**, as our conversations seemed natural and nothing was ever forced.*

*Close to the end of my BA degree, I decided to pay my family and old friends a visit to Oregon. I did not feel hesitant to use either language (English or Spanish), or a mixture of the two with any person who I interacted with. I believe that **I also gained further pragmatic knowledge, and I had a better understanding of how to use my language in certain social settings**.*

*Today, I feel that **I may still have an accent in both languages, but I am now embracing it as part of my identity**. After all, I believe we all have an accent depending on many societal factors in which we learned and are faced to using the language. I feel that I can develop more or less proficiently in both languages, regardless of having an accent in both. I feel equally confident in using either language, and **I am proud of having my background reflected in the usage of my full linguistic repertoire**.*

This insightful *testimonio* echoes themes from *testimonio* #1 of pride, using language to help, intense personal efforts and family language policy to not sound different, and an advanced level of understanding of the processes behind language and identity development. Also bolded in this *testimonio* are times when Isaiah used (perhaps unconsciously) directional metonymy and spatial metaphors to index Mexico as *down*. Part 1, in the following, specifically takes up the often-unconscious influence of these kinds of conceptual language by explicitly highlighting common conceptual metonymy, metaphor, and myth used to talk about the border, the geo-political relationship between the U.S. and Mexico, language about immigration, La Malinche, and transnational youth.

Part 1: False Directional/Spatial and Other Conceptual Thinking: Metonymy, Metaphor, and Myth on the U.S. Side of the Border

Educational discourse on transnationalism in the United States is almost entirely focused on the U.S./Mexico border. This discourse includes language about what is North of the border, what is South of the border, and can often inappropriately be conflated with the cardinal direction North being synonymous with up and the cardinal direction South being understood as directionally down. Although cardinal directions have no correlation to humans' location of being up or down in the universe, Mexico's directional positioning of being south of the U.S. border produces implicit, deficit-based conceptual metonymies regarding what comes from the other side or *below* the border. We argue that conceptual thinking and ideologies linked to quotidian ways of talking about directions are wide-spread, and without analysis and problematization will continue to position transnational youth from Mexico in a negative light on both sides of the border. Highlighting this issue, Narayanaswamy (2007) points out that:

> It has become customary within academic and non-academic circles to distinguish between the developed "North" and the "developing" or "under-developed" "South". These terms reflect very rough geographic generalizations where the developed North, with both wealth and knowledge is contrasted with the financial and intellectual poverty of the South.
>
> (p. 50)

More nuanced discussions regarding the South/North dichotomy have been proposed (Pennycook & Makoni, 2019). Although these have the potential to revert the hegemonic positioning in academia of the North, over the South, such directional and spatial conceptualizations and ideologies remain outside of academia, where it is more common for transnational youth to get swept up in the debate. A quick Google search for some variation of "gone South," produces examples such as, *"The stock market's headed South again"; "The city had the flood under control, then a trickle turned into a stream, then into a full-size breach, and then things went South quickly."* This idea of South being linked to both the direction "down" and the quality "bad," is conceptually linked to Mexico through expressions such as "down South," "South of the border," and "down Mexico way" (see Figure 7.1). Even Isaiah uses some variation of "down in Guanajuato" six times in his truncated *testimonio*.

It's All Gone *South*! 141

Figure 7.1 Section labels at a bookstore in Texas, U.S.
Source: Photograph taken by Steve Daniel Przymus

Both the co-authors of this chapter (2021) have conducted extensive research on the implicit impact of the directional metonymy of WHAT'S FIRST, ABOVE, ON TOP STANDS FOR THE BEST in the linguistic landscape of educational contexts and believe that this is the basis for the spatial metaphors of GOOD IS UP; BAD IS DOWN (Lakoff & Johnson, 1999). We argue that deficit-based identity/language ideologies regarding ethnic-Latinx transnational youth may actually precede these students' attendance in U.S. schools due to the cognitive influence of conceptual metonymy and resulting conceptual metaphors that link the abstract domains of bad, threat, deterioration, decline, etc. with the concrete domain of the direction South. This coupled with current U.S. political discourse of what comes from "down South," expose the directional metonymy of *gone South* as turning bad, going downhill, turning for the worse, things souring, going awry, etc. As educators, we cannot be naïve to the implicit power that language can have on our own ideologies. "North—South is not simply a geographical distinction, but relates to dominance, privilege and elite discourses, and the inequality that these manifest within local, regional or international spaces" (Narayanaswamy, 2007, p. 59)

Once understood for their implicit power, these North/South, up/down, and good/bad conceptual dichotomies are quite evident in how transnational youth are talked about. As we apply Anzalduan frameworks and see these youths as possessing "A bridge/hybrid language . . . one capable of communicating the realities and values" of people who do not identify with either just Spanish nor just English (Anzaldúa, 1999, p. 77), we must be aware of the language used to talk about them; conceptual thinking that could undermine and deteriorate the bridge.

Through further critical discourse analysis, we use conceptual metonymy theory, unearthing other ubiquitous metaphors of transnational youth, such as IMMIGRANTS AS DANGEROUS WATER (Catalano, 2017; Santa Ana, 2002) and due to their bilingualism and cross-border/multi-national experiences, IMMIGRANTS AS TRAITORS/*LA MALINCHE* (Kasun & Mora-Pablo, 2021). Water metaphors that capitalize on phrases such as a new wave, a surge, a flood of immigrants, and streaming across the border are especially powerful for supporting negative ideologies regarding transnational youth (Santa Ana, 2002). The "relentless and overwhelming" (Santa Ana, 2002, p. 73) flow and tide of "illegal" individuals and the destruction that this can have on the "homeland" is built on the metonymies of "flood, streaming (ACTIONS OF WATER FOR ACTION OF PEOPLE), and illegal immigrants (ATTRIBUTE FOR ENTITY)" and lead to the IMMIGRANTS ARE DANGEROUS WATER/CRIMINALS metaphors (Catalano, 2017, p. 4). All of this conceptually justifies the deserving of less than human treatment.

Metonymy and metaphor act as a dangerous one-two punch as metonymy first functions "as a way of highlighting or backgrounding certain aspects of an event, action, or person" (Catalano, 2017, p. 4) and then the resulting metaphor "draws on the unconscious emotional associations of words and assumed values that are rooted in cultural and historical knowledge" (Charteris-Black, 2014, p. 160). It is this cultural and historical knowledge that we turn to, now to understand how transnational youth are positioned upon return to Mexico.

On the Mexican Side of the Border

Although directional/spatial conceptual metonymies and metaphors underlie how these youths are viewed in Mexico, as well, it is the link to their language practices as broken, poor, and their bilingualism as being a mark of treason that is most evident throughout their experiences. "If language and political identity are seen to be inherently, essentially linked, then multilingualism and shifting language use must be an icon of equally shiftable, therefore shallow, political allegiances and unreliable moral commitments" (Gal & Irvine, 1995, p. 982). Due to this strong connection of language-political identity-nationality, these students' bilingualism, which could be viewed as strength, is often used against them, positioned as the split forked tongued serpent, and they are at times made to feel like they have done something wrong. These themes of linguistic insecurities, not fitting it, and feeling like another, are evident in this chapter's *testimonios*. We can also see evidence of much distrust in the multilingualism of transnational students who return to live in Mexico through the myth of linking them to the historical figure *La Malinche*.

Myth Today. In the introduction, we stated that before metaphors, metonymy drives conceptual thought, and after metaphor, myth carries ways of thinking into the future. Myth uses all suitable existing signs as its signifiers: not only written speech, but also pictures, artistic representations, cultural phenomena, etc., that already have some meaning (Barthes, 1972). Many images, such as the famous Diego Rivera mural on the Palacio Nacional, have *La Malinche* facing to the left, as a conceptual representation of the past, the conquered, the colonized, the non-trustworthy (see Kress & Van Leeuwen, 1996 for "zone" and "framing"). Another famous depiction of *La Malinche* is the mural by José Clemente Orozco, in *el Colegio de San Ildefonso en la Ciudad de México*, where again she is depicted second, on the right side of Cortés, looking down and to the left, the past, the conquered, the submissive.

Drawing this link to how the daily present existence of transnational youth conjure up the conquered past, Kasun and Mora-Pablo (2021) share, "*El malinchismo es un recuerdo que pervive en los colectivos sociales en México y que éstos prefieren reprimir*" (p. 41). *Reprimir* is a verb in Spanish that in English means to repress or to directionally push down. Spatial metaphors of GOOD IS UP and BAD IS DOWN (Lakoff & Johnson, 1999) and the conceptual directional metonymies that underlie these metaphors are psychologically internalized, self-actualized, and lived each day by colonized people who are repressed, kept down, made to feel inferior, in a subaltern status, and made to believe that what's on top (North) and what is up is good, the best, and superior (Fanon, 1967). As Kasun and Mora-Pablo (2021) explain the anti-malinchismo[2] against the Mexican-Transnational, bringing to light how transnational youth are seen as traitors, we are reminded here that *La Malinche* was plurilingual that this linguistic ability is directly linked to her ability to "sell out her people" (in reality survive, stay alive), and that this cannot be overlooked in the connection to the mistrust and mistreatment of multilingual transnational youth. Finally, Kasun and Mora-Pablo (2021) make the connection between the defenselessness of Malinche as a woman to the defenselessness of young transnational girls, who are bullied at school and whose decision regarding schooling were made by others, beyond their control. They describe how Malinche, "*como mujer, fue incapaz de protegerse a ella misma, y se le personificó más como propiedad que como agente*" (p. 44). We make the connection to how her treatment of being more like a property than a person is similar to how the aforementioned metonymies, metaphors, and myths have converted transnational youth into objects, more like property, than humans, and thus justification for being treated less humane.

Part 1 of this chapter paints a dreary portrait of the way that implicit, conceptual, common language is used to position transnational youth as lower-class and less than human threats. A new consciousness can only come from a change in how metaphors are used, as people, teachers, and even transnational youth themselves "repeat their ideas, enabling the ideas and values behind the language to enter the brains of the public" (Lakoff & Wehling, 2012, pp. 38–39). In Part 2, in the following, we take up Anzaldúa's call for a new language, a new consciousness, and for an appropriation of metaphors that create new myths. First, we share *testimonio* #3 and start to see examples "towards a new consciousness" (Anzaldúa, 1999, p. 99). *Testimonio* #3 tells the story of Mexican-born Pablo, who grew-up in New York and Florida, moved to the central Mexican state of Guanajuato at the age of 16, and now teaches high school and is studying a Master's degree in Mexico.

Testimonio #3: Pablo

*My experience as a Mexican-American transnational has been one of **personal growth** and discovery when it pertains to the matter of **identity and culture**. Growing up, the only contact that I had to my Mexican culture was through my family and their acquaintances from our church. But even then, reflecting upon it now, it was **only a surface level connection** I had to my Mexican heritage that didn't go past eating typical Mexican food and speaking Spanish. The Spanish-speaking **community that took us in** upon migrating to the U.S. was varied in terms of ethnicity,* *and Mexican families were scarce where we settled. When I was 16 going on 17, I was offered by my parents to visit my family in Mexico. I was interested in learning more about them since I was only four when I last saw them, and to be honest, I had **no real recollection of them or even having lived where I was born**, San Luis de la Paz in the state of Guanajuato. Well, my visit has now been a 15-yearlong visit.* **It had been hard to adapt to my new environment in Mexico**, *but with the help of a few good friends, I have made a happy life here.* **It was strange at first** *since* **I was picked on for being completely clueless** *to how kids here get on, to some of the jokes, and the type of humor that we Mexicans are known for. Although, I must admit* **I still have a hard time fitting in at times** *since* **I'm still seen as a bit of an outsider.** *My way of speaking and acting has changed since I moved, but* **I still sort of stick out** *when people hear me speak. There's a certain something that people can't put their finger on, or so I've been told.* **It's strange being in between identities, not quite American and not quite Mexican.** *It's been interesting* **helping the ex-pats here in Mexico** *since I can now see* **from an outsider's perspective** *how similar our adaptation process has been, and this enables me* **to help them through the adaptation process as my friends from school did for me.** *I must admit that* **being bilingual has opened many doors for me.** *I have been teaching English since I was 18 at all grade levels, from first grade to university levels. I have held managerial positions at a couple companies without any prior experience, as well as being an in-house translator at a Silicon Valley company. And not only* **has it opened doors for me, but it has expanded my understanding of the world. I feel like I have a solid understanding of the Mexican perspective of the world as well as an American one.**

Beyond the struggles of being othered, Pablo relates a strong sense of growing up/maturing through this process and how he has leveraged his transnational experience/bilingualism to help others and for opportunities. The "opened doors for me" is a positive house-based conceptual metaphor that differs from the negative house/homeland being destroyed by destructive waters metaphor shared earlier. This is a concrete example of how one conceptual metaphor (NATION AS HOME being destroyed) can be re-appropriated to become positive (TRANSNATIONAL FUNDS OF KNOWLEDGE AS OPENED DOORS). Part 2 takes up similar re-appropriations of metaphors and myths.

Part 2: A New Language for Dismantling the Mythologies of Transnational Youth

Not only must we be aware of and resist the use of implicit deficit-based language about transnational youth, but we must also use new words, phrases, and ways of talking about these youth's experiences. As

Anzaldúa points out, "The counter stance refutes the dominant culture's views and beliefs, and, for this, it is proudly defiant" (1999, p. 100). From *"ni de aquí, ni de allá"* to *"de aquí y de allá"* or *"de aquí y también de allá"* (Kasun & Mora-Pablo, 2021, pp. 45–46). If we do not push back on negative rhetoric about transnational youth on both sides of the border, this rhetoric becomes normalized through the power of an accepted myth. As Barthes (1972) explained:

> Myth is experienced as innocent speech . . . A reader does not see it as a semiological system, but as an inductive one, an equivalence, a causal process, the signifier and the signified, have in the eyes of the reader, a natural relationship . . . The myth consumer takes the signification for a system of facts . . . Myth is historical reality, defined. (p. 242)

However, anything can be a myth, provided that it is conveyed by a discourse. The work cited earlier, especially from Catalano (2017), Kasun and Mora-Pablo (2021), and Santa Ana (2002), has demonstrated that indeed deficit-based myths about transnational youth are prevalent in public discourse and that this is not lost on the youth themselves who are directly impacted by these myths. If myths are experienced as innocent speech, how then can they be changed and be re-experienced in ways that benefit transnational youth? This requires rewriting the discourse and creating a new reality.

How to Push Back: Carving Out New Myths

Barthes (1972) claims that attempts to push back against myths with truth and data may only strengthen the myth. The only way to vanquish a myth is to mythify the myth. In doing so, we rob the myth and create a third semiological chain (or complete associative total of a concept and an image). As illustrated in Table 7.1, the associative total of a concept and form/image results in a sign. The first order semiological chain is the most literal and then myth is formed by creating a second semiological chain. The first (literal) chain still exists, creating an alibi for the myth. In order to mythify the myth, we must create a third semiological chain, whereas the first (literal), the second (original myth), still exist, but the last, most recent ideological association of concept/form/thought is the third, and in our case the most positive sign/signification (the new myth).

Mythifying the Malinche Myth on the Mexican Side of the Border. Let us take for example the link that some have made between the historical figure *La Malinche* and transnational returnees to Mexico (Kasun & Mora-Pablo, 2021). By following the semiological chains, in the following, we can see how the first order is simply the literal, historic/popular

Table 7.1 Mythifying the Malinche myth with three semiological chains

1. Signifier (Form of La Malinche)	2. Signified (Mental concept of La Malinche, as understood through history)	
	3. Sign (Understanding or meaning of La Malinche as a traitor)	
I. SIGNIFIER (Form of transnational youth compared with La Malinche)	II. SIGNIFIED (Concept of combining and understanding the similarities of transnational youth and La Malinche)	
	III. SIGN (SIGNIFICATION/MYTH) (Understanding or believing that transnational youth are indexed as traitors)	
A. SIGNIFIER (Form of saying/hearing that like La Malinche, transnational youth are multilingual, multicultural, and resilient survivors)	B. SIGNIFIED (Concept of understanding transnationals and La Malinche as multilingual, multicultural, and resilient survivors)	
	C. SIGN (NEW MYTH) (La Malinche and transnational youth become synonymous with survival, intelligence, multilingualism, interculturalism)	

understanding of *La Malinche* as a figure who sold out her people. The second order links transnational youth's experiences to that of *La Malinche*, creating the myth that they are similarly traitors. The third semiological chain and order of understanding does not try to deny either the first or second chain, nor attempt to disassociate transnational youth from *La Malinche*, but rather builds off of the second signification with a new association; one of seeing the multilingualism, multiculturalism, and resiliency of *La Malinche* and in turn having those qualities, as Kasun and Mora-Pablo (2021) have suggested, indexed onto transnational youth.

Embracing the connection with *La Malinche*, we re-appropriate what this relationship means, creating a new consciousness of both transnational youth and the historical figure "*Malinali Tenepat*, or *Malintzín* ... Not me sold out my people but they me" (Anzaldúa, 1999, p. 44), and in turn a new language for talking about transnational youth.

Mythifying the Water Myths on the U.S. Side of the Border. In Table 7.2, we do the same with the ubiquitous water metaphors used to talk about immigrants and transnational youth.

This new water myth, created in the third semiological chain, works well with Gloria Anzaldúa's work toward a new consciousness. Anzaldúa (1999) points to the writing of José Vasconcelos who called for

> a cosmic race ... one of inclusivity. At the confluence of two or more genetic streams, with chromosomes constantly "crossing over," this mixture of races, rather than resulting in an inferior being, provides hybrid progeny, a mutable, more malleable species with a rich gene pool.
>
> (p. 99)

Table 7.2 Mythifying the common water metaphors/myths

1. Signifier (flood, wave, stream, etc.)	2. Signified (great amounts of rushing water)	
3. Sign (the danger, destructive nature of rushing water on property and home) I. SIGNIFIER (a flood, wave of immigrants streaming across the border)	II. SIGNIFIED (a swelling number of constant, un-ending immigrants entering the country)	
III. SIGN (MYTH) (relentless, overwhelming surge of immigrants as dangerous, destructive water to the U.S. homeland)		
A. SIGNIFIER (a flood, wave of immigrants streaming across the border)		B. SIGNIFIED (water as replenishing, invigorating, refreshing)
C. SIGN (NEW MYTH) (Large amounts of immigrant youth replenishing, invigorating, and refreshing the knowledge, experience, and strength of the U.S. [body] country.)		

We see in this description of *una raza mestiza*, how water-like words (confluence, streams, crossing over, and rich gene pool) are used in an almost enviable manner, making this vision of this new race/new consciousness, one to be sought-after. Perhaps even a better way to understand this new way of talking about transnational youth is Anzaldúa's (2002) vision for a new tribalism that "defines who we are by what we include," (p. 3) instead of exclusionary, dichotomous thinking and deterministic language.

Other metaphors and myths ripe for being re-appropriated and mythified might include the word "*pocho*," which literally is defined as ripe, being used to describe transnational experiences as a chance to "grow up," mature, "a *madurar*" (Kasun & Mora-Pablo, 2021, p. 45). *Entonces, no pocho, sino madurado*; and the house metaphor being re-appropriated from an attack on the house/country/homeland (security) to new doors and windows of opportunity being opened, through centering multilingualism and leveraging multicultural funds of knowledge.

Finally, *Testimonio* #4 is from Aslan, a Mexican-born transnational individual who *grew up* in Los Angeles, California. Prior to finishing his education, Aslan moved back to the central Mexican state of Guanajuato, where he currently teaches at a university. His *testimonio* highlights the strengths of the transnational experience and is an example of some of the aforementioned metonymies, metaphors, and myths starting to be re-appropriated with a new consciousness.

Testimonio #4: Aslan

Having been brought up in a multi-cultural city, bilingualism played an important part in my family's life. Since I can remember, I always helped my mother with interpretation and translation in a myriad of contexts. I think that the environment in which I grew up allowed me to be more tolerant toward conceptualizations from other cultures. I think that growing up bilingual gives you the tools to be accepting of new ideas without foreignizing them. Therefore, I think multilingualism or bilingualism should be centerpiece in education since it allows you to see things that a monolingual just could not grasp. When I decided to return to Mexico, bilingualism and bi-culturalism (under God's direction) opened many doors for me. I was quickly able to find a job and develop a career path because of it.

Aslan's testimonio provides an ideal vision of how to live in a multilingual, multicultural world and serves as a manifestation of the attributes of a new tribalism. When he speaks of tolerance "toward conceptualizations from other cultures," "being accepting," and how being bilingual and bicultural has "opened many doors" for him, he describes the strengths, resources, and resilience that it takes to live *entre dos mundos*, perhaps *creando un nuevo mundo, un Mundo Zurdo* (a Left-Handed World), or a bridge from an old way of thinking and talking about transnational youth, to a new *tierra* and lived reality.

Conclusion

The new dialogue, a reappropriation of language, and new myths proposed in this chapter, all facilitate a reimagination of and a new way of thinking about transnational youth. Perhaps Diego Rivera's mural and José Clemente Orozco's painting, both depicting *La Malinche* looking down and to the left, are really putting forth *La Malinche* as looking toward *El Mundo Zurdo*, and an example of how to create and live in a world where the marginalized, othered, and mis-understood struggle together, share strength, and teach the rest how to exist in borderland spaces. In their helping others, learning how to accept differences, increased tolerance, heightened perspective, multicultural understanding, and gained academic achievements through leveraging their bilingualism, Serna, Isaiah, Pablo, and Aslan are bridges for other transnational youth to walk *entre dos mundos*.

The Muslim historian, philosopher, and writer, Ibn Khaldun, wrote that "geography is destiny" (circa 1377) "and one cannot run away from it. It could be a curse or a blessing. It all depends on what one makes of it. We bring our own blessings and carry our own curses" (Kalin, 2016). In describing Chicano Spanish, Gloria Anzaldúa states that, "Due to geography, Chicanos from the Valley of South Texas were cut off linguistically from other Spanish speakers," resulting in a distinct form of speaking, and have internalized the message, myth, belief that they speak a broken, poor, or bastard Spanish (p. 80). Considering what is known about how language works, any idea of "a spoken standardized language can only be understood as an abstraction" (Lippi-Green, 1997, p. 53) or a myth. Yet, standard language-myths and the metonymies and metaphors that underlie them have been used as tools to oppress marginalized populations on both sides of the Mexico/U.S. border, including Black students' English in U.S. schools (Delpit & Dowdy, 2008), Indigenous students' Spanish in Mexico (Przymus et al., 2019), and transnational students' English and Spanish on both sides of the border. We must not only "prepare teachers for the dialectal diversity that characterizes U.S. classrooms but is often framed through racialized deficit ideologies" (Bacon, 2017, p. 341), but also direct educators to pay closer attention to language and to purposefully act to dismantle deficit-based metaphors that relay messages that there is something wrong with transnational youth.

This is a call to action for educators on the U.S. side of the border. Imploring white society, Anzaldúa voices, "We need you to own the fact that you looked upon us as less than human, that you stole our lands,

It's All Gone *South!* 151

our personhood, our self-respect . . . you strive for power over us" (1999, p. 108). Looking down upon, striving for power over, keeping down, repressing that which comes from "down South," "down Mexico way" are all linguistic insights into attitudes and ideologies that need to change. Changing our language is the first step.

This is a call to action for educators on the Mexican side of the border. Transnational youth are not the *gabacho* who has fallen down from the pinnacle *norte, sino el pocho que ha madurado*, who has grown *up*, and carries within the maturity of a resilient, multicultural, multilingual, cosmic racial identity of inclusivity and strength. These youths are not looking *down*, to the left, to the past, but rather lifting *up*, "*hacia el nuevo Aztlan*" (Anzaldúa, 1999, p. 46). In order to counter these North/South, up/down, better/worse, etc. conceptual dichotomies, we offer another orientation (Figure 7.2), one that is influenced by the new myth mentioned

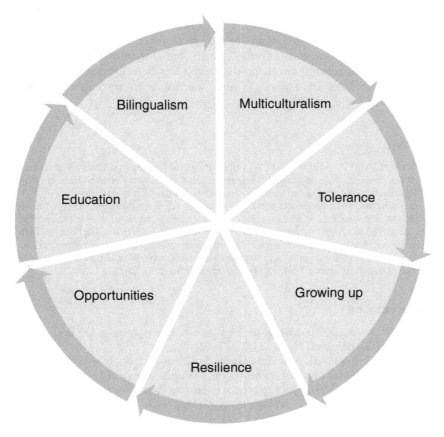

Figure 7.2 Transnational funds of knowledge water cycle

earlier (Table 7.2), based on the reconceptualization of water metaphors as replenishing, invigorating, refreshing the knowledge, experience, and strength of the U.S. and Mexico homelands. Pulling attributes from each *testimonio*, we represent the internal multidirectionality of transnational funds of knowledge, flowing in a circle, giving new life and sustaining a vision of an inclusionary multicultural U.S. and Mexico.

Not only does this transnational funds of knowledge water cycle begin to reconceptualize the water metaphors in relation to the conceptual metonymy of NATIONS AS HOMELANDS that are replenished and reinvigorated, but also the conceptual metonymy of NATIONS AS BODIES that are given new life and sustained via this water cycle.

In responding to this call to action, we arrive once again at Anzaldúa's bridge metaphor and become inspired by the action of transnational youth, the new *mestizo, las nepantleras*, through Anzaldúa's words, "Where others say borders, these nepantleras saw links; where others saw abysses, they saw bridges spanning those abysses. For *nepantleras*, to bridge is an act of will" (2002, p. 4). It is possible that a bridge metaphor could rise above the waters, create a place to meet halfway, and rewrite the discourse about transnational youth, but not until we address the ubiquitous conceptual language that implicitly deteriorates that bridge. "The possibilities are numerous once we decide to act and not react" (Anzaldúa, 1999, p. 101).

Notes

1. Since Lakoff & Johnson's 1980 publication on conceptual metaphor theory, style guidelines in conceptual metaphor and metonymy theory indicate that abstract conceptual domains are represented with caps.
2. Equally negative reaction to malinchismo, or rejection/mal treatment of those whose experiences metonymically conjure the memory of being conquered/colonized through the impurity of mixing with the oppressor, via bilingualism, transnationalism, and treason. (Extreme) anti-malinchismo is a more combative, overt reaction/treatment toward one's own, who would threaten to make the most pure, noble Mexican feel inferior (Hurtado, 2020).

References

Aigner-Varoz, E. (2000). Metaphors of a mestiza consciousness: Anzaldúa's Borderlands/La Frontera. *Melus, 25*(2), 47–62.

Anzaldúa, G. E. (1983). El mundo zurdo. In C. Moraga & G. Anzaldúa (Eds.), *This bridge called my back: Writings by radical women of color.* Suny Press.

Anzaldúa, G. E. (1993). Chicana artists: Exploring Nepantla, el lugar de la frontera. *NACLA Report on the Americas, 27*(1), 37–45.

Anzaldúa, G. E. (1999). *Borderlands/La frontera: The new mestiza* (2nd ed.). Aunt Lute Books.

Anzaldúa, G. E. (2002). (Un)natural bridges, (un)safe spaces. In G. E. Anzaldúa & A. Keating (Eds.), *This bridge we call home: Radical visions for transformation* (pp. 1–5). Routledge.
Bacon, C. K. (2017). Dichotomies, dialects, and deficits: Confronting the "Standard English" myth in literacy and teacher education. *Literacy Research: Theory, Method, and Practice, 66*(1), 341–357.
Barthes, R. (1972). *Mythologies*. Paladin.
Beverley, J., & Zimmerman, M. (1990). *Literature and politics in the Central American revolutions*. University of Texas Press.
Catalano, T. (2017). When children are water: Representation of Central American migrant children in public discourse and implications for educators. *Journal of Latinos and Education, 16*(2), 124–142.
Charteris-Black, J. (2014). *Analysing political speeches*. Palgrave Macmillan.
Delpit, L., & Dowdy, J. K. (Eds.). (2008). *The skin that we speak: Thoughts on language and culture in the classroom*. The New Press.
Fairclough, N. (2013). Critical discourse analysis. In J. Gee & M. Hanford (Eds.), *The Routledge handbook of discourse analysis* (pp. 9–20). Routledge.
Fanon, F. (1967). *Black skin white masks*. Grove Press.
Gal, S., & Irvine, J. (1995). The boundaries of languages and disciplines: How ideologies construct differences. *Social Research, 62*(4), 967–1000.
Gándara, P. (2020). The students we share: Falling through the cracks on both sides of the US-Mexico border. *Ethnic and Racial Studies, 43*(1), 38–59, https://doi.org/10.1080/01419870.2019.1667514
Hawthorne, N. (1850). *The scarlet letter: 1850*. Infomotions, Incorporated.
Hurtado, G. (2020). Malinchismo y anti-malinchismo. *La Razón de México*. www.razon.com.mx/opinion/columnas/guillermo-hurtado/malinchismo-anti-malinchismo-400670
Ibn Khaldun. (1377, translation, 1967). *The Muqaddimah: An Introduction to History*. Princeton University Press.
Jacobo, M., & Jensen, B. (2018). *Schooling for US-citizen students in Mexico*. Civil Rights Project, UCLA. https://tinyurl.com/yxcaynrx
Kalin, I. (2016, April 30). From Baku to Zagreb: In search of the lost wisdom. *Daily Sabah*. www.dailysabah.com/columns/ibrahim-kalin/2016/04/30/from-baku-to-zagreb-in-search-of-the-lost-wisdom
Kasun, G. S., & Mora-Pablo, I. (2021). El anti-malinchismo contra el mexicanotransnacional: Cómo se puede transformar esa frontera limitante. *Anales de Antropología, 55*(1).
Kress, G. R., & Van Leeuwen, T. (1996). *Reading images: The grammar of visual design*. Psychology Press.
Lakoff, G., & Johnson, M. (1980). *Metaphors we live by*. University of Chicago Press.
Lakoff, G., & Johnson, M. (1999). *Philosophy in the flesh: The embodied mind and its challenge to western thought* (Vol. 640). Basic books.
Lakoff, G., & Wehling, E. (2012). *The little blue book: The essential guide to thinking and talking democratic*. Free Press.
Lippi-Green, R. (1997). *English with an Accent: Language, Ideology, and Discrimination in the United States*. Routledge.

Littlemore, J. (2015). *Metonymy: Hidden shortcuts in language, thought and communication*. Cambridge University Press.

Moll, L. C., Amanti, C., Neff, D., & Gonzalez, N. (1992). Funds of knowledge for teaching: Using a qualitative approach to connect homes and classrooms. *Theory into Practice, 31*(2), 132–141.

Narayanaswamy, L. (2007). The power to subvert?: Beyond North—South dichotomies in gender and development discourse. *Narrative Inquiry, 17*(1), 49–67.

Pennycook, A., & Makoni, S. (2019). *Innovations and challenges in applied linguistics from the global South*. Routledge.

Przymus, S. D., & Huddleston, G. (2021). The hidden curriculum of monolingualism: Understanding metonymy to interrogate problematic representations of raciolinguistic identities in schoolscapes. *International Journal of Multicultural Education, 23*(1), 67–86.

Przymus, S. D., Jiménez, F. R., & García, V. P. (2019). Mensajes de los abuelitos: Reclaiming Zapotec ways of knowing and community-based biliteracy practices in Oaxaca, México. *Bilingual Review/Revista Bilingüe, 34*(1).

Santa Ana, O. (2002). *Brown tide rising: Metaphors of Latinos in contemporary American public discourse*. University of Texas Press.

Chapter 8

Malinche's Move From Traitor to Survivor

Recasting Mexico's First Indigenous Woman to Reframe Mexican-Origin Transnationals Returning Home

G. Sue Kasun and Irasema Mora-Pablo

Introduction

In this chapter, we look retrospectively at Mexican-origin youth who returned from the United States to Mexico. We employ a lens on how Malinche/Malintzin—the Indigenous woman who bore a child to Mexico's first conqueror, Hernan Cortés—has been understood and used in the national state-building/mythmaking of the project of Mexico. Her very name has been used as an insult against Mexicans who show a preference for things outside of Mexico as if Malinche had had a choice about giving birth to Cortés's son; we call this phenomenon *anti-malinchismo*. Anzaldúa (1993), among other feminist scholars (e.g., De Alba, 2005, 2014; Elenes, 2011), reframes this key historical figure in ways that help unlock restricting narratives about who gets to be Mexican and who is allowed to employ other aspects of their identities. In our prior research (Hidalgo & Kasun, 2019; Kasun et al., 2020; Mora-Pablo et al., 2015, 2019), we have carefully explored the childhood and adolescent stages of return migrants to Mexico. This chapter aims to provide a decolonial set of ideas about how to embrace the multiple cultural repertoires of returning Mexicans to Mexico.

We interpret the *anti-malinchismo* toward returnees as a postcolonial reaction of rejection of the colonizer, who, by definition, always rejects the native. The native Mexican appears with or without the nopal en la frente, translated as the cactus on their forehead (an expression used throughout and beyond Mexico to indicate that a person physically appears Mexican). During our years of study, we have heard many testimonies from non-migrant Mexicans who reject their pochos/mochos/agringados co-nationals. The painful rejections that we find in the returnees' stories often arise in the returnee's immediate family and social circle. These include the ways returning children's teachers treat them, some of whom are even relatives of these return migrants, with gestures of displeasure when they listen to a transnational child speak English. To

DOI: 10.4324/9781003191575-12

illustrate one example of such disclosure, young children are often told by such teachers not to be showoffs just because they're speaking English.

This chapter probes betrayal, language, and identity through a postcolonial perspective in order to clarify a social phenomenon that consists of the deformation by Mexicans who reside in Mexico, of their frustration toward the betrayal of their own compatriots, those Mexicans who have spent time living in the United States. We present an amalgam of experiences embodied in young returned migrants located and settled in Mexico, thereby establishing other social bonds which transcend borders. The central objective we propose revolves around the concept of the unintentional "traitor," the soul who returns after having stayed and inhabited the United States, and the way in which they are generally understood socially, from a material perspective, through his physical appearance, in addition to being stereotyped for the use of language and discriminated against for being considered a traitor. Gabacho, mocho, and pocho are part of the qualifiers that are attributed to the returned transnational to point him out, denigrate him and marginalize him; these terms are synonymously and specifically used only against those who have spent significant amounts of time in the U.S. This work focuses on the situation experienced by young people who have returned to Mexico from the United States and who are disqualified in their country of origin with terms that portray them as "sons of the *chingada*," the fucked/raped one herself, Malinche/Malintzin. We recognize and describe a continual decolonial resistance to colonization alongside the attraction of satisfying the need for belonging through national identity.

Transnational Returnee Context

As multicultural subjects (Kleyn, 2017), these young people returning to Mexico with a vast repertoire of knowledge, practices, and cultural experiences are unaware of the anger to which they will be subjected. It will be a different anger from the one they suffered during their stay in the United States. Returnees (including children) recall life experiences in a more "modern" system, paying bills electronically, learning in a different educational system, and facing the cultural challenges this entails. In addition, they forged friendships with African–Americans, Asians, whites, etc., some of them fractured; others, more intimate, all relationships emerged from social and cultural interactions. They have also nearly constantly exceeded racist expectations about their academic performance (Kasun, 2016; Basch et al., 1994; Galván, 2005; Mercado, 2015). Most retain the memory of their territory and the Mexican environment while they were in the United States, often wondering if they would return to their home country. They recall having exceeded racist expectations within the host country and return marked—in their imagination—by the need to know if they succeeded in a certain way, thereby giving meaning to their stay in the United States (Kasun, 2016). Upon their return to Mexico, they realize that almost everyone left something behind and that they return differently, with something else to offer.

Return migrants may not be aware that they represent a taboo and the impure mix of something so challenging for the community's mentality that surrounds them. This taboo only serves to repress the community and, in particular, the newcomer to it (Kasun, 2016; Van den Braembussche, 2002). In this way, upon their return, transnational migrants form the basis for the hateful expression of the *malinchistas*, becoming those who sold themselves to outsiders. The transnational's return threatens to remind the other that he also runs the risk of mixing, of leaving, and of betraying.

Anti-malinchismo is an echo of a collective memory that survives in Mexico and that Mexicans generally prefer to repress. This situation is not a complete or totally Mexican repression. It becomes a national affair because it takes place in the nation's project to forge a republic, as nation-building is always an ongoing project. Immigrants to the United States and returnees to Mexico represent a social phenomenon that must be addressed to contribute to the project of creating a homeland.

In this chapter, we invite the reader to consider the following questions:

- What do we do with a community member who returns unexpectedly? What if we consider that this member is a young person?
- What do we think when someone leaves and, in some way, his departure is caused by us (because we well know most Mexicans do not leave Mexico because they don't love where they are from—and we were unable to give them the material resources they needed to stay)?
- What are the discourses constructed by those who return to distinguish themselves and highlight their own presence?
- What happens if a family group returns, be it a whole family or just a part of it?

The expression commonly used to designate someone who returns from another place to Mexico is "retornado" (Kasun, 2019; Bybee et al., 2020), which is a neutral term, analogous to a bird that can return to the nest later of his first flight, but also that he could be forced to return, perhaps for "being defective" and, therefore, legally deported. The shadow of the reasons why migrants have returned is seemingly ever-present. Yet, in the daily discourse of Mexicans, how much is discussed about returnees? And in what way?

In reviewing the studies on education in Mexico, we notice that returnees, in some situations, do not exist (although we know they are physically present in the schools under examination in these studies) (Hamann &

Zúñiga, 2011; Tacelosky, 2018). Schools and educators continue to minimize the social phenomenon and, when returnees are recognized, they are generally seen as foreigners and often mistreated. Where does this abuse originate?

Our research locates this phenomenon in the states of Hidalgo and Guanajuato, where we find cases of which we present some concrete examples in order to highlight and clearly show their life experiences and the challenges they face. However, we are aware this happens all over Mexico. We turn now to an amalgam example shared commonly by our participants and which demonstrates this painful phenomenon.

Interlude: The Little Gabacho Boy

The intense semi-desert sun penetrates the open window of the green and white combi van carrying 12 passengers, churning up the dust of months of land that has been waiting for the rainy season in the mountainous highlands. Now accustomed to the chalky air after months of being back in Mexico, Tomás looks at his brother and asks him about the errand they just ran, in fluent English: "Hey, did you also buy the socks Mom asked for at the *tianguis*?" "Nah, bro, shit. I forgot," replies Luis, the brother, realizing that they are halfway home. Luis wants to continue toward home, and they argue about the possibility of going back while the market is still open. They may have enough *pesos* to pay the round-trip fare, but he says nothing. He feels contempt nearby. The eyes of a nearby passenger narrow and penetrate the older brother. "Oh, who do you think you are, gabachito boy?" she asks him. Tomás does not know how to answer, not for lack of language, but for lack of words.

A Braiding of Postcolonial/Decolonial and Anzalduan Theories as Conceptual Framework

The Mexican is as aware of having been conquered by the Spanish, as all those who have lived experiences of colonization in the last five centuries. This has been part of their learning both in schools and in national holidays that mark, year after year, the independence for the conqueror, as well as part of the official process of creating the myths of the Mexican homeland and of *mestizaje*; (Anzaldúa, 1987; Basave, 2011; González, 2002; Gutiérrez Chong, 2012). In this chapter, we rely on postcolonial and decolonial theory, underscoring the role of women. Universally, and in this particular case in Mexico, women have been the most inferior as a result of colonization. Despite centuries of oppression, women have persisted and resisted. Malinche/Malintzin can be an example of how women can survive, persist, and help others survive at the same time.

We turn to the first moment of how colonization sets about a domino effect of pains and oppressions on all parties involved in colonizing projects. Cesaire (2000) explains that the colonizer self-dehumanizes in the process of colonizing. You cannot enslave, condemn, and rape, without dehumanizing yourself. As a psychological consequence, the colonizer is obliged by circumstances to defend his warped internal psychology even more because of the evil that he inflicts on the colonized. With a diminishing sense of power and the repression the colonized feel, the colonized lose their power to defend themselves against a previously obvious truth to them of their own efficacy. The way the colonized lived on the land before the arrival of the colonizer was no worse than the colonizer's fiction of how the colonized needed the colonizer's support (e.g., Glissant, 1999); in fact, they probably lived much better.

Fanon (1967) was a postcolonial theorist who explored the psychological wounds in non-white people brought about by the colonization process, particularly the sense of inferiority that they developed as a result of the imposition of white colonizers. He explains, "The inferiority complex can be explained as a double process. First, the economic one. Then the internalization or rather epidermisation of this inferiority" (1967, pp. xiv–xv). Just as white supremacy is perceived as dominant in the world, Mexicans often take part in the colonization process by assuming that "white" is better. It is considered that "white" refers to the characteristics of the European population and, by extension, to the characteristics of the United States' predominant population, as well as everything that Whiteness carries with it (Bonilla-Silva, 2010).

As brutalizing and genocidal as colonization is, the resistance of those who are colonized becomes productive in some ways. Postcolonial theory, in addition to providing the critical analysis of the history of the victors, also leads us to heal ourselves from these historical tragedies born out of greed, conquest, and in many of the pre-texts that try to justify that colonization was necessary. For example, Anzaldúa (1987) and Bhabha (1994), among others, investigate how hybridity can be a response to the evils of colonization in order to create something new from the collision of cultures, something in which the "other" (the colonized) creates their own agency. For example, Spanglish can be understood as a hybrid way of speaking, though it has been made out to be "subordinate" to one's own Spanish or English (Anzaldúa, 1987; Sánchez Muñoz, 2013). This mixture is widely recognized in linguistics as being as rich in meaning as any other language or dialect, and in neurology as a more complex brain process than monolingualism. At the same time, Bhabha (2004) recognizes the ambivalences one can feel about identity, and this can open the way to the creation of new meanings related to identity and cultural practices.

We turn now to the special role women take as the colonized. In an interview on the 50th centenary of the Conquest, Inés Hernández-Ávila (2000) explains in a conversation with Gloria Anzaldúa "the Conquest is tied, as you said, to women's bodies. There's a relationship with that whole issue of right of conquest and the fact that people don't challenge it" (p. 182). Colonization occurs from a larger territory to the interior, to the body, the heart, and the mind. In this case, we see the feminization of the victims of the Conquest, despite the power that women do have. Her power is manifested not only in the physical, which comes as an "advantage" for man as long as he wants to conquer her.

Furthermore, when conquering, the victim is raped and even blamed for her own tragedy, as Hernández Ávila suggests: "If someone has overwhelming power . . . does that give them the right to violate, penetrate, terrorize, and overtake someone else . . . Does it give you the right to say also that the victim wanted it?" (2000, p. 182).

Although there are many Mexican female archetypes (such as the Llorona and the Virgin of Guadalupe, also known by her Aztec name of Tonantzin), in this study, we focus on the one that generates the most discussion as an actual historical figure: Malinche, Malintzin, Marina. This mythical figure, of whom little is known in the written historical record, is perhaps best understood in light of the historical moments in which she lived, as explored in detail by one of her main researchers, Sandra Messinger Cypess (2010). Malintzin was the interpreter of the conqueror Hernán Cortés, the bearer of his son. As already stated in this chapter, she has been portrayed and understood nationally as the original traitor to Mexico.

We echo Cypess (2010) when we argue that special attention should be paid to how Malinche survived different roles into which she was forced and how she differs from the popular understanding. She was sold at an early age by one Indigenous group to another, and later she was given in tribute to the Spanish along with 19 other women. Historical records indicate she helped prevent the Cholula massacre and interpreted languages, like Nahuatl and Mayan for the Spanish Conquerors, which influenced the success of colonization in Latin America. There are no records that Malintzin wanted to be with Cortés or that she did not love her own people (González, 2002). We pause here to invite the reader to imagine having to endure any of these events. If you had to choose one, which would be? Being sold from one group to another? Having to translate for the conqueror? Having to save an entire group of people in a prestigious and well-run city?

Malinche is considered the first woman to be screwed or raped by the conquerors, in this case, described in Mexican Spanish as the "woman of Cortés." In Mexican popular wisdom, and even in contemporary discourse, this turns Mexicans into sons of the chingada (the raped/fucked)

(Anzaldúa, 1993). However, only one Mexican is the original traitor: the woman who "sold herself" to the Conqueror, Malinche, the original and Indigenous mother. Being a traitor is the lowest and breaks all social codes. Cypess (2010) explains, "La Malinche comes to signify the traitor to national goals; the one who conforms to her paradigm is labeled malinchista, the individual who sells out to the foreigner, who devalues national identity in favor of imported benefits." (p. 7).

The representation of renowned Mexican thinker Octavio Paz's Malinche as a traitor in "The labyrinth of solitude" (1950) has been considered a distinctive hallmark and a key reference to understand the symbolism of Malinche in Mexican culture. The symbol of surrender is Malinche, Cortés's mistress.

> It is true that she voluntarily gives herself to the conqueror, but he, as soon as it ceases to be useful to her, casts her aside. Doña Marina has become a figure that represents the Indian women, fascinated, raped or seduced by the Spanish. And as a small boy will not forgive his mother if she abandons him to search for his father, the Mexican people have not forgiven La Malinche for her betrayal. . . . By repudiating Malinche—Eva Mexicana, as represented by José Clemente Orozco in his mural of the National Preparatory School—the Mexican breaks his ties with the past, denies his origin and enters only in historical life.
>
> (Paz, 1950 [1992], pp. 125–126)

The postcolonial lens of Fanon (1967) helps understand how Mexicans could frame this woman as a traitor: "All colonized people . . . position themselves in relation to the civilizing language, i.e. metropolitan culture" (p. 2). Historically, many Mexicans have sided with the colonizer, condemned Malinche, and allied with the colonizer, even if he was a rapist, as in this case. La Malinche was a woman with two roles: that of perpetrator and that of victim. She is a curious figure of disgust who evokes a visceral rejection. When Mexicans who "sell themselves" are called "*malinchistas*," with such derision by their compatriots, they are rarely invited to discuss why or how they chose what is meant by being Mexican or what choice they made to have to "sell themselves."

Malinche has been partially rebuilt since Paz's seminal (we use this word with some irony) text in multiple ways. Malinche as archetype can be understood through understanding Mexicans and their historical choices. Duncan, quoted in Cypess (2010), asserts "only . . . through a mythic reevaluation of the past can the Mexican come to terms with his identity in the present and break out of the oppressive cycle of history which haunts him in the modern world" (p. 162). In fact, in this chapter, we tried to steer the conversation in that direction by reframing the colonized, hyper-masculinized and old-fashioned version of who La Malinche was.

Anzaldúa (1993) astutely points out Malinche is abandoned by us, even after she has been raped. This interpretation then puts the burden on us. Why have we left her behind? We recognize Malinche and her newly cast interpretations make her, as an intelligent woman, committed to her fight for the survival of her people and her descendants. De Alba emphasizes her intelligence and her linguistic abilities to collaborate with distinct Indigenous groups and with the Spanish, as well as her "dramatic qualities" (González, 2005). Cypess echoes that admiration and also notes her physical abilities to navigate difficult terrain through a complex awareness of her diplomacy (2010). Although Malinche was described as if she was part of Eve's paradigm for having given herself to the first of the seven deadly sins in the more masculinist and colonizing portrayals of the past, she has also been recognized as someone who can be imagined outside of this patriarchal paradigm. De Alba (2005) acknowledges that while she made impossible decisions, she somehow survived in ways that may have been necessary, evocative of the difficult decisions we face as colonial subjects in this world. The same author explains:

> Malinche's rebellious "Shadow Beast" dares us to look in the mirror and experience what Gloria Anzaldúa called "the knowing", the inner power that results from our underworld journeys into consciousness. "Suddenly the repressed energy rises, makes decisions, connects with conscious energy and a new life begins.
> (De Alba, 2005, p. 58)

In fact, it is time to turn our gaze to many brave women of Mexico, not just to the exceptions (Taylor, 2009). Our intention is to take Malinche as an example of what many transnationals—men and women—do and how they reconstruct their stories throughout their lives. We turn now to concrete examples from our research.

Participants From Our Prior Research in Mexico

The stories presented here are those of 31 university students currently undertaking undergraduate studies in English teaching programs at two Mexican public state universities. All of them lived a large part of their lives in the United States, and most were brought to that country by their families at an early age. The reasons for their return to Mexico were diverse: some for deportation, others for the impossibility of continuing with their university studies in the United States, and others for family reasons. All agreed to be part of the study on which this chapter is based, and their experiences were collected through semi-structured interviews, autobiographies, and life biograms. It should be noted that these stories are part of two investigations carried out by the authors of this chapter, one in the state of Hidalgo and the other in the state of Guanajuato. For the purposes of this chapter, we present excerpts from the stories of Martha, Paty, Yolanda, Laura, Eloy, and Gemma. The names of the participants have been changed to protect their identities.

How the Returned Transnationals Experience *Anti-Malinchismo*

People return from the north, a territory that is a source of conflict in many ways. Due to proximity, Mexico exchanged one oppressor for another, Spain for the United States, that neighbor hungry for power and devouring work. The first colonizer was an obvious acquaintance; the new one is neocolonial in its hegemony of asserting itself over Mexico in political matters [for example, in a poorly negotiated "free" trade agreement (Durand et al., 1999; Esteva, 2019), and with a militarized border on the rise that turns the corpses of those who cross into symbols of colonizing power (De León, 2015)].

How does the Mexican who resides in Mexico react when the returnee arrives? We recognize how dangerous it is to generalize, but we appeal to national discourses and empirical evidence in our research. First, the Mexican myth includes Malinche as the national traitor and, at the same time, as the mother of the country. In this part, we give some examples of the ways in which young people, through a retrospective look, present their stories. These young people were singled out as traitors and later related to postcolonial demonstrations of rich people with hybrid identities. Next, through the empirical evidence obtained, we demonstrate how, sometimes in a visceral and unthinking way, Mexicans can reject what evokes a sense of betrayal, which shows the validity and internalization of *malinchismo* in the citizenry. We also analyze several fundamental ideas that we collect under the headings of humiliation within the family, bullying of students and teachers, being a teacher of my classmates, hybrid identity, and being between two worlds.

Humiliation Within the Family

It is not an exaggeration to say that humiliation can manifest itself within the same family that took that child at an early age "to the other side," to the United States. Martha, currently a 21-year-old university student from a small town in Hidalgo, who commutes daily to the Autonomous University of the State of Hidalgo, explains:

> My family in general made fun of me because they said "Ahh! You think you're a gringa, how can you forget Spanish if you're Mexican"; as if they were saying "You slept with the traitor and now you think you are Spanish, over and above us who could not or chose not to have contact with the invader."

Unlike Malinche, Martha had lost those valid reasons for using her mother tongue, in this case, Spanish, and she had lost many of her oral communication skills. Even her father, who had come and gone to the United States with her, doubted Martha's identity and the way in which, supposedly, he had chosen not to speak Spanish. Her father believed, as did her family, that she was being *"malinchista"* or was leaning toward the colonizer's way of being, in this case, linguistically.

Many of the participants reported having relatives who made negative comments about them by calling them gabachos, making them feel less because they had lived in the United States, even when they did not have the opportunity to choose, since they were brought in at a very young age. Although families represent a space in which *malinchismo* develops, where returnees are branded as "traitors," this also increasingly extends to formal education spaces: schools. Our participants commented that many of them were constantly subjected to bullying just because they lived in the United States and, upon their return, they joined Mexican schools. To be clear, we recognize that there are caring and loving teachers who help many of these young people to adjust to a new life in Mexico; however, the phenomenon of bullying just for being a returnee is too visible not to discuss it. We recognize that it is a major violation of the treatment they should receive from society, simply for having crossed the border, but it is even worse if it is the most vulnerable individuals in society: children.

Bullying From Students and Teachers

The humiliations received by teachers were frequent, and almost all the students we interviewed had at least one uncomfortable story to tell about a teacher who made comments about them for being transnational returnees in Mexico. Many had repeat episodes with more than one teacher. We argue that while this type of bullying becomes common among classmates in a school (when it is committed by adults whose job it is precisely to educate their students), a deeper imbalance of perception is generated among returnees. We believe that this imbalance is due, in part, to the feeling of anger for the *malinchismo* that many Mexicans express. For example, Paty describes her experience during the completion of a Spanish language test, at the age of ten, after her recent arrival in the state of Hidalgo:

> A teacher was very mean to me, like, "How is it possible that you don't know this in Spanish?" "---I don't know Spanish," [I told her] . . . [and I had to take] an exam . . . and I was like, "I don't understand anything. Nothing!" And I would look at the clock, and think, "Do I have to put what time it is?" So I just put it on and stood up. And she told me, "Do whatever you understand," and I said, "I just know that." She couldn't believe it and said "No, that can't be possible. You need to know more," but I didn't know. She was very frustrated and I started crying.

A teacher humiliated Paty in front of the whole class for not knowing Spanish which she was not responsible for. Her humiliation at school was so severe that her parents transferred her to a private bilingual school. Paty was fortunate, as her parents knew how to avoid further humiliating situations and also had the money to do so, which is not the case with other students returning from the United States and at the mercy of abuses of power.

We add a more tragic case, that of a young woman, Yolanda, also ten, who arrived in the state of Hidalgo and experienced a similar situation. "It was more like a culture shock, language shock, it was all a shock. The most difficult thing was that she didn't know any Spanish." Yolanda explained: "I was the perfect target for bullying." She commented that she received the nickname "Manteca" [chubby], since she returned to Mexico weighing 80 kilos at the age of 10, but the worst part for her was the pain caused by her aunt. "It was a bit tough for me to face the reality that my aunt was going to fail me and send me back to kindergarten for not knowing Spanish." After two months of suffering an intense period of bullying and having lost 30 kilos her mother made the decision to remove her from the school. Here we can see parallels with Malinche. Malinche, as a woman, was unable to protect herself and was personified more as property rather than as agent.

"Being a Teacher of My Classmates"

A complex sphere within the Mexican educational system that is related to transnational youth is the subject of English in the national curriculum. In some instances, the returnee transnational becomes a class assistant, which sometimes allows them to feel good about mastering the language being taught (English). However, it is also true that there are times when the transnational returnee is conditioned to give the entire class, instead of the teacher. Laura carried out part of her studies in Mexico and the United States when she was in primary school, so she reached an outstanding level of English. When she returned to Guanajuato, her teacher realized this, so he took advantage and gave her the class, not without first reminding her that in order for her to pass, she had to teach the class to her classmates because she even spoke better English than the teacher (Mora-Pablo & Basurto, 2019).

> I would not treat [my students] like they treated me. For example, I would not ask them to teach my [English] class and send them a message that I could identify them as returnees or as native speakers. I would put them aside and say to them—If you feel like saying something, say it, or if you want to participate more and help me, go ahead, do it and you know? Just do it if you want to do it, if you can, and if not, that's fine, maybe we can work on and give you more advanced [English] material. And I would never give my returning students the burden of teaching my class. That is completely unprofessional. It happened to me and it is not pleasant for the student at all.
>
> (pp. 86–87)

Feeling displaced in the group, with this responsibility for having greater linguistic competence than her peers and even the teacher, could have been an advantage for her; however, it was very uncomfortable. Now that she is an English teacher, she mentions how she would react to the possibility of having students with the same characteristics as her.

Hybrid Identity

The young people we interviewed were able to adapt in hybrid ways to their complex realities, articulating different languages, developing a skill set and even streamlining their identities. It is true that many of our participants decided to identify themselves more as "Mexican" or "American," but when we explicitly asked them about this, the vast majority said they live with two identities, like Malinche, who was able to identify with multiple ways of being and knowing, including their language skills. Identities are difficult to build and require a careful analysis of the characteristics of the subjects that make up society. It seems that the life of these young people resembles the type of experiences that Malinche lived and that could be associated with the concept of survival of the Mexican.

Eloy shares a concrete example that demonstrates the complex nature of the experiences resulting from this hybridity. He mentions: "Sometimes you can think of some things in English, and you can't think of them in Spanish, or vice versa . . . or maybe there are things that you did in the United States, for example, that you lived a year alone, and that's kind of unusual for young Mexicans, right?" Although difficult life experiences are remembered, such as complications to use each language in its corresponding socio-linguistic environment, enriching experiences are also remembered. Eloy explains that he has had the experience of living alone for a year in another country and that this has allowed him to mature, something unusual for Mexicans, who generally stay with family until they get married. We do not say that one experience is better than another, but they are definitely different and allow different ways of understanding life.

Finally, another example is explained through the experience of Gemma, from Guanajuato, who is torn between ambivalence and passion for her identity. This is a hallmark of the hybrid way of living, the sense of being "between two worlds," being able to perform in both, or living in what Anzaldúa refers to as "nepantla" (1987). For Anzaldúa, nepantla represents a paradigm of liminality and transition, living "between two worlds" of diverse border crossings, where it is possible to explore and forge new creative, literary, linguistic, psychological, sociocultural and geopolitical identities. Gemma represents the aforementioned concept:

> When I'm here, it depends on the situation. I'm kind of very undecided about who I am. I have a very Mexican side: oh, I'm Mexican! And I'm as proud as I am of my American side. Just like when someone says something bad about the United States, I get defensive, but when they say something bad about Mexico, I also get defensive. So I am very indecisive in who I am. So I always say that from here to the border I am Mexican, from the border to there I am American.

It is clear that Gemma shows loyalty to the two countries, that she is not "a sell-out" to either of the two cultures, something that is generally attributed to Malinche or the returnees. She has developed the ability to care from both sides of the border. In fact, she demonstrates a somewhat ideal vision of what we expect from multicultural and intercultural education, developing the capacity and flexibility to love more than one place, person, or culture. We believe that having this openness to embody more than one national identity would allow Gemma, and other transnationals like her, to express in a more spontaneous and timely way that she is from both countries without feeling bad. We recognize, as the Mexican saying ni de aquí ni de allá, "neither from here, nor from there" goes, that there are few discourses of acceptance of multiple identities by those who surround them, these being "from here and there."

Implications

As we have shown, the returnee assumes the role of being the target of *anti-malinchismo* by many non-migrant Mexicans. In this sense, the returnees assume/embody Malinche as enemies and threats. From a gender perspective, we see that the returnee is attributed a lower role, just as the figure of women throughout the world, in the logic of gender inequality. Like many women reading their contexts, the returnee perceives the anticipated expectation that they will not excel in what they set out to do in their environment.

We present three ideas to address this history of colonial violence, which is part of a repetitive cycle. To begin with, the person's history should be reinterpreted in order to represent the lived reality of returning transnationals more objectively. Subsequently, it would be convenient to foster awareness in the broader population that encourages the idea of experiencing more than one identity. Finally, it would be necessary to leave space to live and experience the hybridity of identities so that returnees can decide whether or not to resist said hybridity. We want to reclaim the history of La Malinche and the life history of transnational returnees. This allows for Anzaldúa's (1987) Shadow Beast first to be recognized as existing and then acknowledged for its incredible creative power. Instead of negating and repressing the powerful experiences and strength returnees bring back, we can engage them toward creating new myths.

"*Malinchista*" has to stop being an insult. What we want is that the idea of being an intercultural *malinchista* is synonymous with survival, intelligence, and interculturality. In the same way, all the nicknames attributed to returnees, such as gabacho, gringo, and pocho, should be transformed. In this sense, we pose a series of questions related to transnational returnees, who are the actors in this phenomenon: How many of them could not finish their formal education due to bullying? How much talent and communal growth has Mexican society lost by discriminating against transnational returnees? How many more will be victims of abuse by the returnees themselves as a way of transmitting the traumas of what they themselves experienced? How many opportunities to *convivir* with returnees have been wasted? And what would happen if instead of abusing the experiences that transnational corporations bring with them, although difficult, also enriching, were valued?

We consider it necessary to raise awareness among Mexican citizens to avoid discriminating against returnees from an *anti-malinchista* perspective. We recommend different strategies for this that do not necessarily have to be developed in the order in which they are presented. History should be taken up again, just as Taylor (2009) suggests. It would be necessary to understand that Malinche was not an evil and horrible traitor, but a woman who was handed over as property. It is here where we argue that decolonization shows that, after surviving colonization, the possibility of experiencing an unknown but liberating future opens up, taking up stories that may well be shared in the educational context such as the one that concerns us here.

An inclusive discourse would also have to be constructed and put aside expressions such as *ni de aquí ni allá*, "neither from here nor from there" (an expression commonly used as a descriptor of young people who have lived in the U.S.) to replace them with others such as "from here and there" in relation to the belonging and identity of the returnees. You do not always have to belong to one side or the other if you have lived in both worlds, if you have had experiences on both sides, why then you cannot speak of "here and also there." It is very easy to blame someone for preferring to be associated more with one side than the other. It would be desirable to seriously reflect on the experiences lived by the returnee before trying to define it a priori, in a negative way.

We consider that an answer to this phenomenon could be found by associating it with the concept of hybridity. We cannot expect the returnees to go back to being "pure Mexicans." We must appreciate the skills they bring with them, from their bilingualism to their ability to function in different cultures. The returnees managed to live in different environments. They learned to blend in multicultural settings in schools and in many institutions, such as the churches, hospitals, and other spaces. They managed to travel and maintain close ties in both countries. They knew how to deal with different people at work and also among their friends. They have a lot to share with the rest of the community; therefore, they should stop being seen as a threat and consider them as part of a multicultural society.

One Last Hope and the Resistance of the Transnationals

In the end, the returnees will continue to be themselves. In their the case, we have presented in this chapter those who have had the strength to live transnationalism. Following De Alba (2014), we encourage them to enjoy it, which is the "best revenge."

If the best revenge, as they say, is to live well—and we interpret the aforementioned state of being not only as economic well-being but also as the well-being of the spirit and mind as well as the soul and the body (Anzaldúa, 2015, p. 24), which comes from loving ourselves and living according to our nature instead of commodifying it. The "inert heap of bones, blood and dust" is what Octavio Paz called "the cruel incarnation of the feminine gender" (Paz, 1950 [1992], p. 208). The revenge of Malinche's bones and blood is upon us, and there is no turning back. As we shuffle toward the new Aztlán of the 21st century, the "Shadow Beast" of the rebel Malinche challenges us to look in the mirror and experience what Gloria Anzaldúa (1987) calls conocimiento as "knowledge," the innate power that results from our trips to the underworld of consciousness. "Suddenly, repressed energy emerges, makes decisions, connects with conscious energy and a new life begins" (p. 78).

We thus recognize the possibility of reversing the colonization imposed by the logic of colonization, if we observe and learn lessons from the paths lived by transnationals. Many of them have had to make their own trips to the underworld during their experiences as survivors, which has allowed them to become aware of what we have described above. We wonder how many returnees will have to complete these underworld journeys in the hope that the discourse will change and their stories will spread. It would be better if the change arose from the dialogue between Mexicans and those who returned after living incredible experiences in the other country.

References

Anzaldúa, G. E. (1987). *Borderlands/La frontera: The new mestiza*. Spinsters/Aunt Lute.

Anzaldúa, G. E. (1993). Chicana Artists: Exploring nepantla, el lugar de la frontera. *NACLA Report on the Americas, 27*(1), 37–45. https://doi.org/10.1080/10714839.1993.11724648

Anzaldúa, G. E. (2015). Flights of the imagination: Rereading/rewriting realities. In A. Keating (Ed.), *Light in the dark luz en lo oscuro: Rewriting identity, spirituality, reality* (pp. 23–46). Duke University Press.

Basave, A. (2011). *México mestizo*. Fondo de Cultura Económica.

Basch, L., Glick Schiller, N., y Sztanton Blanc, C. (1994). *Nations Unbound: Transnational Projects, Postcolonial Predicaments, and Deterritorialized Nation-States*. Gordon and Breach Science Publishers.

Bhabha, H. (2004). *The location of culture. 1994* (pp. 5–6). Routledge.

Bonilla-Silva, E. (2010). *Racism without racists: Color-blind racism and the persistence of racial inequality in the United States* (3rd ed.). Rowman & Littlefield Publishers.

Bybee, E. R., Feinauer Whiting, E., Jensen, B., Savage, V., Baker, A., & Holdaway, E. (2020). "Estamos aquí pero no soy de aqui": American Mexican youth, belonging and schooling in rural, Central Mexico. *Anthropology & Education Quarterly, 51*(2), 123–145.

Cesaire, A., y Kelley, R. D. G. (2000). *Discourse on colonialism*. Monthly Review Press.

Cypess, S. M. (2010). *La Malinche in Mexican literature: From history to myth*. University of Texas Press.

De Alba, A. G. (2005). Malinche's revenge. In R. Romero y A. N. Harris (Eds.), *Feminism, nation and myth: La Malinche* (pp. 44–58). Arte Público Press.

De Alba, A. G. (2014). *[Un]framing the "Bad Woman": Sor Juana, Malinche, Coyolxauhqui, and Other Rebels with a Cause*. University of Texas Press.

De León, J. (2015). *The land of open graves: Living and dying on the migrant trail.* University of California Press.
Duncan, G. J., Ziol-Guest, K. M., Kalil, A. (2010). Early-childhood poverty and adult attainment, behavior, and health. *Child development,* 81(1), 306-325.
Durand, J., Massey, D. S., y Parrado, E. A. (1999). The new era of Mexican migration to the United States. *Journal of American History,* 86(2), 518–536.
Elenes, C. A. (2011). *Transforming borders: Chicana/o popular culture and pedagogy.* Rowan & Littlefield Publishers.
Esteva, G. (2019, 1 de julio de 2019). Qué hacer. *La Jornada.* www.jornada.com.mx/2019/07/01/opinion/018a1pol
Fanon, F. (1967). *Black skin white masks.* Grove Press, Inc.
Galván, R. T. (2005). Transnational communities En La Lucha: Campesinas and grassroots organizations "Globalizing from below". *Journal of Latinos and Education,* 4(1), 3–20.
Glissant, E. (1999). *Caribbean discourse: Selected essays* (J. M. Dash, Trans. 3rd ed.). University of Virginia Press.
González, C. (2002). *Doña Marina (La Malinche) y la formación de la identidad mejicana.* Ediciones Encuentro.
González, D. J. (2005). Malinche triangulated, historically speaking. En R. Romero y A. N. Harris (Eds.), *Feminism, nation and myth: La Malinche* (pp. 6–12). Arte Público Press.
Gutiérrez Chong, N. (2012). *Mitos nacionalistas e identidades étnicas: los intelectuales indígenas y el Estado mexicano.* UNAM-Instituto de Investigaciones Sociales.
Hamann, Edmund T., y Zúñiga, Víctor (2011). Schooling and the everyday ruptures transnational children encounter in the United States in Mexico. En C. Coe, R. Reynolds, D. Boehm, J. M. Hess, y H. Rae-Espinoza (Eds.), *Everyday Ruptures: Children and Migration in Global Perspective* (pp. 141–160). Vanderbilt University Press.
Hernández-Ávila, I., & Anzaldúa, G. E. (2000). Quincentennial: From victimhood to active resistance. En *Interviews/Entrevistas/Gloria E. Anzaldúa* (pp. 177–194). Routledge.
Hidalgo Aviles, H., & Kasun, G. S. (2019). Imperial language educators in these times: Transnational voices from Mexico on nationalisms and returnee transnationals. *Educational Studies.* https://doi.org/10.1080/00131946.2019.1570932
Kasun, G. S. (2016). Interplay of a way of a knowing among Mexican-origin transnationals: Chaining to the border and to transnational communities. *Teachers College Record,* 119(9), 1–32.
Kasun, G. S., Hernández, T., & Montiel, H. (2020). The engagement of transnationals in Mexican university classrooms: Points of entry towards recognition among future English teachers. *Multicultural Perspectives,* 22(1), 37–45.
Kleyn, T. (2017). Centering transborder students: Perspectives on identity, languaging and schooling between the US and Mexico. *Multicultural Perspectives,* 19(2), 76–84. https://doi.org/10.1080/15210960.2017.1302336
Mercado, A. (2015). Medios indígenas transnacionales: el fomento del cosmopolitismo desde abajo. *Comunicación y sociedad,* 171–193. www.scielo.org.mx/scielo.php?script= sci_arttext&pid=S0188-252X2015000100008&nrm=iso

Mora-Pablo, I., & Basurto, N. M. (2019). Experiencias educativas y de vida de migrantes de retorno: ¿Una creciente generación de maestros de inglés en México? *Publicaciones, 49*(5), 75–91. https://doi.org/10.30827/publicaciones.v49i5.11441

Mora-Pablo, I., Lengeling, M. M., & Basurto Santos, N. M. (2015). Cruzando fronteiras: Narrativas de transnacionais tornando-se professores de língua inglesa no México./Crossing borders: Stories of transnationals becoming english language teachers in Mexico. *Signum Estudos da Linguagem, 18*(2), 326–348. ISSN 2237-4876. www.uel.br/revistas/uel/index.php/signum/issue/view/1082

Paz, O. ([1950] 1992). *El laberinto de la soledad*. Fondo de Cultura Económica.

Sánchez Muñoz, A. (2013). Who soy yo? The creative use of "Spanglish" to express a hybrid identity in Chicana/o heritage language learners of Spanish. *Hispania, 96*(3), 440–441.

Tacelosky, K. (2018). Teaching English to English speakers: The role of English teachers in the school experience of transnational students in Mexico. *MEXTESOL Journal, 42*(3), 1–13.

Taylor, A. (2009). Introduction. En *Indigeneity in the Mexican cultural imagination* (pp. 1–11). University of Arizona Press.

Van den Braembussche, A. (2002). The Silence of Belgium: Taboo and Trauma in Belgian Memory. *Yale French Studies*, (102), 35–52. https://doi.org/10.2307/3090591

Conclusion

Expanding Transnational Bridges for a World Where Many Worlds Fit

Irasema Mora-Pablo and G. Sue Kasun

> In nepantla we hang out between shifts, trying to make rational sense of this crisis, seeking solace, support, appeasement, or some kind of intimate connection. En este lugar we fall into chaos, fear of the unknown, and are forced to take up the task of self-redefinition. In nepantla we undergo the anguish of changing our perspectives and crossing a series of cruz calles, junctures, and thresholds, some leading to a different way of relating to people and surroundings and others to the creation of a new world. Nepantleras such as artistas/activistas help us mediate these transitions, help us make the crossings, and guide us through the transformation process—a process I call conocimiento.
> (Anzaldúa, 2015, p. 17)

In *Applying Anzalduan Frameworks to Understand Transnational Youth Identities: Bridging Culture, Language, and Schooling at the US-Mexican Border*, we recounted and analyzed different testimonios with transnationals about their journeys between Mexico and the United States as well as their accomplishments and challenges across borders. This book resonates with previous work on return migration and transnationalism in the fields of education, linguistics, anthropology, and sociology. Contributors analyzed the lives of transnational youth through Anzalduan lenses. Using various methodologies in harmony with Anzaldúa's work (testimonios, narrative inquiry, case studies, life history), the chapters provided examples of how transnational youth engage the complexity of identities and fight for their visibility on a daily basis.

This book has blended research-based and theoretical contributions regarding transnational youth. Throughout, the authors engaged several of Anzaldúa's main theoretical constructs to recommend interventions to facilitate the journey of transnationals. We present our work as scholars/activists with the intention that readers become more spacious in their interpretations of young people and less clinical in the research. As Anzaldúa and her colleague Cherrie Moraga (1981) have explained

DOI: 10.4324/9781003191575-13

that they have written Chicana feminism as "theory in the flesh," we believe that the authors of this volume have enfleshed and theorized by showing how and why young transnationals engage resistances, in-betweenness, and movement toward transformations. While it may be obvious to state, we believe it merits repeating—all lives are rich, complicated, and individuals' stories are valuable. The authors of this text have, we believe, honored young people in ways research does not always do of its "subjects."

Contributions to Transnational Youth: Anzaldúa's Constructs to Understand the Complexities of Living Multiple Identities

The authors of the chapters designed their work to reflect the languages that our participants, the authors, us, and our audiences live wholly and fully. Therefore, each contribution has adopted a particular variety of language that reflects the participants' voices and displays the authors' work. We find in-text full English translations to no translations. This reflects the bilingualism and translanguaging our authors and participants live daily, or as Anzaldúa (1987) would argue, as we write with an accent to finally free and legitimate our wild tongues "when writing in academic spaces" (Caldas, 2021, p. 2). This resonates with Anzaldúa's work in Borderlands/La Frontera: the New *Mestiza* (1987), a mestizo text. Her linguistic diversity (Spanish, English, Náhuatl, northern Mexican Spanish, Tex-Mex, Chicano, and Pachuco, among others), shows her critical discourse that celebrates the multiplicity of identities and the linguistic variation of those *fronterizos*, what she portrays as the new Mestiza. As Saldívar (2006) states, "we meet in Anzaldúa's autohistoriateoría[1] a braided, mestiza consciousness, and a feminist writer fundamentally caught between various hegemonic colonial and postcolonial languages and subaltern dialects, and vernacular expressions" (p. 162). In this sense, we urge the audience to acknowledge transnational youth's culture and languages as additive resources, and not as a threat on the playground, at work, or in the school. This in turn takes us to look at the historical relationship between Mexico and the Unites States and the need to provide access to opportunities historically denied, wherein certain kinds of bodies and languages are more valuable than others, depending on which side of border one finds oneself. It is time to start working toward the creation of more spaces for youth to share who they are and question what is happening around them.

Anzaldúa's concept of *frontera* becomes crucial in understanding the testimonios presented in this book. She referred to this not as a geographical border, but a cultural border, in constant transition, where many live, especially those who cross the limits of the "normal" (Anzaldúa,

1987). La "frontera" then is resignified as that ideological place of identity resistance and political position. This is where we need to understand the different vision of the *fronterizo* and her ways of resisting, but also the vision of the State and the Other. Anzaldúa (1987) stated that:

> To live in the Borderlands means that you are neither hispana india negra Española ni gabacha, eres mestiza, mulata, half-breed caught in the crossfire between camps while carrying all five races on your back not knowing which side to turn to, run from.
>
> (p. 194)

The chapters presented here show how transnational youth have lived in two nations, speak two languages (or more, as in the case of some Indigenous transnational youth), live in two (or more) worlds, but still are not recognized as bi- or mutli-cultural. Instead, they live in danger, in constant questioning by others. Anzaldúa's form of nepantilism is often manifested by the transnational youth in these chapters as a violent cultural in-betweenness. The participants in the chapters presented here live in-between, in two opposing cultures, where they do not feel either completely Mexican or U.S. American. This was represented in many testimonios in this book, and it shows the need to give voice to those who experience these hybrid identities wherein young people are not forced to use a negative identity category (the famous indictment of *"ni de aquí ni de allá"*) but rather a positive identity, as offered here, such as *"de aquí y de allá."*

We believe we have an ethical responsibility to promote spaces for open discussions to engage in critical consciousness and el *mundo zurdo*, Anzaldúa's vision of the "left-handed" world, similar, we believe, to the Zapatista vision of a world wherein many worlds fit. For instance, in this text, we have included a range of predominantly Latinx voices, the majority of whom originate from and/or reside on the southern side of the border as well as those who reside to the north. The young people in these chapters and the theoretical contributions in the final section argue for the need to shift discourse, historic understandings, and daily understandings. What would it mean to start studying transnational histories as opposed to national histories? What does it mean to insist on mutli-sited research to more robustly engage how we work with transnational young people? For those who are more mono-national in their backgrounds, what can they come to understand from taking these perspectives?

This is where the New Mestiza concept becomes crucial in Anzaldúa's work and which has been engaged throughout this book. The new *mestiza* faces the dilemma of what Anzaldúa called being of "mixed race." We take this as an invitation to reflect on the cultural categories (*fronteras*) that help define transnational youth and restrict their freedom. The new tribalism term was coined to include nations while modernize the term "tribe," allowing for the incorporation of other categories of identity. In Anzaldúa's words,

> In my rationale for using the "new tribalism," I use the word nos/otras (us/them, we/they) to signify how we are in each other's worlds and how we are each affected by the other and how we are all dependent on the other. Pure categories don't exist. Categories attempt to contain, imprison, limit, keep us from growing. We have to constantly disrupt those categories and invent new ones.
> (Blake & Ábrego, 1995, p. 15)

With this, Anzaldúa refers to the constant fluidity and transition of those categories related to identity. This is what happens with the transnational youth we refer to in this work. They are in constant transitions, in constant change and mobility.

Extending the Bridges

The chapters of this text call for more institutional support on both sides of the border, more recognition of the transnational youth and more empathy toward increasing spaces for hybridity of identity and ways of being. The Anzalduan constructs used here help us to understand and talk about resistance as part of ethnic and identity studies which can serve all youths toward empowerment and mutual understanding. Furthermore, what if schools took the new tribalism seriously? Not only would we perhaps achieve robust ethnic studies at the institutional level, but we could find spaces of empathy, caring, and the schools where many worlds could fit. We conclude this chapter with some questions to encourage the audience to join us in our vision of extending Anzaldúa in the discussions surrounding transnational youth:

- How do we engage the complexities of identity and extend Anzaldúa even further when there were components that were not as well-developed (e.g., the importance of engaging indigeneity among Indigenous youth and beyond)? How can we hybridize her theorizing with others and transnationalism?
- What do we need to do to shift these youths from *nepantla* into being able to work toward personal and social transformation as *nepantleras*, as activists and artists and more?
- How can we build upon the experiences of these youths toward breaking down barriers and even borders?
- How can we reframe painful myths, oppressive language, and metaphors toward social transformation?

- What can we harness from these dually conscious young people toward all of us being able to use *la facultad* as part of mestiza consciousness? Anzaldúa (2015) did, after all, say even non-women of color can have women of color consciousness.

As we mentioned at the beginning of this book, we offer this work as a corrective—a corrective to the misunderstandings of who transnational youth, especially Mexican-origin transnational youth, are. It is our hope that this book provides new insights and stimulates productive engagement with transnational youth in both sides of the border.

Note

1. Gloria Anzaldúa writes in "Border Arte: Nepantla, El lugar de la Frontera," that border art

    depicts both the soul of the artist and the soul of the pueblo. It deals with who tells the stories and what stories and histories are told. I call this form of visual narrative autohistorias. This form goes beyond the traditional selfportrait or autobiography, in telling the writer/artist's personal story, it also includes the artist's cultural history.

    (113)

    In a conversation with me at the University of California, Santa Cruz, on October 17, 1990, Anzaldúa described the form of Borderlands/La Frontera with the neologism, autohistoriateoría (Saldívar, 2006, p. 170).

References

Anzaldúa, G. E. (1987). *Borderlands: The new mestiza. La frontera*. Aunt Lute Books.

Anzaldúa, G. E. (2015). Let us be the healing of the wound. In A. Keating (Ed.), *Light in the dark Luz en lo oscuro: Rewriting identity, spirituality, reality* (pp. 9–22). Duke University Press.

Blake, D., & Ábrego, C. (1995). An interview with Gloria Anzaldúa. *Iowa Journal of Cultural Studies*, (14), 12–22.

Caldas, B. (2021). Hablando Pa'tras: Developing critical conscious bilingual teacher education programs in Mexican-American/Latinophobic Times. *Journal of Language, Identity & Education, 20*(1), 1–3. https://doi.org/10.1080/15348458.2021.1864202

Moraga, C. (1981). Chicana feminism as theory in the flesh. In G. Anzaldua & C. Moraga (Eds.), *This bridge called my back: Writings by radical women of color*. Aunt Lute Press.

Saldívar, J. D. (2006). Border thinking, minoritized studies, and realist interpellations: The coloniality of power from Gloria Anzaldúa to Arundhati Roy. In *Identity politics reconsidered* (pp. 152–170). Palgrave Macmillan.

Index

academic language 96, 100, 107
American-Mexicans 8
Anzalduan theories 2
aquí or *allá* 103
atravesado 26
autohistorias 2, 4, 5
autohistoriateoria 174, 177n1
Aztlán 23

Barthes, R. 136, 143,
   146, 153
Borderlands/La Frontera
   19, 67
bullying 163–164, 168

Chicana/Chicano 1, 3, 4, 75, 77,
   87–89, 104, 108
circular migrants 93
Coatlicue 3
Coatlicue state 117, 120–121, 127
conocimiento 3, 4, 10, 13, 38, 39, 42,
   44, 48, 50
conocimientos 54
Cypess, S.M. 160–162, 170

Deferred Action for Minor Arrivals
   (DACA) 114–115, 122–123, 125,
   129, 130–131

El camino de la Mestiza/The Mestiza
   Way 19
El destierro 22
el mundo zurdo 4
emotional transnationalism 74
English class 166
ethnic identity 98

Fanon, F. 159, 161, 171
funds of knowledge 96, 107

generation 1.5 114, 127, 129

hybridity 159, 166, 168–169, 176

ideological practices 103
in-between 37, 40, 42, 44, 46–49
Indigenous communities 53, 56,
   58–59, 62, 64–66
In-service Certificate in English
   Language Teaching (ICELT) 105
interculturality 168

la Raza Cósmica 64, 66n1
la resistencia 20, 23, 26, 28, 32
Latinx/a/o 71–73, 81, 86, 87n1, 88
linguistic terrorism 80

Malinche 140, 142–144, 146, **147**,
   148, 150
Malinche/Malintzín 155–156, 158
malinchistas 161, 164, 168
Mestiza consciousness 71, 74–75, 79,
   80, 83, 85–88
mestizaje 114, 116–119, 128
metaphor 133–134, 136, 140,
   142–143, 145, 149, 152n1
metonymy 133–134, 136, 139, 140
multicultural 156, 167, 169, 171
Mundo Zurdo 113–114, 117–119,
   124–125, 129–130, 135,
   150, 152
myth(s) 136, 139–140, 143, 146,
   147–148, 150, 151, 158, 168, 176

nepantla 21, 31, 37–39, 40, 42, 48–49, 51, 134–135, 152
nepantleras 106
new *mestiza* 116, 118, 125, 130, 174–175, 177
new tribalism 4, 13, 16, 176
ni de aquí ni de allá 146, 169

pláticas 77, 88
positionality 23, 77
poststructuralist view 103
Programa Binacional de Educación Migrante (PROBEM) 37–38
Programa Nacional de Inglés en Educación Básica (PNIEB) 99

Schmelkes, S. 33, 36
Secretaría de Educación Pública 99, 108
Shadow-Beast 162, 168–169
switching modes 102

testimonio 38–39, 42, 48–49, 50
traitor 155–156, 160–161, 163–164, 168
transnational learning community 31
transnationalism 71, 73–74, 77, 86–87, 89
transnationals 102–103

Vasconcelos, J. 116, 132

Zentella, A. C. 6

Taylor & Francis eBooks

www.taylorfrancis.com

A single destination for eBooks from Taylor & Francis with increased functionality and an improved user experience to meet the needs of our customers.

90,000+ eBooks of award-winning academic content in Humanities, Social Science, Science, Technology, Engineering, and Medical written by a global network of editors and authors.

TAYLOR & FRANCIS EBOOKS OFFERS:

A streamlined experience for our library customers

A single point of discovery for all of our eBook content

Improved search and discovery of content at both book and chapter level

REQUEST A FREE TRIAL
support@taylorfrancis.com

Printed in the USA
CPSIA information can be obtained
at www.ICGtesting.com
LVHW020825170924
791293LV00003B/486